Developing Large Web Applications

Developing Large Web Applications

Kyle Loudon
foreword by Nate Koechley

O'REILLY®

Beijing · Cambridge · Farnham · Köln · Sebastopol · Taipei · Tokyo

Developing Large Web Applications

by Kyle Loudon

Published by O'Reilly Media, Inc., 1005 Gravenstein Highway North, Sebastopol, CA 95472.

O'Reilly books may be purchased for educational, business, or sales promotional use. Online editions are also available for most titles (*http://my.safaribooksonline.com*). For more information, contact our corporate/institutional sales department: (800) 998-9938 or *corporate@oreilly.com*.

Editor: Andy Oram
Production Editor: Sumita Mukherji
Copyeditor: Amy Thomson
Production Services: Newgen North America, Inc.

Cover Designer: Karen Montgomery
Interior Designer: David Futato
Illustrator: Robert Romano

Printing History:

March 2010:   First Edition.

RepKover.™   This book uses RepKover™, a durable and flexible lay-flat binding.

ISBN: 978-0-596-80302-5

[M]

1267033559

Table of Contents

Foreword

As a little kid, I wondered if I would be big and strong when I grew up. There were a lot of aspects to growing well. Would I be healthy? Useful? Productive? Successful?

Websites start out small, too. But these humble sites share my childhood dreams. They want to help more people in more ways; they want to be durable and reliable; they want to be indispensable and to live forever. In short: they want to be large and successful.

But growing up is hard to do. Challenges accumulate and complexity snowballs.

> Expansion means complexity and complexity decay.
>
> —C. Northcote Parkinson

I've seen it. The inevitable challenges of growth in websites—data management, performance—become crippling if mishandled. Things you thought were straightforward, like HTML, start giving you headaches. From front to back, JavaScript to PHP, harmony is displaced by dissonance.

> Fools ignore complexity. Pragmatists suffer it. Some can avoid it. Geniuses remove it.
>
> —Alan Perlis

I've worked hand-in-hand with Kyle on some of the Web's largest applications. I've watched him craft CSS systems to make sprawling sites skinable and design Ajax architectures that adapt to and enhance the sites. He emerges from the trenches on top every time. He's a perpetual teacher, and, like the best in any discipline, also a perpetual student. We all benefit from his expertise.

Kyle shares his genius and hard-won expertise in this valuable book that will prepare you and your application for scale and success. The book is well structured and readable, with memorable tenets supported by savvy insights, sound philosophy, and fully functioning code examples. Complexity is inevitable, but success rewards the prepared.

> The way to build a complex system that works is to build it from very simple systems that work.
>
> —Kevin Kelly

During this book's deft tour of the complete web application stack, Kyle, the perfect guide, converts lines of explanatory code from one context into insightful tips in another. Build big by thinking small. Build new by thinking old. Manage scope. Boost signal and reduce noise. Resist breakage...these things are easy to rattle off, but it takes an author like Kyle, and a book like this, to make them practical and real.

If you're ready to build a finely crafted large site, this is the book for you. Learn what it takes, because today's compromise is tomorrow's constraint. Start today, because the world is waiting for your application.

Grow large and prosper.

—Nate Koechley
San Francisco, January 2010

Preface

It's been a while since I first worked on a book with O'Reilly in 1997. That book was a practical guide to data structures and algorithms, a subject that, for the most part, had been defined many years before by some of the early giants of computer science (Dijkstra, Hoare, Knuth, to name a few). By comparison, I've been able to witness the rapid evolution of the subject of this book from the front lines, and I have had the good fortune to help refine it myself while working as a web developer at one of the largest web applications in the world, Yahoo!.

Web developers have a fascinating role. We work just as closely with user experience designers as with engineers, and sometimes we're the designers, too. In many ways, we are guardians of the user experience as a web design goes from its mockup to its implementation. But we also have to write exceptionally good code that performs well in the challenging environment of web browsers. Today, more than ever, engineers recognize that web development must be carried out with the same rigor as other types of software development.

This book presents a number of techniques for applying established practices of good software engineering to web development—that is, development primarily using the disparate technologies of HTML, CSS, JavaScript, and server-side scripting languages. Whereas there are many books on how to use languages, how to use libraries, and how to approach software engineering, this is the first book to codify many of the techniques it presents. These techniques will make the components of your own web applications more reusable, maintainable, and reliable.

Audience

The primary audience for this book is software developers and managers interested in large web applications; however, you'll find that the techniques in this book are equally useful for web applications of any size. Although it's especially important to follow good development practices in large web applications, smaller web applications benefit from many of the same techniques, too.

To get the most out of this book, you should already be very familiar with HTML, CSS, and JavaScript; this book does not teach these languages, although it covers many interesting aspects about them. This book uses PHP as the scripting language for server-side examples. Many readers will have a good understanding of PHP as well, but even those who don't should find the examples easy to follow. PHP is known for its flexibility, ubiquity, and ease of use, so it works well. Most examples can be translated to other server-side scripting languages fairly easily, if you desire.

Organization of This Book

This book is organized into three types of material: background (e.g., Object Orientation in Chapter 2), techniques associated with specific languages (e.g., Large-Scale HTML in Chapter 3, Large-Scale CSS in Chapter 4, Large-Scale JavaScript in Chapter 5, and Large-Scale PHP in Chapter 7), and techniques related to other aspects of development (e.g., Data Management in Chapter 6, Large-Scale Ajax in Chapter 8, Performance in Chapter 9, and Application Architecture in Chapter 10). Each chapter begins with a tenet presented from Chapter 1. These tenets act as assertions about the topic for each chapter to provide a concisely articulated direction.

Throughout the book, there are numerous examples in real code to demonstrate many of the techniques presented. Some of the numbered examples work together to create larger, more complete examples that extend across multiple chapters. While the focus of this book is not on teaching the specific languages addressed, the examples do demonstrate a number of aspects of each language that will help make you more proficient with each as you master them.

Conventions Used in This Book

The following typographical conventions are used in this book:

Italic
> Indicates new terms, URLs, filenames, and Unix utilities.

`Constant width`
> Indicates command-line options, variables and other code elements, HTML tags, the contents of files, and the output from commands.

`Constant width bold`
> Shows commands or other text that should be typed literally by the user.

`Constant width italic`
> Shows text that should be replaced with user-supplied values.

This icon signifies a tip, suggestion, or general note.

There are some other conventions to be aware of in this book:

...
> Indicates something that is missing (for you to fill in) in a line of code or a path (e.g., `require_once(.../navbar.inc);`).

`<?php ... ?>`
> Wraps PHP examples that contain the complete code for a file. Most PHP examples don't have this, because they show only a code snippet.

Using Code Examples

This book is here to help you get your job done. In general, you may use the code in this book in your programs and documentation. You do not need to contact us for permission unless you're reproducing a significant portion of the code. For example, writing a program that uses several chunks of code from this book does not require permission. Selling or distributing a CD-ROM of examples from O'Reilly books *does* require permission. Answering a question by citing this book and quoting example code does not require permission. Incorporating a significant amount of example code from this book into your product's documentation *does* require permission.

We appreciate, but do not require, attribution. An attribution usually includes the title, author, publisher, and ISBN. For example: "*Developing Large Web Applications*, by Kyle Loudon. Copyright Yahoo!, Inc., 978-0-596-80302-5."

If you feel your use of code examples falls outside fair use or the permission given here, feel free to contact us at *permissions@oreilly.com*.

We'd Like to Hear From You

Every example has in this book has been tested on various platforms, but occasionally you may encounter problems. The information in this book has also been verified at each step of the production process. However, mistakes and oversights can occur and we will gratefully receive details of any you find, as well as any suggestions you would like to make for future editions. You can contact the author and editors at:

O'Reilly Media, Inc.
1005 Gravenstein Highway North
Sebastopol, CA 95472
(800) 998-9938 (in the United States or Canada)
(707) 829-0515 (international or local)
(707) 829-0104 (fax)

We have a web page for this book, where we list errata, examples, and any additional information. You can access this page at:

http://www.oreilly.com/catalog/9780596803025

You can find additional information about this book, including electronic versions of the examples at:

http://kyleloudon.com

To comment or ask technical questions about this book, send email to the following address, mentioning its ISBN number (978-0-596-80302-5):

bookquestions@oreilly.com

For more information about our books, conferences, Resource Centers, and the O'Reilly Network, see our website at:

http://www.oreilly.com

Safari® Books Online

Safari Books Online is an on-demand digital library that lets you easily search over 7,500 technology and creative reference books and videos to find the answers you need quickly.

With a subscription, you can read any page and watch any video from our library online. Read books on your cell phone and mobile devices. Access new titles before they are available for print, and get exclusive access to manuscripts in development and post feedback for the authors. Copy and paste code samples, organize your favorites, download chapters, bookmark key sections, create notes, print out pages, and benefit from tons of other time-saving features.

O'Reilly Media has uploaded this book to the Safari Books Online service. To have full digital access to this book and others on similar topics from O'Reilly and other publishers, sign up for free at *http://my.safaribooksonline.com*.

Acknowledgments

This book is the result of having worked with outstanding people both at O'Reilly and in many projects leading up to the book. For this, I offer my heartfelt thanks.

First, I thank my editor at O'Reilly, Andy Oram. Andy and I worked together on my first book with O'Reilly, and I had hoped for a long time that working on another book together would not be a matter of if, but when. Having finished this book, I hope that another book will be a matter of when again. Andy inspires me with his ability to always find ways to make things better. His insights appear in one form or another on nearly every page of this book. Andy also kept our project moving along while being patient and understanding of the struggle that writers doing other jobs constantly face.

I also extend my sincere thanks to the entire production team at O'Reilly, who constantly impress me with their ability to handle the numerous aspects of production so smoothly. The ease with which it all seems to take place belies the work that it really requires. I would also like to thank Amy Thomson, my copyeditor, for having worked under such tight time constraints at the end of the book.

I send my heartfelt thanks to Nate Koechley for writing the foreword. Nate was one of my earliest colleagues at Yahoo! to turn me on to the truly awesome potential of web development. Much of what I've tried to capture in this book came from ideas that Nate worked passionately to instill at Yahoo! and across the Web. I couldn't have asked for a more fitting person to write the foreword.

I am grateful to have had outstanding technical reviewers for this book as well. Christoph Dorn, Steve Griffith, and Nate Koechley each provided an impressive level of detail and thought in their reviews. The book benefited greatly from their comments.

I would also like to acknowledge the influence of my many colleagues at Yahoo! and other projects before this. I especially thank Bryce Kujala and Vy Phan, who helped refine many of the ideas in the book by putting them to the test in practice early on. I'm also grateful to the exceptional user experience designers with whom I've had the honor to work closest: Veronica Gaspari, Cathy Tiritoglu, and Sasha Verhage.

Finally, I thank Shala, my wife, for her encouragement on another book project; my parents, Marc and Judy, for their support from afar; Shala's parents, Elias and Maria, for their frequent assistance at a moment's notice; and Julian, who has been my late-night companion—just too young to know it yet.

CHAPTER 1

The Tenets

As applications on the Web become larger and larger, how can web developers manage the complexity? In many ways, we need to turn to some of the same good practices used in other types of software development. Generally speaking, these practices are not yet pervasive in web development—that is, in software development primarily using HTML, CSS, JavaScript, and various server-side scripting languages (we'll use PHP for the server-side scripting in this book, but the same principles apply to many other languages). Furthermore, the uniqueness of these technologies poses a challenge for developers trying to apply good practices in a cohesive way.

One of the themes that you'll see repeated in this book is the importance of extending modular development practices to web development. This book presents concrete, practical techniques to achieve modularity in large web applications. In the process, we'll explore many of the finer aspects of HTML, CSS, JavaScript, and PHP. You'll find that most of the techniques are relatively simple to apply, and none rely on the use of specific frameworks. That said, it's important to realize that they don't preclude you from using various frameworks, either; to the contrary, these techniques create a better landscape in which to use many frameworks. As a case in point, we'll look at several examples that utilize the Yahoo! User Interface (YUI) JavaScript library.

At the outset, it's important to establish why the techniques that we're going to explore in this book are especially useful for web developers working on large web applications. We'll begin by looking at some of the factors that contribute to the complexity of many large web applications. Then we'll explore how modularity plays an important role in managing this complexity. Last, we'll examine a list of tenets that will guide our discussions throughout the rest of the book.

Managing Complexity

If you consider how different the Internet is today from just 10 years ago, it's clear how complicated web applications have become and just how quickly the changes have taken place. Far too often, this complexity makes large web applications difficult to

1

maintain, less reliable, and more costly over their lifetimes. Let's examine some factors that contribute to the complexity of many large web applications. Typically, large web applications have the following characteristics:

Continuous availability
Most large web applications must be running 24/7. In addition, response times have to be fast at any moment, even at peak load times. Web developers need to write code that is especially robust.

Large user base
Large web applications usually have large numbers of users. This necessitates management of a large number of simultaneous connections or layers of caching. Web developers often need to write code to manage these situations.

Piece-by-piece delivery
Whereas many types of software are distributed as complete units, web applications have many parts delivered page by page, or connection by connection via Ajax. As a result, large web applications operate within an environment effectively shared by a huge number of users.

Diversity
It's hard to think of a business or service that doesn't have at least some sort of web interface. For example, we see financial applications, ticketing sites, applications that organize massive amounts of data (e.g., search engines), media systems (e.g., news sites), and the list goes on. Web developers need to write code that may be reused in unexpected places.

Longevity
The largest web applications today, even those that have been around many years, are just at the beginning of their lifetimes. Web developers need to write code under the assumption that it will have to stand up to years of changes and maintenance.

Multiple environments
The Web is a fast-changing landscape littered with old browsers and other devices that can be difficult to support. Users access large web applications from all types of environments and with screens of wildly different sizes (including mobile devices). Web developers must write code that can handle the numerous idiosyncrasies that result from this.

Real-time updates
Large web applications are not static; they are constantly fluctuating applications for which changes are typically pushed to servers regularly. Web developers need to write code to address this potential for moving parts.

Over time, web developers often end up addressing complexity in large web applications via one-off fixes and tweaks as their applications reach various breaking points. But there is a better way. This book will show you how to address challenges like the ones above head-on from the start. Mitigating the complexity from these challenges can often be attributed to one or more byproducts of modularity that we'll examine in a moment. For example, I stated above that large web applications need to be available all the time. From the perspective of the web developer, this is an issue of reliability, which modularity plays a key role in addressing.

Modular Components

In a large web application, to address complexity with modular components, or *modules*, you need to encapsulate everything the component needs within small, well-defined pieces of the application. This allows you to divide a large application into more manageable pieces that you can build with a specific focus and reuse wherever needed. In addition, you hide (or abstract) the implementation details of each module and take steps to ensure each module can operate more or less independently of the others. Even relatively small web applications can benefit from such modularity. After all, the small web applications of today are the Googles, Yahoo!s, and Amazons of tomorrow. Building web applications in a modular way at the start provides a solid foundation for future growth.

Modularity seems like a simple thing, but it can be deceptively difficult to attain in a cohesive manner across the HTML, CSS, JavaScript, and server-side scripts that web developers write for large web applications. Let's look more closely at the concept of modularity and some basic ideas to help you achieve it.

Achieving Modularity

You achieve modularity in large web applications, as in other types of software, through *encapsulation*, *abstraction*, and maintaining as much of a *loose coupling* as possible among an application's modules.

Encapsulation

Encapsulation is the process of bundling everything that a module requires within a single, cohesive unit. Modules for web applications need to encapsulate all the HTML, CSS, JavaScript, and PHP that they require. Chapter 7 shows how to accomplish this using object-oriented PHP. We'll also have to employ techniques in the HTML, CSS, and JavaScript itself for a module to support this. These techniques are presented in Chapters 3, 4, and 5, respectively.

Abstraction

Abstraction is the process of hiding details that should not be observable when working with a module from outside its implementation. Defining a good interface is the key to abstraction. Web applications present special challenges because HTML is not built for hiding information in the manner that many languages enforce and because CSS cuts across module boundaries, or *cascades*, and must therefore be managed rigorously. Chapter 7 shows how object-oriented PHP can be used to define interfaces that abstract the details of working with sections of HTML and CSS. Data managers, presented in Chapter 6, are good examples of interfaces that abstract working with dynamic data managed by the backend.

Loose coupling

A loose coupling between modules means that one depends on the other as little as possible and only in clearly defined ways. In Chapter 2, you'll see that it's relatively easy to create a dependency graph that depicts the dependencies among objects in an object-oriented system. When object orientation is used to implement modules in a large web application, it's easier to notice how changes to one part of a system may affect another. The techniques presented for modular HTML and CSS in Chapters 3 and 4 also promote loose coupling.

Benefits of Modularity

Once you create modules that take advantage of encapsulation, abstraction, and loose coupling, you'll have better *reusability*, *maintainability*, and *reliability* across your entire web application. When a module is reusable, it's clear how to make it operate and do new things. You can move it from place to place in the application with the confidence that everything it needs to work properly will come with it, and that you won't experience unexpected consequences when you reuse the module. When a module is maintainable, it's clear which area of the application you need to change to affect certain features and how to make the changes. Modules that are easy to maintain are more reliable because they reduce the risk of side effects when changes take place.

Ten Tenets for Large Web Applications

With an eye toward modularity, we'll use the list of tenets in this section to guide our discussions in the chapters that follow. A tenet is a principle or belief that we will accept as true—that is, it's an assertion. A quick read-through of this list will provide you with a high-level understanding of where we'll be heading. Later, you may find this list to be a concise reminder of the concepts we've discussed. Each tenet is examined in the chapter with the corresponding number. For instance, Tenet 4 describes the robust use of CSS, and Chapter 4 shows how to apply this tenet when implementing your CSS.

Tenet 1
> Large web applications are built from modular components that are highly reusable, maintainable, and reliable.

Tenet 2
> The use of object orientation in JavaScript and server-side scripting languages improves reusability, maintainability, and reliability in large web applications by promoting modularity.

Tenet 3

Large-scale HTML is semantic, devoid of presentation elements other than those inherent in the information architecture, and pluggable into a wide variety of contexts in the form of easily identifiable sections.

Tenet 4

Large-scale CSS forms a layer of presentation that is separate from the information architecture, applied in a modular fashion, and free of side effects as we reuse modules in various contexts.

Tenet 5

Large-scale JavaScript forms a layer of behavior applied in a modular and object-oriented fashion that prevents side effects as we reuse modules in various contexts.

Tenet 6

Dynamic data exchanged between the user interface and the backend is managed through a clearly defined data interface. Pages define a single point for loading data and a single point for saving it.

Tenet 7

Pages are constructed from highly reusable modules that encapsulate everything required (e.g., HTML, CSS, JavaScript, and anything else) to make each module an independently functioning and cohesive unit that can be used in a variety of contexts across various pages.

Tenet 8

Large-scale Ajax is portable and modular, and it maintains a clear separation between data changes and updates to a presentation. Data exchange between the browser and server is managed through a clearly defined interface.

Tenet 9

Large-scale HTML, JavaScript, CSS, and PHP provide a good foundation on which to build large web applications that perform well. They also facilitate a good environment for capturing site metrics and testing.

Tenet 10

The organization of files on the server for a large web application reflects the architecture of the application itself, including clearly demarcated scopes in which each file will be used.

CHAPTER 2

Object Orientation

Object orientation has been at the heart of many types of software for years, but web developers using JavaScript and server-side scripting languages generally haven't been as fast to embrace it. In the early days, websites had fairly simple scripting needs, so object orientation wasn't crucial. Today, with the complexity of software on the Web, an understanding of object orientation is fundamental to approaching the development of large web applications with the same rigor as other types of software.

Throughout this book, we'll explore many examples that use object orientation in PHP and JavaScript, so it's worth spending a little time to examine its importance and how both languages address it. Both PHP and JavaScript have powerful support for object orientation, but each implements it in different ways. One of the fundamental differences is that PHP is a *class-based language*. In class-based languages, you declare and extend classes, which you then instantiate as objects wherever needed. This is object orientation as C++ and Java developers know it. On the other hand, JavaScript is a *prototype-based* (or *object-based*) *language*. In prototype-based languages, there are no classes; you create objects on the fly and derive new ones using existing objects as prototypes. Whatever the language, the following tenet (first described in Chapter 1) articulates what we expect to achieve with an object-oriented implementation:

> Tenet 2: The use of object orientation in JavaScript and server-side scripting languages improves reusability, maintainability, and reliability in large web applications by promoting modularity.

This chapter begins with an overview of object orientation and why it's a good approach in general. To this end, we'll examine the fact that one of the most important reasons for its popularity, often not easily articulated even by experienced developers, is that it helps narrow the semantic gap between real-world problems and the solutions that you build in software. Next, we'll look at an example of how to visualize a web page in an object-oriented way. Finally, we'll explore some of the details behind object orientation in PHP and JavaScript. We won't cover all aspects of object orientation for each, but we'll explore the core features with an emphasis on those used in this book.

The Fundamentals of OOP

The fundamental idea behind object-oriented programming (OOP) is to group together data (called *data members* in object-oriented parlance) with the operations that do things with it (called *methods*). In PHP, you define which data members and methods go together by placing them in a *class*, as shown in Example 2-1. In JavaScript, the details are little different (as you'll see later in the chapter), but the idea is the same.

Example 2-1. A simple class in PHP

```php
class Account
{
    protected $balance;
    protected $minimum;

    public function __construct($amount, $lowest)
    {
        // Initialize the data members when a new object is instantiated.
        $this->balance = $amount;
        $this->minimum = $lowest;
    }

    public function deposit($amount)
    {
        $this->balance += $amount;
    }

    public function withdraw($amount)
    {
        $this->balance -= $amount;
    }
}
```

Note the use of $this in each method. It refers to the particular instance of the object that's currently being manipulated. This way, each account can have a different balance and minimum, and when a deposit or withdrawal is made, it will always affect the correct balance—the one for the account on which the deposit or withdrawal is invoked.

Once you have the data members and methods bundled together, you create an instance of the bundle as an *object* and invoke the methods to carry out various operations, as shown in Example 2-2. In this example, each object is a separate instance of the class, so after depositing $100.75 into $account1, that object has a balance of $600.75, while $account2 still has a balance of $300.00. Of course, there is a lot more behind object orientation than this, but this example illustrates some of the fundamental ideas.

Example 2-2. Using an object in PHP

```php
$account1 = new Account(500, 200);
$account2 = new Account(300, 200);

...

$account1->deposit(100.75);
```

Why Object Orientation?

To understand why object orientation is a good approach to software development, it helps to think about the following:

- What's the natural way in which people tend to think about problems and, as a result, build cognitive models to solve them?
- How can we draw visual models from our cognitive models in a standard way so that we can work with them?
- How can software developers write code to resemble as closely as possible these visual, and hence cognitive, models?
- How can we abstract problems in common ways to allow developers with diverse backgrounds to collaborate?

In programs that are not object-oriented (programs written using traditional procedural languages, for example), the models we create tend to be abstractions of the computer itself: functions are abstractions of processors, data structures are abstractions of memory, etc. Since most real-world problems don't look like a computer, this creates a disconnect. Object-oriented systems more closely resemble our cognitive models and the visual models drawn from them. As a result, object orientation fundamentally narrows the semantic gap between the natural way we think about problems and how we work with them on a computer.

To illustrate how object orientation narrows this gap, we'll need a visual model that we can translate into code. Let's look at a standard approach for drawing visual models from cognitive ones: the *Unified Modeling Language* (UML). Although UML defines nine types of diagrams to describe components and their interactions or relationships in systems, we'll focus on just one: the *class diagram*.

UML Class Diagrams

If someone were to ask you to draw a model of how various components of a banking system were related, you would most likely draw some combination of boxes or circles for the components, and lines or arrows to show their relationships. UML class diagrams standardize this rather natural way to depict things. Stated formally, a UML class diagram is a directed graph in which nodes (boxes) represent classes of objects and edges (lines or arrows) represent relationships between the classes. Two examples of some of the relationships between classes are *generalization* and *association*.

Generalization

Generalization is the relationship between one class and a more general form of it. This type of relationship is sometimes called an "is-a" relationship because one class *is a* more specialized form of the general one. For example, a checking account is a more specialized form of a bank account. In UML, you show generalization by drawing a hollow arrow from a box labeled with the more specialized class to a box labeled with the more general class, as shown in Figure 2-1.

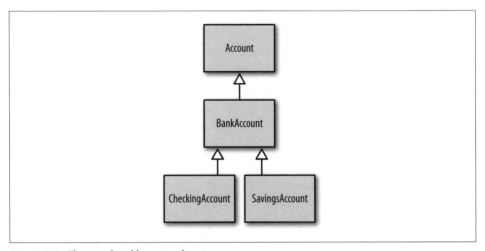

Figure 2-1. Classes related by generalization

Association

Association is the relationship between one class and a class of something it contains. This type of relationship is sometimes called a "has-a" relationship because one class *has a* member within it. For example, a customer at a bank has an account. In UML, you show an association by drawing an arrow from a box labeled with the containing class to a box labeled with the class of its member, as shown in Figure 2-2 (you can omit the arrowheads if both classes contain each other). You can also include a number of instances next to the arrowhead or use an asterisk (*) to indicate any number of instances, if you know these details.

Other items that you may include within the box itself are the operations the class may perform and data members associated with the class that don't aggregate any data themselves (e.g., an account balance that is simply a number). Figure 2-2 shows examples of these items as well.

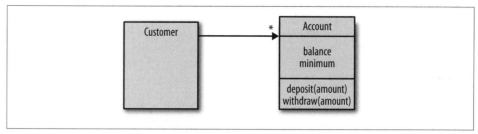

Figure 2-2. Classes related by association

Modeling a Web Page

Now let's turn to the class diagram for a web page, shown in Figure 2-3. This diagram captures the way we're going to think about web pages when we write some PHP code to build them in a modular fashion in Chapter 7. It doesn't capture all the details of the implementation in Chapter 7, but it shows enough to illustrate the resemblance between this type of model and its object-oriented code in Example 2-3. Our diagram has two fundamental entities: *pages* and *modules*.

Defining Page Types

The most general form of a page is represented by a class called `Page`, which represents the data and operations for web pages across all types of web applications. We also recognize the need for more specialized classes of pages on a specific website (e.g., `SitePage`), pages on certain sections of the site (e.g., `NewCarsPage`), and pages for very specific purposes (e.g., `NewCarSearchResultsPage`). The diagram further conveys the fundamental use of modules in pages. Every page is composed of modules, and a module conversely has an association with the page on which it resides. This way, it can add what it needs to the page.

To keep things simple for now, the diagram shows just one data member for `Page`, `js_module`, and one operation, `add_to_js`. In Chapter 7, you'll see that modules need a way to add their JavaScript to a page, and `add_to_js` provides a way to do this. Pages need someplace to collect the JavaScript, and the diagram shows the data member `js_module` for just this purpose.

Defining Module Types

The most general class of module is `Module`, which represents the data and operations common to all modules. We also recognize the need for more specialized classes of modules to implement modules for very specific purposes (e.g., `NavBar`), as well as layouts and containers, which are themselves more specific forms of `Layout`.

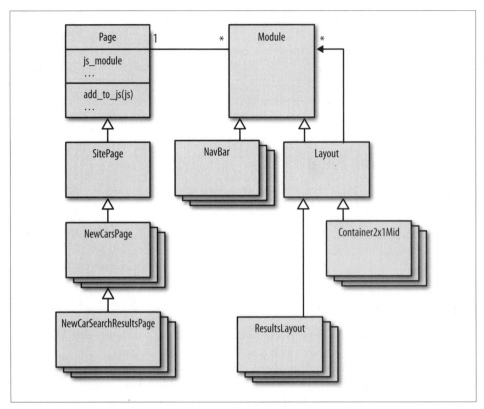

Figure 2-3. A class diagram for modeling a web page

Writing the Code

Once we have this model for a web page, it's relatively easy to use object orientation to write the code that represents it, as shown in Example 2-3. Again, we'll fill in the details for some of these classes in Chapter 7. For now, the important point to recognize is how closely the object-oriented code of Example 2-3 corresponds to the class diagram from Figure 2-3. That is, object-oriented programming has narrowed the gap between our thought process and the computer model.

Example 2-3. PHP from the class diagram

```
// These are the base classes for all pages, modules, and layouts.
class Page
{
    protected $js_module;
    ...
    protected $modules;
    ...
```

```php
    public function add_to_js($js)
    {
        ...
    }

    ...
}

class Module
{
    protected $page
    ...
}

class Layout extends Module
{
    protected $modules;
    ...
}

// The following class supports capabilities across an entire site.
class SitePage extends Page
{
    ...
}

// Page classes like this add capabilities across specific sections.
class NewCarsPage extends SitePage
{
    ...
}

// Page classes like this support capabilities for specific pages.
class NewCarSearchResultsPage extends NewCarsPage
{
    ...
}

// Module classes like this add capabilities for specific modules.
class NavBar extends Module
{
    ...
}

// Layout and container classes are reusable groupings for modules.
class ResultsLayout extends Layout
{
    ...
}

class Container2x1Mid extends Layout
{
    ...
}
```

Achieving Modularity

Another important aspect of object orientation is how well it facilitates modularity, which is essential to improving reusability, maintainability, and reliability over the life of a large web application. To achieve modularity, we need to build large applications from components that are *cohesive* (i.e., neatly *encapsulated* and *abstracted*) and *loosely coupled*.

Objects in object-oriented systems are naturally cohesive because their data and methods are grouped into nicely encapsulated bundles by virtue of being defined within a class (or in object-based languages, added to an object). Furthermore, you can abstract the implementation details for an object by hiding its data members and certain methods with private or protected visibility (see "Classes and Interfaces" on page 15). As a result, the data and methods tend to stick together.

Objects are loosely coupled when they aren't overly dependent on one another and they interact in clearly defined ways. The public and protected methods of an object establish a clear interface for how others may interact with it. You can see the dependencies among objects by visualizing a class diagram as a dependency graph. A dependency exists wherever there is a generalization or association (see Figure 2-4).

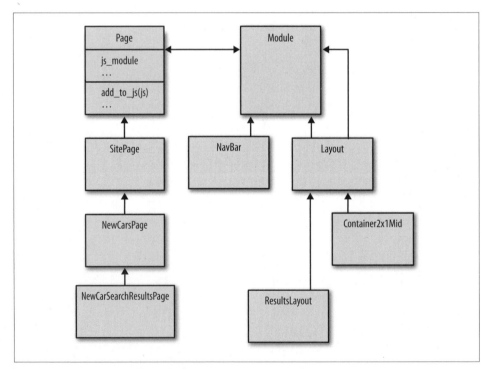

Figure 2-4. The dependencies within a web page

Object-Oriented PHP

This section presents some of the fundamentals behind object orientation in PHP 5. PHP 4 has object orientation as well, but its implementation is quite limited. This section will provide just enough detail to help you understand the examples in this book and to recognize important differences between object orientation in PHP and JavaScript. You can learn more about object orientation in PHP 5 at *http://php.net*.

Classes and Interfaces

As we mentioned at the start of the chapter, PHP is a *class-based language*. This means that you declare classes and create instances of objects from them. PHP also supports interfaces, which allow you to specify the methods that derived classes must implement in the future, without providing an implementation yourself.

Declaring a class

Example 2-4 illustrates declaring a class in PHP. This class has two data members (`$balance` and `$minimum`) and two methods (`deposit` and `withdraw`). It also defines a constructor, which we'll discuss in a moment.

Example 2-4. Declaring a class in PHP

```php
class Account
{
    protected $balance;
    protected $minimum;

    public function __construct($amount, $lowest)
    {
        ...
    }

    public function deposit($amount)
    {
        ...
    }

    public function withdraw($amount)
    {
        ...
    }
}
```

Using objects

To use a class, create an instance of it using `new`. If the constructor for the class accepts any parameters, pass those to the constructor as with any other method you implement:

```php
$account = new Account(500, 200);
```

Within a method of the class, to access data members or other methods, use `$this`, which refers to the invoking object itself:

```php
public function withdraw($amount)
{
    $this->balance -= $amount;
}
```

To call a method (or access a data member) from outside the object, use an instance of the class to invoke the method:

```php
$account = new Account(500, 200);
$account->withdraw(100);
```

Constructors

You can define your own constructor for a class. The constructor is called automatically to initialize the object whenever you create an instance of the class. To define a constructor, implement __construct (one of several *magic methods* in PHP) for the class with whatever parameters you need:

```php
public function __construct($amount, $lowest)
{
    // Initialize the data members when a new object is instantiated.
    $this->balance = $amount;
    $this->minimum = $lowest;
}
```

Information hiding

Every member of a class (data member or method) has a specific visibility that defines where it can be accessed. PHP defines three visibilities: *public*, *protected*, and *private*:

public
> The public members of a class are accessible from anywhere (inside or outside of the class). Use public for members of a class to which users of the class and implementers should have access.

protected
> The protected members of a class are accessible only from the class that defined them as well as within any classes that inherit from the class. Use protected for members of a class to which you are willing to give access to implementers of a class derived from your class.

private
> The private members of a class are accessible only within the class that defined the members. Use private for members to which only implementers of the class should be allowed access.

Give a member a specific visibility by writing `public`, `protected`, or `private` in its declaration:

```
class Account
{
   protected $balance;
   protected $minimum;

   ...

   public function deposit($amount);
   {
      ...
   }
}
```

Class data members

Class data members, also called *static data members*, are shared among all instances of a class. Declare a data member as static with the keyword `static`:

```
class Account
{
   protected $balance;
   protected $minimum;

   // The static member $deposits is shared by all Account instances.
   protected static $deposits = 0;

   ...
}
```

As the example suggests, a good use for class data members is for storing data that pertains to the class rather than to any one instance of the class. Here, the `$deposits` member is the total number of deposits made across all account instances. The number of deposits is a feature of the class itself, not any single account.

Access static data members outside the class (if the visibility permits it) using the scope operator (`::`) prefixed with the name of the class:

```
// You could do this outside of the class if $deposits were public.
$count = Account::$deposits;
```

Access static data members from within the class using the scope operator prefixed with the keyword `self`:

```
public function deposit($amount)
{
   $this->balance += $amount;

   // Count the total deposits made across all instances of Account.
   self::$deposits++;
}
```

Class methods

Class methods, also called *static methods*, are callable without an instance of a class. Declare a method as static with the keyword `static`:

```
class Account
{
    // The static member $deposits is shared by all Account instances.
    protected static $deposits = 0;

    ...

    // The static method here is callable without an invoking object.
    public static function increment_deposits()
    {
        self::$deposits++;
    }
}
```

 Because there is no invoking object for static methods, you cannot use `$this` within a static method.

Invoke static methods outside the class (if their visibility permits it) using the scope operator prefixed with the name of the class:

```
Account::increment_deposits();
```

Invoke static methods from within the class using the scope operator prefixed with the keyword `self`:

```
public function deposit($amount)
{
    $this->balance += $amount;

    // Count the number of deposits made across all Account instances.
    self::increment_deposits();
}
```

Declaring an interface

Interfaces allow you to specify the methods that derived classes must implement without providing an implementation yourself. If we had wanted to leave it up to derived classes to determine how to implement withdrawals and deposits for accounts, we could declare `Account` as an interface:

```
interface Account
{
    public function deposit($amount);
    public function withdraw($amount);
}
```

All methods in an interface must be public, and the class that implements the interface must use the exact same method signatures as defined in the interface. Because an interface doesn't implement anything, you cannot construct an object from an interface; it must be implemented by a class first.

Inheritance in PHP

The real power of object orientation comes from inheritance. A class that inherits from (or extends) a base class has access to the public and protected members of the base class. The class that inherits from the base class can also override the methods that were implemented in the base class.

Extending classes

Example 2-5 shows how to extend a class. The resulting BankAccount class inherits the members of Account that we saw earlier under "Classes and Interfaces" on page 15 and defines some additional members of its own.

Example 2-5. Extending a class in PHP

```
class BankAccount extends Account
{
    protected $interest;

    public function __construct($amount, $lowest, $rate)
    {
        // Call the constructor for the class that this class extends.
        parent::__construct($amount, $lowest);

        // Do anything else that you require to initialize this class.
        $this->interest = $rate;
    }

    public function accrue_interest($period)
    {
        // This class can access the protected members of the base class.
        $this->balance += ($this->balance * $this->interest) / $period;
    }
}
```

The class in Example 2-5 also demonstrates a common practice in PHP: calling the constructor of the base class explicitly using parent::__construct as the first task within the constructor of the derived class. Many object-oriented languages handle this for you, but you have to do it explicitly in PHP. A class may be extended directly from only one class at a time in PHP.

Implementing interfaces

If you declared `Account` as an interface, thereby deferring the implementation of its methods for a class to handle in the future, you implement its interface using the keyword `implements` rather than `extends`. Example 2-6 illustrates implementing an interface.

Example 2-6. Implementing an interface in PHP

```
class BankAccount implements Account
{
    protected $balance;
    protected $minimum;

    protected $interest;

    public function __construct($amount, $lowest)
    {
        ...
    }

    public function deposit($amount)
    {
        ...
    }

    public function withdraw($amount)
    {
        ...
    }

    // You can add you own methods as well as implementing the others.
    public function accrue_interest($period)
    {
        ...
    }
}
```

You can configure a class to implement more than one interface by separating the names of the interfaces with commas.

Abstract classes

Sometimes you want to provide part of an implementation for a class, but you do not want to allow instances of the class to be created until a more specific class extends it. An interface doesn't help with this because you can't include any bodies for methods in an interface. Instead, you can enforce your policy by declaring a class with the keyword `abstract`. You cannot create an instance of an abstract class; you need to extend the class and create instances of the extended classes.

Declare the methods for which you want to provide no implementation with the key-word `abstract`. Any class that contains an abstract method must itself be declared abstract. Example 2-7 illustrates declaring an abstract class.

Example 2-7. Declaring an abstract class in PHP

```
abstract class Account
{
   protected $balance;
   protected $minimum;

   public function __construct($amount, $lowest)
   {
      ...
   }

   abstract public function deposit($amount);
   abstract public function withdraw($amount);
}
```

Final methods

To specify that you do not want to allow a method to be overridden in a derived class, declare the method with the keyword `final`. Example 2-8 illustrates declaring a method as a final method.

Example 2-8. Declaring a final method in PHP

```
class Account
{
   protected $balance;
   protected $minimum;

   public function __construct($amount, $lowest)
   {
      ...
   }

   ...

   final public function withdraw($amount)
   {
      // No other class can override the implementation provided here.
      ...
   }
}
```

You can also specify that an entire class cannot be extended by placing the keyword `final` before the keyword `class`.

Object-Oriented JavaScript

This section presents some of the fundamentals behind object orientation in JavaScript. JavaScript is a powerful language, but many of its features, including object orientation, are not well understood. This is primarily because people just haven't explored them much. Douglas Crockford provides a good description of some of the misconceptions surrounding JavaScript at *http://javascript.crockford.com/javascript.html* and in his book *JavaScript: The Good Parts* (O'Reilly).

This section will provide just enough detail to help you understand the examples in this book and to recognize important differences between object orientation in PHP and JavaScript. A good book for learning more about object orientation in JavaScript is *JavaScript: The Definitive Guide* (O'Reilly) by David Flanagan.

Objects

As mentioned at the start of the chapter, JavaScript is an *object-based language*; it does not have classes. You create an object by adding properties to it. Properties can be data or functions (also technically data in JavaScript).

Creating an object

Example 2-9 illustrates how to define an object in JavaScript. This object defines two properties as data members (`balance` and `minimum`) and two properties as methods (`deposit` and `withdraw`). It also defines a constructor (`Account`), which we'll discuss in a moment.

Example 2-9. Defining an object in JavaScript

```
Account = function(amount, lowest)
{
   this.balance = amount;
   this.minimum = lowest;
};

Account.prototype.deposit = function(amount)
{
   ...
};

Account.prototype.widthdraw = function(amount)
{
   ...
};
```

Yes, those semicolons are supposed to be there after the closing braces. We're doing assignments, so each statement should have a terminating semicolon. Many developers leave them off because these assignments look somewhat similar to method definitions within classes in PHP, C++, etc. (where semicolons do not appear), and one of the bad features of JavaScript is that it does semicolon insertion. Semicolon insertion occurs when JavaScript assumes that you meant to add a semicolon and lets it go instead of generating a syntax error. Semicolon insertion leads to programming errors.

Define data members for an object using `this` in the constructor, which references the instance of the object being created. In other methods, as with the similar PHP construct, `this` refers to the object on which the method was invoked.

Using objects

Create new instances of an object using `new` followed by the object's constructor. If the constructor for the object accepts any parameters, pass those to the constructor just as with any other method you implement:

```
account = new Account(500, 200);
```

Within a method for the object, to access data members or other methods of the object, use `this`:

```
Account.prototype.withdraw = function(amount)
{
   this.balance -= amount;
};
```

To call a method (or access a data member) from outside the object, use an instance of the object to invoke the method:

```
account = new Account(500, 200);
account.withdraw(100);
```

Constructors

Give the constructor the same name as the class of object that it creates and use `this` to initialize whatever data members you need:

```
Account = function(amount, lowest)
{
   this.balance = amount;
   this.minimum = lowest;
};
```

When you invoke the constructor with new, JavaScript sets the prototype property of the created object to the prototype property of the constructor. As a result, properties that you add to the prototype property of the constructor appear to be properties of new instances of the object created with new using that constructor. Since you want to be able to use the same methods with all instances of an object, this makes the prototype property the ideal place to define methods, which is what we did earlier.

Information hiding

JavaScript does not have public, protected, and private keywords like PHP to affect the visibility of members. However, there are patterns you can use to achieve something similar to the private visibility offered by PHP and a visibility somewhat unique to JavaScript that Douglas Crockford calls *privileged*. These constructs, while very enlightening (and good examples of using closures in JavaScript), are not very common in practice, so we won't use them in this book. Most JavaScript developers using object orientation realize that the interfaces they define essentially will have public visibility and therefore need to document which parts of the interface should not be used outside that context. This is similar to what developers using the early support for object orientation in PHP 4 needed to do. You can read more about private and privileged members in JavaScript at *http://javascript.crockford.com/private.html.*

Class data members

Class data members in JavaScript are like class (or static) data members in PHP. They are data members shared among all instances of a class of object. Define a class data member by adding it to the prototype property of the constructor for an object:

```
Account = function(amount, lowest)
{
    // These data members are specific to each instance of the object.
    this.balance = amount;
    this.minimum = lowest;
};

// This counter for the number of deposits is shared by all accounts.
Account.prototype.deposits = 0;
```

Access class data members, whether from inside or outside methods of the object, via the constructor:

```
Account.deposits++;
```

Class methods

Class methods in JavaScript are like class methods in PHP. They provide a way to place methods within the namespace for a class of object, but are not associated with any specific instance of that class of object. Define a class method by adding it to the constructor's prototype property:

```
// This counter for the number of deposits is shared by all accounts.
Account.prototype.deposits = 0;

Account.prototype.incrementDeposits = function()
{
    // Count the total deposits made across all instances of Account.
    Account.deposits++;
};
```

Invoke class methods, whether from inside or outside methods of the object, via the constructor:

```
Account.incrementDeposits();
```

Inheritance in JavaScript

JavaScript implements inheritance using the prototype objects we discussed earlier. Recall that every object you create using new in JavaScript gets its own prototype property set to the prototype property of the object's constructor. To understand inheritance in JavaScript, we need to look in more detail at how this prototype property is used.

The prototype property of an object plays a key role in how JavaScript accesses the various properties (data members and methods) defined for objects. Each time you try to read a property of an object, JavaScript first checks the object itself. If it is not found there, JavaScript checks the object stored in the prototype property for the object. If it is not found there, JavaScript checks the object referenced by the prototype property of that object. This inspection of prototype objects continues up the *prototype chain* until either the property is found or you hit the end of the chain. On the other hand, when you write a property for an object, the value is stored in that object itself, so it does not affect objects up the prototype chain.

Prototype-based inheritance

Once you understand how JavaScript uses prototype chains, inheritance is relatively easy to implement and visualize. For an object to inherit the capabilities of another object, simply set its prototype property to a new instance of the class of object from which you wish to inherit capabilities. Example 2-10 illustrates inheritance using a prototype.

Example 2-10. Inheritance using a prototype in JavaScript

```
BankAccount = function(amount, lowest, rate)
{
    // Call the constructor for the object from which this one inherits.
    Account.call(this, amount, lowest);

    // Do anything else that you need to initialize this type of object.
    this.interest = rate;
};

// Set up BankAccount objects so that they inherit from Account.
```

```
BankAccount.prototype = new Account(0, 0);

// Add this method for handling a task unique to BankAccount objects.
BankAccount.prototype.accrueInterest(period)
{
    this.balance += (this.balance * this.interest) / period;
};
```

In Example 2-10, when we call `withdraw` (defined earlier for `Account`) using an instance
of `BankAccount`, the method will be found in the prototype chain even though
`BankAccount` does not define `withdraw` itself. That is, a `BankAccount` instance *inherits* the
methods of `Account`, its prototype. On the other hand, if you want a different implementation of `withdraw` for instances of `BankAccount`, you can define an implementation
of `withdraw` for `BankAccount`. This would be found earlier in the prototype chain, and
would therefore override `withdraw` in `Account`:

```
BankAccount.prototype.withdraw(amount)
{
    // Do something different here for withdrawing from bank accounts.
    ...
};
```

Example 2-10 also demonstrates calling the constructor of the prototype object explicitly to initialize that object using the `call` method provided by JavaScript. This is
similar to what we did with `parent::__construct` in PHP earlier. The `call` method
invokes `Account` (the `Account` constructor) with the first parameter (`this`) as the invoking
object and the remaining parameters (`amount` and `lowest`) passed as arguments to
`Account`.

Because many web developers are not familiar with prototype-based inheritance, it's
worth noting that in this book you can find more complete examples of prototype-
based inheritance in Chapter 5, where we implement a special type of selection list, and
in Chapter 8, which illustrates a basic implementation of the Model-View-Controller
design pattern with Ajax.

CHAPTER 3

Large-Scale HTML

There was once a time when HTML was king. Browser manufacturers moved hastily to shove it full of features as quickly as web developers demanded them. Unfortunately, these features often fell outside the original purview of HTML, and in many cases they were carried out in proprietary ways. Beyond the well-known problems of interoperability among browsers that bedeviled web pages for many years, the pumping up of HTML seduced web developers into relying on it as more than just a way to describe *what* a page contained. They began to use it for *how* parts of a page should look and behave.

In large web applications, the use of HTML for such commingled responsibilities creates a tangled mess that prevents you from being nimble in structuring your site or guiding visitors through it. Conceptually, this is because doing layout in HTML obscures a page's *information architecture*, a model or concept of data that makes the data more readily understandable and digestible in a variety of contexts. When the information architecture of a large web application is not clear, it adversely affects reusability, maintainability, and reliability. Well-constructed HTML does not obscure information architecture, but instead reflects it.

> Tenet 3: Large-scale HTML is semantic, devoid of presentation elements other than those inherent in the information architecture, and pluggable into a wide variety of contexts in the form of easily identifiable sections.

This chapter addresses Tenet 3, restated here from the complete list of tenets for developing large web applications provided in Chapter 1. This chapter begins by looking at the HTML for a simple module and presenting alternative examples that reflect its information architecture from worst to best. Next, we'll examine a detailed list of reasons why a good information architecture for a module is important, and expound on a set of tags to avoid along with a set of tags with good semantic value (some of which don't see widespread use yet). Finally, we'll look at how the rigor of XHTML (Extensible Hypertext Markup Language) is beneficial to information architecture, and explore RDFa (Resource Description Framework with Attributes) for adding further meaning to our markup. We'll conclude with a bit about HTML 5, the latest version of HTML; however, HTML 5 is still in the working draft stage as this book goes to print, so it's not yet supported across the major browsers.

Modular HTML

When assembling a web page, you should make choices that increase the capability of components and portions of the page to be repurposed and reused in as wide a range of scenarios as possible. Even if you don't plan to reuse pieces, assembling the page from smaller individual components will make it more reliable and easier to maintain. A component can be anything from a small control (e.g., a paginator) to an entire section of a page (e.g., a list of search results).

To determine the potential components on a page, you need to deconstruct the page into a reasonable set of *modules*. Chapter 7 presents a more unified concept of a module as an entity that includes everything you need to make a component independently functioning and cohesive. For now, let's look at one module as an example (see Figure 3-1) and focus on how to make its HTML a good reflection of its information architecture.

Figure 3-1. The New Car Reviews module

A Bad Example: Using a Table and Presentation Markup

Example 3-1 presents an ill-fated but not altogether uncommon attempt to create an information architecture for the New Car Reviews module. The problem in this example is that it uses HTML markup more to define the layout than to reveal the information architecture of the module.

Example 3-1. A bad example of HTML for the New Car Reviews module

```
<table>
  <thead>
    <tr>
      <th>
        <big>New Car Reviews</big>
      </th>
      <th>
        <small>
          <a href="http://...">The Car Connection</a>
        </small>
      </th>
    </tr>
  </thead>
  <tbody>
    <tr>
      <td colspan="2">
        <p>
          <b>2009 Honda Accord</b> <i>(from $21,905)</i>.
        </p>
        <a href="http://.../reviews/00001/">Read the review</a>
      </td>
    </tr>
    <tr>
      <td colspan="2">
        <p>
          <b>2009 Toyota Prius</b> <i>(from $22,000)</i>.
        </p>
        <a href="http://.../reviews/00002/">Read the review</a>
      </td>
    </tr>
    <tr>
      <td colspan="2">
        <p>
          <b>2009 Nissan Altima</b> <i>(from $19,900)</i>.
        </p>
        <a href="http://.../reviews/00003/">Read the review</a>
      </td>
    </tr>
    <tr>
      <td colspan="2">
        <form method="post" action="http://.../email/">
          <p>
            Get our most recent reviews each month:
          </p>
          <small>Email</small><br />
          <input type="text" name="nwcreveml" value="" /><br />
          <p>
            <input type="submit" name="nwcrevsub" value="Sign
              Up" />
          </p>
        </form>
      </td>
    </tr>
```

```
    </tbody>
</table>
```

First, everything has been placed within a table to achieve a presentation in which some elements appear side by side while others appear above or below each other. In fact, the developer has gone to a lot of trouble to create a two-column table simply to left-justify "New Car Reviews" while right-justifying "The Car Connection" on the top line; all the other `tr` and `td` elements are redundant. Naturally, the columns in the `th` header have nothing to do with the "rows" underneath it; the table is being used simply for visual effect.

From a standpoint of information architecture, tables are for tabular data; we'll look at better ways to achieve a side-by-side presentation in Chapter 4. The limitations of misusing table elements will bite you if the page has to be used for new purposes, such as for display on a mobile device or providing information in a web service.

Another problem is the heavy use of the purely presentational elements `b`, `i`, `big`, and `small`. These describe how we want things to appear, not what information the elements enclose. Markup like this is also often accompanied by HTML attributes such as `width`, and `border` that also serve only a presentational purpose (although I have avoided showing them here). The HTML standard has accumulated an astounding number of such attributes, but they have no place in large-scale HTML.

A Better Example: Using CSS

Example 3-2 presents a better attempt to reflect the information architecture for the New Car Reviews module.

Example 3-2. A better example of HTML for the New Car Reviews module

```
<div id="nwcrev">
   <span class="head">
     New Car Reviews
   </span>
   <span class="name">
      <a href="http://...">The Car Connection</a>
   </span>
   <div class="list">
     <div class="item">
        <p>
           <strong>2009 Honda Accord</strong>
           <em>(from $21,905)</em>.
        </p>
        <a href="http://.../reviews/00001/">Read the review</a>
     </div>
     <div class="item">
        <p>
           <strong>2009 Toyota Prius</strong>
           <em>(from $22,000)</em>.
        </p>
        <a href="http://.../reviews/00002/">Read the review</a>
```

```
      </div>
      <div class="item">
        <p>
          <strong>2009 Nissan Altima</strong>
          <em>(from $19,900)</em>.
        </p>
        <a href="http://.../reviews/00003/">Read the review</a>
      </div>
    </div>
    <form method="post" action="http://.../email/">
      <p>
        Get our most recent reviews each month:
      </p>
      <span class="label">Email</span>
      <input type="text" id="nwcreveml" name="nwcreveml" value="" />
      <p class="action">
        <input type="submit" id="nwcrevsub" name="nwcrevsub" value=
          "Sign Up" />
      </p>
    </form>
</div>
```

First, we have replaced the various table-related elements with div and span elements. These immediately reveal a more systematic hierarchy that reflects the true relationship between the elements. In addition, we have added IDs and classes with good, semantic names that tell us a bit more about what the elements enclose. These also provide the hooks that we will require to achieve the desired presentation using CSS. Finally, we have changed the purely presentational elements b and i to strong and em because the meanings of "strong" and "emphasis" avoid specific connotations of presentation whereas "boldface" and "italic" do not. A good example of the fact that strong is better than b is that if we were to change the presentation of the strong element from boldface to red in the future, we could do it in just one place using CSS and wouldn't have to touch the HTML at all.

The Best Example: Semantically Meaningful HTML

In the previous section, Example 3-2 leverages the power of CSS to overload generic div and span elements. But div and span don't indicate that we're delivering a heading followed by a list, which HTML allows us do. Example 3-3, therefore, presents the best example of how we can use HTML to reflect the information architecture of the New Car Reviews module.

Example 3-3. The best example of HTML for the New Car Reviews module

```
<div id="nwcrev">
    <h3>
        New Car Reviews
    </h3>
    <cite>
        <a href="http://...">The Car Connection</a>
    </cite>
```

```
<ul>
    <li class="beg">
        <p>
            <strong>2009 Honda Accord</strong>
            <em>(from $21,905)</em>.
        </p>
        <a href="http://.../reviews/00001/">Read the review</a>
    </li>
    <li class="mid">
        <p>
            <strong>2009 Toyota Prius</strong>
            <em>(from $22,000)</em>.
        </p>
        <a href="http://.../reviews/00002/">Read the review</a>
    </li>
    <li class="end">
        <p>
            <strong>2009 Nissan Altima</strong>
            <em>(from $19,900)</em>.
        </p>
        <a href="http://.../reviews/00003/">Read the review</a>
    </li>
</ul>
<form method="post" action="http://.../email/">
    <p>
        Get our most recent reviews each month:
    </p>
    <label for="nwcreveml">Email</label>
    <input type="text" id="nwcreveml" name="nwcreveml" value="" />
    <p class="action">
        <input type="submit" id="nwcrevsub" name="nwcrevsub" value=
        "Sign Up" />
    </p>
</form>
</div>
```

First, we have replaced the span elements at the top of the module with an h3 element for the header and a cite element for the name of the provider of the reviews. These elements carry more meaning about your information than simply calling the elements "spans." In addition, we have used a ul element and multiple li elements to construct the list of reviews, since these also are a better reflection of what the elements really contain. Finally, we have used a label element for the label associated with the email address input. The label element in HTML is often overlooked, but is an important element that conveys valuable information and enables useful features in many browsers; its for attribute specifies the ID of the element to which the label pertains, in this case the input element for the email address.

We have also added IDs and classes to several of the elements to add more meaning about their roles and to provide the hooks that we may require to achieve a desired presentation using CSS. For example, we have added beg, mid, and end to the list items based on their places in the list. The hooks are also useful in JavaScript.

One way to test how well we have reflected the information architecture for a module is to observe how a browser renders it, with none of our styles applied. Figure 3-2 shows how the New Car Reviews module of Example 3-3 is rendered by most browsers by default. As you can see, the default appearance reveals the information architecture of the module rather well.

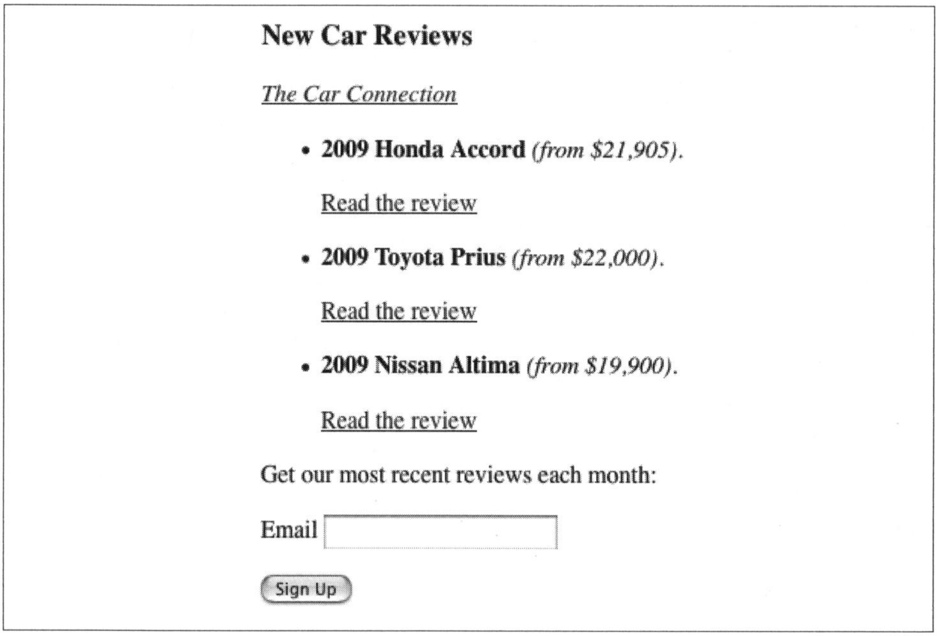

New Car Reviews

The Car Connection

- **2009 Honda Accord** *(from $21,905)*.

  Read the review

- **2009 Toyota Prius** *(from $22,000)*.

  Read the review

- **2009 Nissan Altima** *(from $19,900)*.

  Read the review

Get our most recent reviews each month:

Email [   ]

[Sign Up]

Figure 3-2. The default rendering of Example 3-3

The original developer of Example 3-1 may have rejected the use of a ul list because she didn't think the bullet-list layout style was appropriate. But all browsers have supported powerful enough CSS for several years to let you make a list look almost any way you want.

Example 3-4 presents the CSS that makes the New Car Reviews module look like Figure 3-1. It assumes you have first applied the browser reset and font normalization CSS presented at the end of Chapter 4.

Example 3-4. CSS for adding presentation to the New Car Reviews module

```
#nwcrev
{
    position: relative;
    width: 280px;
    padding: 9px;
    border: 1px #333 solid;
}
#nwcrev h3
```

```
{
   position: absolute;
   font: normal 123.1% arial;
}
#nwcrev cite
{
   display: block;
   width: 280px;
   margin-top: 3px;
   font: normal 85% verdana;
   text-align: right;
}
#nwcrev cite a
{
   color:#999;
}
#nwcrev ul
{
   margin: 10px 0;
}
#nwcrev li.beg
{
   margin-bottom: 8px;
}
#nwcrev li.mid
{
   margin-bottom: 8px;
}
#nwcrev li p
{
   text-align: left;
}
#nwcrev li em
{
   color: #999;
   font-style: italic;
}
#nwcrev li a
{
   color: #999;
   font: normal 85% verdana;
}
#nwcrev label
{
   display: block;
   margin: 5px 0 2px;
   font: normal 85% verdana;
}
#nwcrev #nwcreveml
{
   width: 274px;
}
#nwcrev .action
```

```
{
  margin-top: 10px;
  text-align: right;
}
```

Benefits of Good HTML

A module whose HTML reflects its information architecture is more reusable, maintainable, and reliable because it is more descriptive and honest. The following list, adapted from research at Yahoo! by Nate Koechley et al., describes why well-constructed HTML offers these benefits, and lists a number of others. Well-constructed HTML has the following characteristics:

Modularity

A module built using well-constructed HTML does not have to be enclosed by certain other structures. It encapsulates everything it needs within a single outer `div`. As such, the module can be used safely in a variety of contexts.

Lighter

Many web developers report seeing savings of 70 to 80 percent in page weight. When Microsoft made the transformation away from tables on its home page in 2004, for example, it saw an improvement of over 72 percent. When Yahoo! made this transformation, it found a savings of around 30 percent, since many pages were already optimized. A savings of 50 percent seems to be more common.

Faster rendering

A pure reflection of information architecture means less for the browser to download, less to parse, and generally fewer elements to organize in the DOM (Document Object Model), another model of a page's information architecture. In addition, when you avoid tables for the primary layout of a page, the perceived time to load a page is faster, because the browser does not need to delay rendering until the entire table is processed (although you can also make tables render without delay in modern browsers by setting `table-layout` to `fixed` via CSS).

Support for Ajax development

The terseness of well-constructed HTML directly affects the browser's creation of the page's DOM. A DOM that is smaller and easier to map to your information architecture helps you access and manipulate the page more easily using JavaScript, which is especially important for Ajax.

Backward compatibility

Backward compatibility means that you can be reasonably certain that things you build today will work for browsers of yesterday. All browsers support a core subset of HTML fairly consistently. At the very least, a good information architecture that uses these core elements can help your applications work reasonably well in browsers that you haven't been able to test and fully support, even if the presentation has some inconsistencies. In the worst cases, you can disable parts of the presentation more easily because it is isolated in its own layer.

Forward compatibility

Clean, concise HTML is more likely to continue working as visitors upgrade their browsers or adopt new ones.

Reduced bandwidth requirements

A lighter page weight, the normal outcome of making HTML a pure reflection of the information architecture, reduces bandwidth requirements. In addition, a good information architecture makes it easy to place most JavaScript and CSS in separate files that browsers can cache. When these files are shared across many pages, the bandwidth savings across a large web application can be very significant.

Better internationalization support

Internationalization touches many part of an application. By writing clean, concise HTML, you can be confident that the changes needed to support different locales will have fewer and more predictable effects on other parts of your application.

Support for multiple types of media

A good information architecture lets you apply the `media` attribute using CSS to delineate the types of media to which various presentations apply. The two most common types of media are computer screens (browsers) and print. A common approach is to provide one set of styles for all media types and hide certain presentational aspects (e.g., large graphics, ads, etc.) for printed pages.

Better search engine optimization

Search engines are primarily concerned with information architecture because it ought to describe what a page contains. The less you do to obscure your information architecture through the use of HTML for presentation, the more accessible your pages are to various search engines, which can find the key elements that your potential readers search for.

Better accessibility

Accessibility describes the extent to which any visitor can use your website, particularly visitors with difficulty seeing or scrolling around. Assistive devices, such as screen readers, rely on good information architecture to communicate effectively about what a page contains, especially as visitors navigate a page.

Visual consistency

A good information architecture provides more options to layer presentation across many elements in a consistent way. CSS selectors and stylesheets, which require a good information architecture to be effective, help you apply certain presentational elements to entire sets of elements as easily as to individual ones. This promotes visual consistency across a large web application.

Precise visual control

Presentation was always a hack in HTML; CSS is the modern and powerful means of providing presentation in browsers. When you use HTML to try to do more than just reflect information architecture, you risk inconsistency in support and absent features within the major browsers, as well as information architecture and presentation that are difficult to untangle when you want to reuse modules in different contexts. In short, you lose visual control.

More efficient redesigns

Better efficiency means that you can produce redesigns faster, more cheaply, and with less bug fixing. Clean, concise HTML helps you predict the ways you'll have to change your modules as you redesign your application's information architecture for new purposes and content.

Expanded audience

A good information architecture degrades gracefully and is accessible to more users operating in more environments. Even today, there are still plenty of people around the world accessing sites from old browsers. With a good information architecture in place, upon which you can layer other capabilities, your site has more reach, even if in a slightly degraded form. When your HTML tries to do too much, you risk your site appearing completely broken and unreadable.

A competitive edge

Taken together, the characteristics of well-constructed HTML presented in this section make large web applications easier to use, easier to maintain, and more accessible to a wide variety of visitors. This gives you an advantage in the market.

HTML Tags

Although all web developers are thoroughly familiar with HTML, many of us can benefit from a simple review of tags that offer sound, semantic descriptions for what they enclose. When we think about large-scale HTML primarily as a means of describing a module's information architecture, it becomes clear that there are some tags that we should avoid as well.

Bad HTML Tags

Table 3-1 presents a list of HTML tags to avoid; these tags are generally either presentational in nature or deprecated. We could present a number of tag attributes as well (e.g., `bgcolor`, `border`, etc.), but that list would be very long indeed, given the formatting options that have made their way into HTML over the years. Suffice it to say that if you find yourself considering any attribute with more presentational implications than uses for information architecture, you can be sure there is a better option in CSS. To learn more about any of the tags in Table 3-1, look at the index of detailed descriptions provided by the W3C at *http://www.w3.org/TR/html401/index/elements.html*.

Table 3-1. Bad HTML tags

Tag	Explanation
b	Presentational. Use `strong` instead.
basefont	Deprecated.
big	Presentational. Use CSS instead.
center	Deprecated.
dir	Deprecated.
font	Deprecated.
hr	Presentational. Use CSS instead.
i	Presentational. Use `em` instead.
isindex	Deprecated.
menu	Deprecated.
s	Deprecated.
small	Presentational. Use CSS instead.
strike	Deprecated. Use `del` instead.
tt	Presentational. Use CSS instead.
u	Deprecated.

Good HTML Tags

Table 3-2 presents a list of HTML tags that offer sound, semantic descriptions about what they enclose along with brief explanations of where to apply them. Examples of useful tags that tend to be forgotten include `label`, `cite`, `dl`, `dt`, and `dd`. By making good use of meanings that HTML provides for tags intrinsically, you can take advantage of the markup itself to provide meaning where you may have otherwise needed to use a class name. A rich use of tags also frequently can give you the uniquely identifiable hooks on which to hang your CSS. To learn more about the tags in Table 3-2, look at the index of descriptions provided by the W3C at *http://www.w3.org/TR/html401/index/elements.html*.

Table 3-2. Good HTML tags

Tag	Explanation
a	Anchor for linking to another page or a point within a page.
abbr	Abbreviations of any type. If an acronym, use the `acronym` tag.
acronym	Abbreviations that are acronyms (i.e., pronounceable words).
address	Address information about the document author or company.
area	Client-side image map area.
base	Document base URI (Uniform Resource Identifier). Relative URIs are resolved from this point.

Tag	Explanation
blockquote	Long quotation.
body	Document body.
br	Line break. Avoid for presentation; may be a semantic separator.
button	Button in a form.
caption	Caption for a table.
cite	Citation or reference to a source.
code	Computer code fragment.
col	Column for a table. Allows attribute specification for columns.
colgroup	Explicit grouping of columns for a table.
dd	Definition description within a dl tag.
del	Deleted text with respect to another version of the document.
dfn	Defining instance of a term or phrase.
div	Generic, block-level container. Be more specific if possible.
dl	List of definitions constructed using dt and dd tags.
dt	Definition term within a dl tag.
em	Emphasis. Rendered by default as italics, but do not treat as such.
fieldset	Group of form fields. Give a title with a legend tag.
form	Form for data entered by the user via input, select, etc. tags.
head	Document head section. Use exactly one per document.
html	Document root element. Use exactly one per document.
h1 ... h6	Section headers. Ideally, nest in order from h1 to h6 with one h1.
iframe	Inline subwindow containing its own document.
img	Embedded image.
input	Input for a form, which can be of many different types.
ins	Inserted text with respect to another version of the document.
kbd	Literal text to be typed by the user.
label	Label for a form input. Every input should have one with for set.
legend	Gives a title to a fieldset tag.
li	List item within an ol or ul tag.
link	Link conveying relationship information, typically for stylesheets.
map	Client-side image map.
meta	Metadata for the document, typically keywords, a description, etc.
noscript	Alternate content for nonscript rendering.
object	Embedded object that may be rendered by an external application.
ol	Ordered list of items constructed using li tags.

Tag	Explanation
optgroup	Group of options within a `select` tag.
option	Selectable option within a `select` tag.
p	Paragraph.
param	Named property value.
pre	Preformatted text (via indentation). Can be overridden in CSS.
q	Short quotation.
samp	Sample text.
script	Text to be interpreted as a script for dynamic control in a browser.
select	Selection list in a form.
span	Generic, inline container. Often, a more specific tag is better.
strong	Strong text. Rendered by default as bold, but do not treat as such.
style	Embedded CSS.
sub	Think of this in a semantic way. Avoid using it just to lower text.
sup	Think of this in a semantic way. Avoid using it just to raise text.
table	Table for data that is truly tabular in nature. Avoid for layout.
tbody	Body, or main content, of a table.
td	Table data cell (cells other than those in the header of the table).
textarea	Text input with multiple lines.
tfoot	Footer for a table.
th	Table header cell.
thead	Header for a table.
title	Document title.
tr	Row within a table.
ul	Unordered list of items constructed using `li` tags.
var	Instance of a program argument or variable.

IDs, Classes, and Names

You can assign any element in HTML an ID using the `id` attribute and a class using the `class` attribute. Because you should use an ID only once per page, they provide a great way to create a unique scope of sorts for working with a module. For instance, refer to the outermost `div` element with the ID of `nwcrev` for the New Car Reviews module in Example 3-3. By giving this module an ID, you can focus specific CSS on that module, as shown in Example 3-4, and easily access the module's elements in the DOM via JavaScript (see Chapter 5). Classes let you do the same for collections of semantically similar elements all at once. This is because classes are intended to be used on a page any number of times.

Don't confuse the `id` attribute with the `name` attribute. In various form inputs, the `name` attribute lets you give names to input values; these names are passed along with the values for scripts on the server side.

Conventions for Naming

There are a lot of opinions about naming conventions for IDs, classes, and names, but everyone can agree that establishing some sort of convention is important. In large-scale HTML, a good naming convention is key to modularity. One convention, demonstrated earlier in Example 3-3, is to use short groups of three to six characters for naming (e.g., `nwcrev` is the ID for the New Car Reviews module). From here, you can append other name segments of three or four characters to create further qualified names for use deeper within the module (e.g., `nwcreveml` for the `id` and `name` attributes of the email address text field).

Using fully qualified names like this promotes modularity because you can be assured that anywhere you use this module, its names will not conflict with those used by other modules. For example, if you were to place the New Car Reviews module on a page with another module that also contained a similar form input field for an email address, this naming convention would ensure that the inputs of the two modules would be passed to the server-side script with different names.

Because using short, augmentable name segments is compact and works well, it's the convention that we employ throughout this book. That said, the exact convention is not what is important here; whatever conventions you prefer, establishing a system of unique qualification that ensures modularity is the key.

XHTML

For quite some time, HTML has implied HTML 4.01, but browsers have been very forgiving of code that did not meet precisely with this specification. In fact, many egregious transgressions are politely rendered by the browsers in a reasonably elegant way. That said, this forgiving attitude by browsers has been a double-edged sword. On the one hand, it plays an essential role in ensuring that older documents can survive on the Web with little or no modification. On the other hand, it gives web developers a lot of room to be sloppy. XHTML establishes a more rigorous definition of HTML that formally helps web developers alleviate some of this sloppiness.

Benefits of XHTML

XHTML 1.0, the latest version of XHTML from the W3C to advance past the working draft stage, is a reformulation of HTML 4.01 in XML 1.0. This reformulation provides additional rigor and formality that earlier versions of HTML were never intended to have. Because XHTML conforms to XML, it offers web developers several benefits.

First and foremost, XHTML's strictness results in cleaner, more consistent code that promotes better maintainability and reliability. Next, XHTML is readily viewed, edited, and validated with standard XML tools. In addition, XHTML can utilize applications that rely upon either the HTML DOM or the XML DOM. Finally, XHTML is more likely to interoperate within various XHTML environments in the future should XHTML continue to advance. Since XHTML can be written to operate in older browsers as well as in XHTML-conforming browsers, there are few reasons not to start writing HTML using this higher standard.

XHTML Guidelines

Fortunately, it is relatively easy to make the HTML that we write conform to the higher standards of XHTML. The examples of HTML in this chapter, as well as in the rest of the book, are actually XHTML, for the most part. Most HTML is compatible with XHTML, but there are a few guidelines that you need follow to ensure your code conforms to XHTML while continuing to render properly in older and XHTML-conforming browsers alike. A list of these guidelines is presented below.

Proper nesting of tags

In XHTML, tags must be nested in such a way that tags are closed in the exact reverse order that they were opened. For example, Example 3-3 contains the following, where the tags are properly nested:

```
<!-- Yes, XHTML -->
<strong>2009 Nissan Altima</strong>
<em>(from $19,900)</em>.
```

Consider, in contrast, the following example, where the strong tag is closed before the em tag. This does not conform to XHTML:

```
<!-- Not XHTML! -->
<strong>2009 Nissan Altima<em>
(from $19,900)</strong></em>.
```

End tags and empty tags

In XHTML, every tag must have a corresponding end tag. In HTML, web developers frequently leave off closing tags for elements such as list items and paragraphs because browsers can infer where these tags should be closed. In XHTML, you must provide the end tags explicitly. Example 3-3 includes the following text, where we have correctly closed all list items:

```
<!-- Yes, XHTML -->
<li class="mid">
    <p>
        <strong>2009 Toyota Prius</strong>
        <em>(from $22,000)</em>.
    </p>
    <a href="http://.../reviews/00002/">Read the review</a>
```

```
    </li>
    <li class="end">
      <p>
        <strong>2009 Nissan Altima</strong>
        <em>(from $19,900)</em>.
      </p>
      <a href="http://.../reviews/00003/">Read the review</a>
    </li>
```

Contrast that with the following example, where there are no end tags for the list items. This does not conform to XHTML:

```
    <!-- Not XHTML!-->
    <li class="mid">
      <p>
        <strong>2009 Toyota Prius</strong>
        <em>(from $22,000)</em>.
      </p>
      <a href="http://.../reviews/00002/">Read the review</a>
    <li class="end">
      <p>
        <strong>2009 Nissan Altima</strong>
        <em>(from $19,900)</em>.
      </p>
      <a href="http://.../reviews/00003/">Read the review</a>
```

The requirement for every tag to have a corresponding end tag can make tags like br rather tedious to use; you would need to use `<br></br>` in XHTML wherever you had been using `<br>` in HTML. Fortunately, there is a shorthand for tags that enclose no content: include a forward slash before the closing bracket. Although XHTML allows a construct such as `<br/>` to accomplish this, it is advisable to put a space between the tag and the forward slash, like `<br />`, to protect against compatibility problems in HTML browsers.

In Example 3-3, we use an input tag (which always has no content), correctly terminated with a space and a forward slash:

```
    <!-- Yes, XHTML -->
    <input type="submit" id="nwcrevsub" name="nwcrevsub" value="Sign Up" />
```

Contrast this with the following example, where there is no forward slash before the closing bracket. This does not conform to XHTML:

```
    <!-- Not XHTML! -->
    <input type="submit" id="nwcrevsub" name="nwcrevsub" value="Sign Up">
```

Using the shorthand notation can be a handy way to denote empty content for any tag. For example, if you had an empty paragraph, you could write `<p />` instead of writing `<p></p>`. The following HTML tags appear in Table 3-2 and never have content:

```
<area />
<base />
<br />
<col />
<img />
<input />
<link />
<meta />
<param />
```

Case sensitivity

In XHTML, every tag and tag attribute is case-sensitive and defined in lowercase. In Example 3-3, we have the following for the `label` tag, where we see lowercase for the tag and its `for` attribute:

```
<!-- Yes, XHTML -->
<label for="nwcreveml">Email</label>
```

In contrast, the following example puts the tag and its attribute in uppercase. This does not conform to XHTML:

```
<!-- Not XHTML! -->
<LABEL FOR="nwcreveml">Email</LABEL>
```

Attribute values

In XHTML, all attribute values must be quoted using double quotes. In Example 3-3, we have the following, where we used double quotes:

```
<!-- Yes, XHTML -->
<input type="text" id="nwcreveml" name="nwcreveml" value="" />
```

In the following example, the attribute values use apostrophes (single quotes) or omit the quotes around the values altogether. These practices do not conform to XHTML:

```
<!-- Not XHTML! -->
<input type=text id=nwcreveml name=nwcreveml value='' />
```

Furthermore, you must specify an explicit value for all attributes that you use. This means that attributes that often are shown without values in HTML must be assigned something in XHTML, even though this may feel pedantic. Set these attribute values to a value the same as the name of the attribute (e.g., `checked="checked"`).

JavaScript, CSS, and special characters

JavaScript, CSS, and the special characters that these may contain require some special treatment in XHTML. Whereas in HTML you can wrap sections of embedded Java-Script and CSS between `<!--` and `-->`, XML browsers may ignore the sections. On the other hand, if you place these sections in a `CDATA` block, HTML browsers will ignore the `CDATA` contents. The ideal solution is to link JavaScript and CSS via external files, which is a good practice anyway. However, there may be times that you cannot do this entirely. In these cases, your document will not conform to XHTML.

XHTML is also sensitive to certain special characters. In XHTML, you need to replace greater-than signs, less-than signs, and ampersands wherever they appear in text nodes, JavaScript, and CSS with their character entities (e.g., `&lt;`, `&gt;`, and `&amp;` or their numeric equivalents).

As a result of these issues, many developers set their document types to the HTML 4.01 Strict DTD, even if coding to take advantage of XHTML's benefits. This lets you continue to validate your document using HTML validators while coding to the higher XHTML standard, albeit with a few compromises for now.

RDFa

Even when you have created a good information architecture for a module in HTML, there is only so much meaning that you can communicate in a standard way using the small collection of elements that HTML provides. RDFa (Resource Description Framework with Attributes) is an emerging technology for extending your HTML to provide additional meaning. It has special significance for the *Semantic Web*. The Semantic Web is an evolving extension of the World Wide Web in which web developers define the semantics of information and services so that the Web can understand and satisfy requests for content made by people *and* machines.

A key characteristic of RDFa is that it defines a standard way for web developers to annotate information further within pages that have been built for visual consumption. In this sense, RDFa attempts to unify the "human Web" (the one we see published as web pages) and the "data Web" (the one increasingly consumed by applications via web services). If we are part of the growing web community that believes that websites should be open for humans and machines to consume alike, we should consider extending the information architecture of our modules with RDFa.

 Microformats were an earlier attempt to add meaning beyond what HTML was able to provide. Microformats define standard structures using HTML tags and classes to represent certain commonly occurring data structures. RDFa has much loftier and more extensible goals in mind.

RDFa Triples

RDFa is fundamentally about creating triples that consist of a *subject*, *predicate*, and *object* to form statements. The subject is what you are making a statement about. The predicate is the relationship that the statement defines. The object is the resource with which the subject forms a relationship. You form these triples by adding attributes to your HTML. Some attributes are already defined as part of XHTML (see Table 3-3), while others are specific to RDFa (Table 3-4).

Table 3-3. XHTML attributes relevant to RDFa

Attribute	Explanation
rel	A predicate URI used for expressing a relationship between two resources.
rev	A predicate URI used for expressing a relationship between two resources in reverse.
content	An object literal used for supplying machine-readable content for a literal.
href	An object URI used for expressing the partner resource of a relationship.
src	A URI object used for expressing the partner resource of a relationship when the resource is embedded (e.g., an image).

Table 3-4. Attributes specific to RDFa

Attribute	Explanation
about	A URI subject used for expressing what the data is about. By default, the base URI for the document is the root URI for all statements.
property	A URI predicate used for expressing a relationship between the subject and some literal text.
resource	A URI object used to express a resource that is not visible in the document.
datatype	A URI for expressing a literal's datatype. The datatype is defined as part of a vocabulary.
typeof	A URI for expressing the type of a subject. The type is defined as part of a vocabulary.

Because XHTML is extensible while HTML is not, RDFa has only been specified in the working draft for XHTML 1.1. Web developers can use RDFa markup inside HTML 4.01 without experiencing adverse effects in various browsers, since the designers of RDFa expected this use case. However, RDFa will not validate in HTML 4.01. RDFa attributes validate using the XHTML1.1+RDFa DTD.

RDFa statements built from a subject, predicate, and object are based on a vocabulary to help convey certain meanings. You can define a vocabulary yourself or use existing vocabularies that RDFa processors are likely to understand. One such vocabulary is the *Dublin Core* vocabulary. This vocabulary defines properties about common resources found in documents, such as *title*, *creator*, and *subject*.

Applying RDFa

Example 3-5 uses RDFa to enhance the information architecture that we presented in Example 3-3 for the New Car Reviews module. In Example 3-5, we have added RDFa attributes to annotate the three new car reviews. This produces three triples (see Table 3-5). For each statement, the subject (a URI) is defined by the about attribute added to each list item. The property attribute for each strong element specifies dc:title for each statement's predicate. The object for each statement is the literal enclosed within each strong element itself. The value dc:title for the predicate comes from the Dublin Core vocabulary. To use this vocabulary, we have to define a namespace and refer to it using the xmlns:dc attribute, typically within a higher-level element of the page, such as the body element (see Example 3-6).

Example 3-5. The New Car Reviews module annotated using RDFa

```
<div id="nwcrev">
    <h3>
        New Car Reviews
    </h3>
    <cite>
        <a href="http://...">The Car Connection</a>
    </cite>
    <ul>
        <li class="beg" about="http://.../reviews/00001/">
            <p>
                <strong property="dc:title">2009 Honda Accord</strong>
                <em>(from $21,905)</em>.
            </p>
            <a href="http://.../reviews/00001/">Read the review</a>
        </li>
        <li class="mid" about="http://.../reviews/00002/">
            <p>
                <strong property="dc:title">2009 Toyota Prius</strong>
                <em>($22,000)</em>.
            </p>
            <a href="http://.../reviews/00002/">Read the review</a>
        </li>
        <li class="end" about="http://.../reviews/00003/">
            <p>
                <strong property="dc:title">2009 Nissan Altima</strong>
                <em>($22.95)</em>.
            </p>
            <a href="http://.../reviews/00003/">Read the review</a>
        </li>
    </ul>
    <form method="post" action="http://.../email/">
        <p>
            Get our most recent reviews each month:
        </p>
        <label for="nwcreveml">Email</label>
        <input type="text" id="nwcreveml" name="nwcreveml" value="" />
        <p class="action">
            <input type="submit" id="nwcrevsub" name="nwcrevsub" value=
                "Sign Up" />
        </p>
    </form>
</div>
```

Example 3-6. Namespace definition for the Dublin Core vocabulary

```
<body xmlns:dc="http://purl.org/dc/elements/1.1/">
.
.
.
```

.
```
</body>
```

Table 3-5. Triples from the RDFa attributes in Example 3-5

Subject	Predicate	Object
http://.../reviews/00001/	dc:title	2009 Honda Accord
http://.../reviews/00002/	dc:title	2009 Toyota Prius
http://.../reviews/00003/	dc:title	2009 Nissan Altima

Example 3-7 presents a further enhancement to the information architecture presented in Example 3-3 for the New Car Reviews module. In Example 3-7, we have annotated the title and creator for the reviews as a whole. In addition, we have used the content attribute to change the object of the triple for each review. By doing so, we can provide something more descriptive than what appears in the markup. Altering the content like this can be useful when you need to use different representations of information in the human Web and the data Web (the human Web did not require this clarification in the title, for example). The enhancements in Example 3-7 produce five triples (see Table 3-6).

Example 3-7. The New Car Reviews module annotated further using RDFa

```
<div id="nwcrev" about="http://.../reviews/">
   <h3 property="dc:title">
      New Car Reviews
   </h3>
   <cite property="dc:creator">
      <a href="http://...">The Car Connection</a>
   </cite>
   <ul>
      <li class="beg" about="http://.../reviews/00001/">
         <p>
            <strong property="dc:title" content="Review for 2009 Honda
               Accord">2009 Honda Accord</strong>
            <em>(from $21,905)</em>.
         </p>
         <a href="http://.../reviews/00001/">Read the review</a>
      </li>
      <li class="mid" about="http://.../reviews/00002/">
         <p>
            <strong property="dc:title" content="Review for 2009 Toyota
               Prius">2009 Toyota Prius</strong>
            <em>(from $22,000)</em>.
         </p>
         <a href="http://.../reviews/00002/">Read the review</a>
      </li>
      <li class="end" about="http://.../reviews/00003/">
         <p>
            <strong property="dc:title" content="Review for 2009 Nissan
               Altima">2009 Nissan Altima</strong>
            <em>(from $19,900)</em>.
```

```
        </p>
        <a href="http://.../reviews/00003/">Read the review</a>
    </li>
  </ul>
  <form method="post" action="http://.../email/">
    <p>
      Get our most recent reviews each month:
    </p>
    <label for="nwcreveml">Email</label>
    <input type="text" id="nwcreveml" name="nwcreveml" value="" />
    <p class="action">
      <input type="submit" id="nwcrevsub" name="nwcrevsub" value=
        "Sign Up" />
    </p>
  </form>
</div>
```

Table 3-6. Triples from the RDFa attributes in Example 3-7

Subject	Predicate	Object
http://.../reviews/	dc:title	New Car Reviews
http://.../reviews/	dc:creator	The Car Connection
http://.../reviews/00001/	dc:title	Review for 2009 Honda Accord
http://.../reviews/00002/	dc:title	Review for 2009 Toyota Prius
http://.../reviews/00003/	dc:title	Review for 2009 Nissan Altima

In the end, both Example 3-5 and Example 3-7 provide additional meaning for our module because they go beyond the HTML markup to add annotations that tell a processor exactly what certain pieces of the markup are. So, instead of having to make an assumption about what the cite element represents in Example 3-7 (e.g., *The Car Connection* has been cited as having something to do with the division that encloses it), you now know specifically that *The Car Connection* is the creator of the content at *http://.../reviews/*, which is a resource with the title *New Car Reviews*.

The value of RDFa depends on the presence of processors that do something useful with the RDFa statements in web applications. With a groundswell of interest in using RDFa data at major websites such as Yahoo! and Google, it's possible that modern web applications will soon be expected to provide relevant annotations as a matter of course.

HTML 5

As mentioned previously, at the time of this book's publication, HTML 5 is still in its working draft form, so a consistent implementation hasn't been agreed upon. However, it's worth keeping in mind that HTML 5, whenever it does settle down, is likely to bring with it a new set of semantic tags for creating good information architecture using HTML. Table 3-7 presents some of the structural tags being proposed.

Table 3-7. Tags proposed for HTML 5 to help with structure

Tag	Explanation
article	Independent piece of content of a document.
aside	Content only slightly related to the rest of the page.
dialog	Marks up a conversation between multiple parties.
figure	Associates a caption with content.
footer	Groups content that typically appears at the bottom of a section.
header	Groups content that typically appears at the top of a section.
hgroup	Groups parts of a header when it has multiple levels.
nav	Section of a document intended for navigation.
section	Generic document or application section.

HTML 5 proposes a number of other important changes to elements. Some examples of these changes include the following:

- New elements for common types of data (e.g., `canvas`, `meter`, `progress`, and `time`)
- New values for the `type` attribute of `input` elements to support common user interface components (e.g., `url`, `email`, and `datetime`)
- New attributes for many elements
- Changes in meanings for some elements and attributes to help reflect how they are used today
- The removal of many elements and attributes that were deprecated in earlier HTML versions

HTML 5 also proposes a number of changes and additions to various interfaces. For example, it introduces useful APIs (application programming interfaces) for creating web applications. These include a drawing API for use with the `canvas` element, an API for controlling audio and video, and an API for drag and drop, among others. HTML 5 also proposes extensions to some of the existing DOM interfaces.

Unfortunately, the lack of support for HTML 5 in the major browsers at this time makes it primarily something to keep an eye on for later. Even as it may be tempting to start to use some of the new elements in your markup, the pitfalls regarding potential inconsistencies among the major browsers in the future are still too much of a question to employ these for now. However, look forward to it in the future, because it is likely to include many features that will help you make an information architecture created in HTML more descriptive.

CHAPTER 4

Large-Scale CSS

In Chapter 3, you saw how a good information architecture based on well-constructed HTML provides a solid foundation on which we can layer other capabilities for modules within a large web application. In this chapter, we explore techniques for adding a layer of presentation.

The purpose of the presentation layer is to enhance usability and provide an aesthetic user experience by applying principles of good visual design. At its best, a good presentation plays a principal role in making a large web application more usable and appealing. At its worst, a poorly executed presentation can render an otherwise useful and meaningful information architecture completely worthless.

In web development, a well-defined presentation layer is implemented using CSS. This, in fact, was the original purpose of CSS when it first came on the scene in the late 1990s: it allowed for clear separation of a web application's underlying information architecture from its presentation. However, this separation hasn't necessarily guaranteed modularity. Our goal in developing large web applications is defined in the CSS-related tenet from Chapter 1:

> Tenet 4: Large-scale CSS forms a layer of presentation that is separate from the information architecture, applied in a modular fashion, and free of side effects as we reuse modules in various contexts.

In this chapter, we begin by looking at the tradeoffs between the various ways to include CSS. We explore important techniques with selectors, standard module formats, and CSS scoping that help you apply CSS in a modular way. Next, we view some useful methods by which we can position elements outside the normal document flow. These are especially important in the creation of layouts and containers, which are reusable enclosures that allow you to organize modules across a large web application. Finally, we examine a few examples of layouts and containers, and discuss some practices to provide a clean, consistent slate on which to layer a presentation.

Modular CSS

Once you have divided the components of a web page into reusable modules that reflect the information architecture (see Chapter 3), you can focus on how to give the modules the desired presentation through CSS. As mentioned earlier in Tenet 4, the CSS should:

- Have distinct modules of its own that apply to specific parts of the architecture (in other words, it should be well targeted), and
- Not produce unexpected consequences as a module is reused in various contexts (in other words, it should be free of side effects).

In practice, you may need to alter your information architecture slightly over time to accommodate highly stylized presentations. But even when making such adaptations, always try to maintain a meaningful HTML structure upon which you can layer modular CSS.

Including CSS

Let's look at three ways to include CSS in a web application: *linking*, *embedding*, or *inlining*. Although linking is generally the most desirable of these options, it is common to find some combination of these methods in use across a large web application, even within a single page, since each method has some benefits, depending on the specific situation.

Linking

Linking allows you to place CSS in a file, which you then apply by placing a `link` tag in an HTML file. This has desirable effects: architecturally, multiple pages can share the same CSS, while in terms of performance, the browser can cache the file after downloading it the first time. The following example links a CSS file:

```
<link href="http://.../sitewide.css" type="text/css" rel="stylesheet" />
```

Linking also allows you to specify a media type so that you can direct certain CSS rules at specific media (e.g., screens, printers, etc.). For example, when displaying a file for printing, you can remove nonessential items that would consume a lot of printer ink. To achieve this flexibility, specify `media="all"` as an attribute for the main stylesheets, then conceal certain parts of the page during printing by including specific styles for this purpose in a second stylesheet with the attribute `media="print"`. For example:

```
<link href="http://.../sitewide.css" type="text/css" rel="stylesheet"
    media="all" />

<link href="http://.../printers.css" type="text/css" rel="stylesheet"
    media="print" />
```

Once you modify a file that browsers may have already cached, you need to make sure browsers know when to bust the cache and download the new copy. Version numbers help you manage this. Incorporating a date stamp into the CSS file's name works well, and you can add a sequence number when updating the CSS file more than once a day (or you could use the version number from your source control system instead of the date stamp). For each new copy, simply bump up the version number as shown here:

```
<link href="http://.../sitewide_20090422.css" type="text/css"
    rel="stylesheet" />
```

Of course, each page that includes a link to the CSS file must also be updated to refer to the new version. Chapter 7 presents information on managing this in a centralized way.

Embedding

Embedding places CSS directly within a **style** block on a web page. One benefit of this method is that you can generate and include CSS programmatically. For example, PHP can generate CSS directly as it generates the HTML for the page. It also provides an easy way to override the styles in a linked CSS file on a per-page basis. Because browsers apply CSS rules in order as they encounter them (after taking into account the rules of specificity), the embedded styles must come after the **link** tags in order to override them. Example 4-1 defines a CSS rule for an element with the ID **nwcrev** using embedded CSS.

Example 4-1. Embedding CSS

```
<head>

...

<style>
#nwcrev
{
  ...
}
</style>

...

</head>
```

You can specify a media type with embedded CSS, just as when linking CSS. Example 4-2 illustrates embedding CSS for different media types.

Example 4-2. Embedding CSS with different media types

```
<head>

...
```

```
<style media="all">
#nwcrev
{
   /* Add styling normally needed for the element. */
   ...
}
</style>
<style media="print">
#nwcrev
{
   /* Avoid displaying this element when printing. */
   display: none;
}
</style>

...

</head>
```

Inlining

Inlining sets CSS styles for an individual element of an HTML page using its `style` attribute. You should use inlining very sparingly, because it requires the most effort to override and provides little opportunity for reuse. That said, you can make a good case for inlining in situations where CSS serves more than just a purely presentational purpose. Some examples include pop-up menus or tabbed interfaces in which certain elements need to be concealed by default. Because the CSS in these situations is more tightly coupled to the markup and behavior to begin with, it may make sense to communicate this situation by inlining the CSS. Another benefit in these situations is that inlining CSS also prevents concealed menus or tabs from being revealed briefly in the event that network latency keeps the linked CSS from being downloaded immediately.

Example 4-3 illustrates inlining CSS to conceal a pop-up menu. This technique is useful in that you can hide or show the menu by simply toggling the CSS `display` property of its enclosing `div` from `none` to `block` via JavaScript rather than reconstructing the menu in the DOM each time.

Example 4-3. Inlining CSS

```
<div id="msgpop" style="display: none;">
   <ul>
      <li>
         <a href="http://...">Contact via Email</a>
      </li>
      <li>
         <a href="http://...">Contact via IM</a>
      </li>
      <li>
         <a href="http://...">Add to My Contacts</a>
      </li>
```

```
      </ul>
   </div>
```

Applying CSS

However you include your CSS, you apply its rules to specific elements in the HTML markup with CSS *selectors*. A thoughtful use of CSS selectors is essential to the creation of modular CSS. Let's review the basic, most widely supported selectors so that we can then see how to best use them in large web applications.

IDs

IDs are unique identifiers for elements specified using an element's `id` attribute. You select an element based on its ID by preceding the element's identifier with a pound sign (#). For example, to apply CSS to an element with `id="nwcrev"`, specify the following:

```
#nwcrev
{
   /* Add styling for the element with the ID nwcrev. */
   ...
}
```

In large web applications, selection by ID plays a particularly important part in scoping CSS so that it is applied only within certain modules or certain pages (see "Scoping with CSS" on page 58).

Classes

Classes are identifiers for collections of semantically similar elements and are applied to HTML elements using the `class` attribute. You select an element based on its class by preceding the class identifier with a dot (.). For example, to apply CSS to all elements with `class="action"`, do the following:

```
.action
{
   /* Add styling for elements with the class action. */
   ...
}
```

Example 4-4 illustrates how you can use classes to apply different styles to items that appear at various positions within a list. Unlike with IDs, it is possible to assign multiple classes to an HTML element. In addition to beg, mid, and end, the example adds the classes odd and even for styling the list items based on this distinction as well. You could use the odd and even classes to create a striped list.

Example 4-4. Classes within a module

```
<div id="msgpop" style="display: none;">
   <ul class="menu">
      <li class="beg odd">
```

```
        <a href="http://...">Contact via Email</a>
    </li>
    <li class="mid even">
        <a href="http://...">Contact via IM</a>
    </li>
    <li class="end odd">
        <a href="http://...">Add to My Contacts</a>
    </li>
  </ul>
  <ul class="more">
    <li class="beg odd">
        <a href="http://...">View More Options</a>
    </li>
  </ul>
</div>
```

In large web applications, selection by class plays an especially important role in presentation switching (see "Scoping with CSS" on page 58).

Descendants

The descendants of an element are all the elements it encloses. For instance, a ul element has all its li elements as descendants, as well as all the elements they enclose. You specify descendants in CSS by placing them after the ancestor element, with one or more spaces between them, as shown here:

```
#msgpop .beg
{
    /* Add styling for elements with class beg enclosed by msgpop. */
    ...
}
```

In large web applications, a good understanding of selection using descendants is especially important when working with standard module formats (see "Standard Module Formats" on page 63).

Elements

Elements can be selected based just on their type. CSS selects elements this way simply by listing them without any additional punctuation, as shown here:

```
a
{
    /* Add styling for all links wherever they appear. */
    ...
}
```

Pseudoclasses, which let you specify a state for the element, are appended to element selectors with a colon:

```
a:visited
{
    /* Add styling for all links that have been visited. */
```

```
   ...
}
```

You should use element selectors sparingly on their own in a large web application, because they potentially affect such a large number of elements, unless that is truly your intention and all developers are aware of that intent. A better option is to use them as part of a contextual selector that targets a specific pattern of descendants:

```
#msgpop ul .odd a
{
   /* Only style odd links within unordered lists inside msgpop. */
   ...
}
```

Appending a class selector to an element selector (using no space between the element and class) lets you achieve even further qualification, as shown here:

```
#msgpop ul.menu .odd a
{
   /* Only style odd links in uls with the class menu in msgpop. */
   ...
}
```

In large web applications, selection by element is primarily useful when you have done a good job creating reasonably small, well-constructed modules that each have a clearly defined scope (see "Scoping with CSS" on page 58). You can also qualify an element selector further by requiring the element to have a specific ID (e.g., div#nwcrev).

Grouping

Grouping selectors provides an easy syntax to help you achieve visual consistency in a large web application. To group selectors, separate them with commas:

```
#nwcrev h3, #nwcrev h4
{
   /* Add styling for h3 and h4 elements enclosed by nwcrev. */
   ...
}
```

Specificity and Importance

Specificity is a value calculated to determine the winner when multiple selectors in a cascade of styles end up addressing the same element. For example, specifying an element by ID is more specific than using its class; specifying an element by its class is more specific than using an element selector. Because the rules for calculating specificity are often not at the top of a web developer's mind (although not difficult to learn), it is good to avoid relying on them too heavily in large web applications.

Declaring a style with !important overrides its selector's specificity. Its use is almost always a bad idea, because it hinders maintainability. In fact, it's usually a sign that you're obscuring a mistake that will bite you later. Instead of using !important, interpret the urge as a warning to look for a brittle section of your code. As the lifespan of the application continues, one use of `!important` inevitably leads to others as developers seek quick fixes in place of understanding the underlying structure of the application. This situation quickly becomes unwieldy.

Scoping with CSS

In a large web application, we expect modules to move around and be used in a variety of contexts over time. To keep your CSS reusable, you must always be aware of the scope in which your CSS applies.

Scoping within a module

In Chapter 3, we discussed the fact that because IDs never should be used on a page more than once, they provide a great way for us to identify modules in a unique way, provided we have a good naming convention. Assuming that a module's ID is unique, we can use it to create a convenient scope of sorts for any CSS that we want to direct only at that module.

Example 4-5 illustrates defining the CSS for two modules, the New Car Reviews module and the New Car Queries module. Because each selector begins with the module ID, each rule is targeted specifically at the module we expect.

Example 4-5. Scoping CSS within modules

```
/*
 *  New Car Reviews
 */
#nwcrev
{
    ...
}
#nwcrev label
{
    ...
}

/* Add more rules here for the New Car Reviews presentation. */
...

/*
 *  New Car Queries
 */
#nwcqry
{
    ...
}
#nwcqry label
{
    ...
}
```

```
/* Add more rules here for the New Car Queries presentation. */
...
```

Scoping at the page level

If you want to apply CSS to a module only where it appears within a specific page, use CSS scoped at the page level. Scoping CSS at the page level is particularly useful when you desire slight differences in the way a module looks on various pages, which is a common issue with reusability in large web applications.

For example, suppose you want a left margin for a module when it appears on the right side of a page and a right margin for the same module when it appears on the left. One solution is to assign the **body** element of each page a unique page ID, which gives you a way to target CSS for modules on specific pages where they appear. Examples 4-6 and 4-7 illustrate adding top and left margins to the New Car Reviews module and top and right margins to the New Car Queries module on the New Car Search Results page.

Example 4-6. New Car Search Results page

```
<body id="nwcsrspage">
...
        <div id="nwcrev">
          ...
        </div>

...

        <div id="nwcqry">
          ...
        </div>
...
</body>
```

Example 4-7. Scoping CSS at the page level

```
#nwcsrspage #nwcrev
{
   /*
      Only apply these margins to the New Car Reviews module on the New
      Car Search Results page.
   */
   margin: 10px 0 0 10px;
}
#nwcsrspage #nwcqry
{
   /*
      Only apply these margins to the New Car Queries module on the New
      Car Search Results page.
   */
   margin: 10px 10px 0 0;
}
```

A good guideline is to apply styles that affect a module's border and everything inside its border at the module level, but leave styles that apply outside a module's border (e.g., margins, floating, etc.) for each page to style based on how and where the module is used. However, if something within the module requires styling on the outermost `div` everywhere it is used (e.g., it needs to be floated), style that at the module level.

Presentation switching

When variations in a module's presentation require multiple rules and when these rules are likely to be reused across a variety of contexts, just relying on a page ID to achieve alternate presentations is cumbersome. In these situations, a better solution is to associate a class with each presentation and switch between presentations by setting the appropriate class on the outermost `div` for the module.

Figure 4-1 illustrates two presentations for the Popular New Cars module. In Examples 4-8 and 4-9, we use the class `default` to switch to the CSS for the default (wider) presentation. If we change the class to `compact`, we end up applying a different set of CSS for the module. CSS that is the same in both presentations is specified without qualifying it further as part of the `default` or `compact` classes. The CSS in Example 4-9 assumes that you have first applied the browser reset and font normalization CSS presented at the end of this chapter.

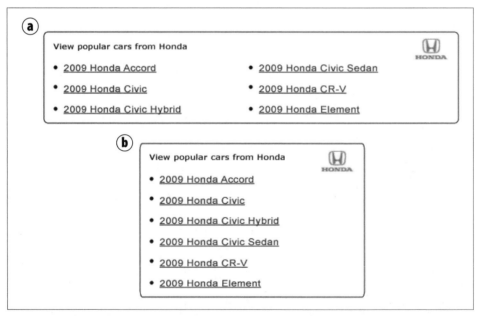

Figure 4-1. The Popular New Cars module: a) default version, and b) compact version

Example 4-8. The Popular New Cars module

```html
<div id="nwcpop" class="default">
    <div class="hd">
        <div class="tagline">
            <cite>
                View popular cars from Honda
            </cite>
        </div>
        <div class="logo">
            <img src="http://.../logo_honda.gif"/>
        </div>
    </div>
    <div class="bd">
        <ul class="pri">
            <li>
                <a href="http://...">2009 Honda Accord</a>
            </li>
            <li>
                <a href="http://...">2009 Honda Civic</a>
            </li>
            <li>
                <a href="http://...">2009 Honda Civic Hybrid</a>
            </li>
        </ul>
        <ul class="sec">
            <li>
                <a href="http://...">2009 Honda Civic Sedan</a>
            </li>
            <li>
                <a href="http://...">2009 Honda CR-V</a>
            </li>
            <li>
                <a href="http://...">2009 Honda Element</a>
            </li>
        </ul>
    </div>
</div>
```

Example 4-9. Presentation switching for the Popular New Cars module

```css
/* Apply this CSS to all presentations of the module. */
#nwcpop .hd
{
    position: relative;
}
#nwcpop .hd .tagline
{
    position: absolute;
    padding: 5px 0 0 15px;
}
#nwcpop .hd .tagline cite
{
    font: bold 77% verdana;
    color: #000;
}
```

```css
#nwcpop ul
{
   list-style-type: disc;
   margin: 0;
   padding: 0;


}
#nwcpop li
{
   margin-left: 15px;
   line-height: 1.3em;
}

/* Apply this CSS to just the default version of the module. */
#nwcpop.default .hd
{
   width: 630px;
   background: url(http://.../top_630.gif) #fff no-repeat;
   padding-top: 8px;
}
#nwcpop.default .tagline
{
   width: 475px;
}
#nwcpop.default .logo
{
   padding: 0 15px 0 0;
   background: url(http://.../mid_630.gif) repeat-y;
   text-align: right;
}
#nwcpop.default .bd
{
   position: relative;
   background: url(http://.../btm_630.gif) no-repeat;
   background-position: bottom left;
   padding: 10px 15px 15px;
}
#nwcpop.default .pri
{
   width: 295px;
}
#nwcpop.default .sec
{
   position: absolute;
   top: 10px;
   right: 15px;
   width: 295px;
}

/* Apply this CSS to just the compact version of the module. */
#nwcpop.compact .hd
{
   width: 300px;
   background: url(http://.../top_300.gif) #fff no-repeat;
```

```
    padding-top: 8px;
}
#nwcpop.compact .tagline
{
    width: 145px;
}
#nwcpop.compact .logo
{
    padding: 0 15px 0 0;
    background: url(http://.../mid_300.gif) repeat-y;
    text-align: right;
}
#nwcpop.compact .bd
{
    background: url(http://.../btm_300.gif) no-repeat;
    background-position: bottom left;
    padding: 10px 15px 15px;
}
```

In Chapter 7, we'll examine how to manage presentation switching in a nicely encap-sulated, programmatic way using PHP. In practice, highly stylized modules often re-quire a combination of presentation switching and programmatic changes to the information architecture.

Standard Module Formats

As a general rule, it may be worthwhile to group parts of modules into some common divisions. Besides adding further elements of structure to your information architec-ture, they can provide additional hooks for styling. For instance, Examples 4-8 and 4-9 apply background images for the rounded borders in the presentation. These are conveniently placed on the hd division (the header) and bd division (the body). Divisions of this type often contain other divisions. For example, an outer division with presen-tation for the header or body encapsulates an inner division that contains the content for either section.

Some examples of divisions applicable to most modules (just as they are to entire pages) are a header, a body, and a footer, to which you might give the classes hd, bd, and ft, respectively. This is the case in Example 4-8. Even when one of these sections is empty, it may be useful to add the section for future use, so we could have also added an empty division with the class ft after the bd division in Example 4-8. Undoubtedly, there are other standard divisions that you may choose to apply to certain modules in certain types of applications. *Microformats* are other examples of standard formats that you might incorporate within some modules. You can read more about microformats at *http://microformats.org*.

Examples 4-10 and 4-11 illustrate the use of standard header, body, and footer divisions for a module. In these examples, a module with the ID nwclst (New Car Listings) is nested within a module with the ID nwcsrs (New Car Search Results). Examples 4-10 and 4-11 also demonstrate that, although standard formats are useful, you do have to be mindful of side effects when applying them within nested modules (in actuality, the same problem exists when you use *any* commonly used class within nested modules). In these situations, when you apply CSS to the outer instance of the class, the cascading nature of CSS applies the same styles to any inner instances as well because the inner instances are descendants, too, just deeper ones.

Example 4-10. Nested modules using a standard module format (with side effects)

```
<div id="nwcsrs">
   <div class="hd">
      ...
   </div>
   <div class="bd">
      <div class="pri">
         <div id="nwclst">
            <div class="hd">
               <!-- This hd gets styling from the outer hd too. -->
               ...
            </div>
            <div class="bd">
               <!-- This bd gets styling from the outer bd too. -->
               ...
            </div>
            <div class="ft">
               <!-- This ft gets styling from the outer ft too. -->
               ...
            </div>
         </div>
      </div>
      <div class="sec">
         ...
      </div>
   </div>
   <div class="ft">
      ...
   </div>
</div>
```

Example 4-11. Applying CSS for a standard module format (with side effects)

```
#nwcsrs .hd
{
   /* Add styling for the header section of the nwcsrs module. */
   ...
}
#nwclst .hd
{
   /* The nwclst module hd gets styles from the nwcsrs hd too. */
   ...
}
```

Fortunately, the solution for guarding against side effects within nested modules is rather simple: use the unique module ID as a prefix for the common classes that may occur within nested modules. Examples 4-12 and 4-13 illustrate how this resolves the issue. Small, self-contained modules generally do not exhibit this issue; therefore, we will leave the shorter classes for the `nwclst` module (the inner one) intact.

Example 4-12. Nested modules using a standard module format (no side effects)

```
<div id="nwcsrs">
    <div class="nwcsrshd">
        ...
    </div>
    <div class="nwcsrsbd">
        <div class="nwcsrspri">
            <div id="nwclst">
                <div class="hd">
                    <!-- This hd gets only its own stlying now. -->
                    ...
                </div>
                <div class="bd">
                    <!-- This bd gets only its own styling now. -->
                    ...
                </div>
                <div class="ft">
                    <!-- This ft gets only its own styling now. -->
                    ...
                </div>
            </div>
        </div>
        <div class="nwcsrssec">
            ...
        </div>
    </div>
    <div class="nwcsrsft">
        ...
    </div>
</div>
```

Example 4-13. Applying CSS for a standard module format (no side effects)

```
#nwcsrs .nwcsrshd
{
    /* Add styling for the header section of the nwcsrs module. */
    ...
}
#nwclst .hd
{
    /* The hd for the nwclst module gets only its own styles now. */
    ...
}
```

Positioning Techniques

When you eliminate presentation from your information architecture, a significant part of how you position your modules now must be accomplished within the presentation layer. The document flow that is inherent in your information architecture will dictate to some extent certain aspects of positioning intrinsically—for instance, by default, modules appear on the page in the order specified—but the rest must be accomplished using CSS. As a result, a good understanding of some basic positioning techniques in CSS is essential. These provide the foundation for creating the layouts and containers in which to arrange your modules. The same positioning techniques are useful for positioning elements within modules as well.

CSS Box Model

Because positioning techniques are often sensitive to the size of our elements, it is important at the outset to have a fundamental understanding of the CSS box model and how it affects an element's size. The parts of an element that figure into an element's size, working from the outermost edge of an element inward, are its *margin*, *border*, *padding*, and *content area* (see Figure 4-2).

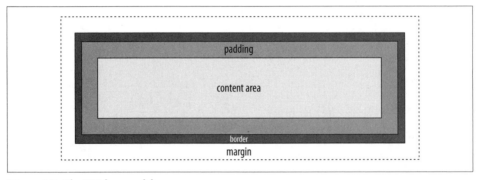

Figure 4-2. The CSS box model

Margin
> The margin is the buffer zone between the element and others around it. You specify how much space to leave around each edge. Even if your element has a background, this margin is empty and transparent.

Border
> The border is the line (or other stylized decoration) that forms a perimeter. You can specify a thickness, style, and color for the border.

Padding
> The padding is the buffer zone that appears inside the border of an element. You specify how much space to leave within each edge before the content begins.

Content area
> The content area is the innermost region of an element, holding your content. You can set its width and height, among other properties.

The size of an element in either direction (width or height) is the space in that direction (horizontally or vertically) occupied by all four of these properties. If you don't specify the size of the content area explicitly (using the `width` or `height` properties), the content area expands in that direction to fit the space required by the content.

Although browsers used to be inconsistent in how they calculated the size of an element, all popular browsers now handle the calculation consistently as just described. Example 4-14 shows the CSS for a module that yields a width of 320 pixels:

- 10 pixels for the left margin
- 2 pixels total for left and right borders of 1 pixel each
- 18 pixels total for left and right padding of 9 pixels each
- 290 pixels for the content area

The overall height of the module expands to whatever height is needed for the content since the height is not specified; however, this height will include an additional 20 pixels (2 pixels total for both the top and bottom borders of 1 pixel each, plus 18 pixels total for both the top and bottom padding of 9 pixels each). In the layouts and containers presented later in the chapter, we will fix the widths and let the heights expand to fit the content as needed, which is a common approach. In Example 4-14, we're setting the margin separately using CSS scoped at the page level to demonstrate margins changing based on where the module is used.

Example 4-14. Setting CSS properties that affect sizing

```
/* Styles for the module set for wherever the module will be used. */
#nwcqry
{
    width: 290px;
    border: 1px solid #fafafa;
    padding: 9px;
}

...

/* Scoping at the page level to target the margin for just one use. */
#nwcsrspage #nwcqry
{
    margin-left: 10px;
}
```

Document Flow

Although the goal is to keep information architecture and presentation separate in a large web application, they are, of course, related. The information architecture is largely responsible for the normal flow of elements on a page, and many CSS rules are applied based on the structure of the HTML markup. In the normal document flow, by default, inline elements (e.g., `span`, `strong`, `img`, etc.) flow side by side; block-level elements (e.g., `div`, `p`, `form`, etc.) appear on their own line. However, you can always alter this using CSS. To make an inline element appear as a block-level element, you can set `display: block` for the element. Similarly, to make a block-level element appear as an inline element, you can set `display: inline`. If you set `display: none`, you remove the element from the document flow altogether, and elements around it are closed up as if the element were never there. To conceal an element without removing it from the document flow, use `visibility: hidden`.

> Even though you can change the CSS `display` property for an element, you must always honor the original HTML-level display of an element within your information architecture. For example, regardless of what you do in CSS, you cannot put block-level HTML elements within inline HTML elements, because it may cause serious bugs in some scenarios.

You can also use CSS to move elements around the page and make them appear out of their normal order. The default, where elements flow down and across the page, is called *static* positioning. The most useful alternatives are *relative* positioning, *absolute* positioning, and *floating*.

Relative Positioning

You specify relative positioning by setting the CSS property `position` to `relative`. Relative positioning lets you position an element relative to where it would have appeared in the normal document flow without disrupting the normal flow of other elements on the page. It's often used to nudge an element slightly into a desired position without affecting neighboring elements. The following CSS uses relative positioning to position a citation within the `nwclst` module five pixels higher than it would appear otherwise.

```
#nwclst cite
{
    position: relative;
    top: -5px;
}
```

Absolute Positioning

You specify absolute positioning by setting the CSS property `position` to `absolute`. Absolute positioning removes an element from the normal document flow and positions it relative to the *containing block*. Because absolutely positioned elements are removed from the document flow, other elements are superimposed on the same location as if the absolutely positioned elements were not there.

The containing block is the first block-level ancestor of the absolutely positioned element that has something other than static positioning itself; if no ancestor qualifies, the absolutely positioned element is positioned relative to either the `html` or `body` element, depending on the browser. This lesser-known nuance of absolute positioning is very important because it has dramatic implications for the actual location where an absolutely positioned element ends up.

The logical choice, then, for establishing the containing block explicitly is to apply relative positioning to a chosen ancestor element. If you avoid specifying coordinates for the ancestor (i.e., using `top`, `left`, etc.), the element remains in its original position within the document flow, visually unaffected.

One important use of absolute positioning is to position block-level elements side by side, especially `div` elements with a set width (you cannot simply set `display: inline`, because for layout purposes, you usually require other benefits that block-level elements provide related to margins, borders, and padding). As long as you know which of the elements will be the tallest, you can use that element to occupy the necessary vertical space in the document flow while you absolutely position the other element or elements beside it. This approach to positioning elements side by side provides you with the benefit of not having to worry about special measures to get the parent element to size itself appropriately, unlike with floating elements (see "Floating" on page 70). Absolute positioning often works well for positioning small sections of HTML markup side by side.

Examples 4-15 and 4-16 show the HTML markup and CSS relevant to absolutely positioning the tagline and logo blocks for the default presentation of the Popular New Cars module presented in Figure 4-1. Notice that the tagline block, the first division in the module's normal flow, is the one that we absolutely position. This is required so that the logo block is superimposed at the same vertical position; otherwise, because the logo division follows the tagline division, the tagline would hog its own vertical block and the logo would get the next block down.

Now that we have positioned the tagline and logo at the same position vertically, the `text-align` attribute, applied to the logo block at the end of Example 4-16, pushes it to the right. Also notice that the `hd` division for the module has `position` set to `relative` so that it becomes the containing block for the tagline block.

Example 4-15. The Popular New Cars divisions for absolute positioning

```
<div id="nwcpop" class="default">
   <div class="hd">
      <div class="tagline">
         <cite>
            View popular cars from Honda
         </cite>
      </div>
      <div class="logo">
         <img src="http://.../logo_honda.gif" />
      </div>
   </div>

   ...

</div>
```

Example 4-16. Absolute positioning in the Popular New Cars module

```
#nwcpop .hd
{
    position: relative;
}
#nwcpop .hd .tagline
{
    position: absolute;
    padding: 5px 0 0 15px;
}
#nwcpop .hd .tagline cite
{
    font: bold 77% verdana;
    color: #000;
}

...

#nwcpop.default .hd
{
    width: 630px;
    background: url(http://.../top_630.gif) #fff no-repeat;
    padding-top: 8px;
}
#nwcpop.default .tagline
{
    width: 475px;
}
#nwcpop.default .logo
{
    padding: 0 15px 0 0;
    background: url(http://.../mid_630.gif) repeat-y;
    text-align: right;
}

...
```

Floating

To float an element, set the CSS property **float** to **left** or **right**. In some ways, floated elements are removed from the normal flow of the document, but they still affect the document's layout. In general, when you float an element, other content flows around it. However, if you float a series of elements in sequence, floating provides a powerful means of arranging block-level elements side by side as well.

The rule with floating is that if multiple elements occupy the same vertical location and all of them have **float** set to **left**, they appear in order from left to right. Therefore, you can use this technique to place two elements side by side. You could float one to the left and one to the right, but floating everything to the left makes for simpler code if you want to expand the layout to include more than two sections.

Compared with absolute positioning for arranging block-level elements side by side, floating has the benefit of not requiring you to know which of the elements is the tallest. This makes floating especially well suited for creating highly reusable, generic layouts and containers, which we will discuss in a moment. Figure 4-3, presented in the next section, shows an example of floating within a layout.

Block-level elements containing floated elements need to be floated as well to ensure that they expand as needed to fit the floated content. Alternatively, you can set `over flow` to `hidden` and `zoom` to `1` for the parent of the floated elements. The next section provides examples of floating in layouts and containers.

Layouts and Containers

Layouts are generic templates that define the overarching structure of pages. Containers are generic groupings of modules that you can place within layouts to support common organizations. Together, layouts and containers play a vital role in fostering reusability, maintainability, and reliability in large web applications. You can use them to define the standard sections in which to place your modules on a page.

Chapter 3 mentions the importance of exploring the design of web pages to find ways to reuse as many components as possible. Ultimately, building a page as a set of individual components makes it easier to maintain and more reliable throughout its lifetime. In addition to developing reusable modules, you should consider reusable traits within the structure of pages across your entire application, which you can exploit through layouts and containers. Not only does this promote maintainability and reliability within the code, but it also fosters a more consistent user experience across the application and contributes to its overall usability. Furthermore, layouts and containers provide a good opportunity for engineers and designers to work together to establish standard guidelines for designing and building large web applications.

In this section, we explore layouts and containers that are fixed width, variable height, and grid-based. These are some of the most common layouts in large web applications. That said, the principles we will discuss apply equally well for other types of layouts (e.g., fluid layouts where sections grow or shrink as the window is resized, free-form layouts, etc.), despite different implementation details.

 No matter what type of layout you choose, it is important to remember the dynamic nature of layout on the Web. Fluid layouts require that you relinquish control to the browser for the sizing and flow of content within any portion of the layout that uses a relative unit (percentage, em, etc.). Fixed-width layouts add a certain amount of control in the horizontal direction, but you still must anticipate the impact of letting content flow as needed in the vertical direction.

Example Layouts

Figure 4-3 presents an example layout well suited to pages containing search results or various types of listings; we'll call it the Results layout. Examples 4-17 and 4-18 present an implementation for the layout using the techniques discussed in "Floating" on page 70. In Chapter 7, we will explore techniques for inserting modules and containers into the layout dynamically. This way, you can reuse the layout for any page that needs the same overall structure. Let's look at some examples of the types of content that might appear within each section of the layout.

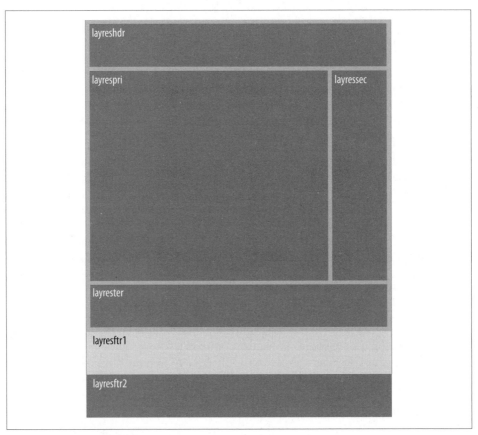

Figure 4-3. The Results layout

`layres` *(outer wrapper)*
    Contains no content directly, but provides overarching structure for the other sections in the layout.

`layreshdr` *(header)*
    Extends across the top of the page and might contain branding, banner advertising, primary navigation, and a query form for narrowing the search results.

layresmaj *(major)*
>   Contains no content directly, but provides overarching structure for the major part of the page containing the `layrespri`, `layressec`, and `layrester` sections.

layrespri *(primary)*
>   Holds the primary content for the page, which is the set of search results or listings.

layressec *(secondary)*
>   Holds the secondary content for the page, such as business partner callouts and additional advertising.

layrester *(tertiary)*
>   Holds tertiary content, which, because of its position well down the page, is intended for less frequently used modules.

layresftr1 *and* layresftr2 *(footers)*
>   Sections for footers. We define two sections to provide slightly different styling options (the second footer does not have the border on the left and right). Both might contain helpful cross-linking to other parts of the site.

Within the CSS, we float all these sections to the left. Because `layrespri` and `layressec` together fit within the width of their container (`layresmaj`), the result is that `layressec` appears to the right of `layrespri`. Our hardcoded widths ensure that the two layers take up the exact horizontal space we have allocated. We float the other elements on the page to ensure each section expands to fit any floated content within it. Recall our earlier discussion about this in "Floating" on page 70.

The `overflow` attribute on the inner elements is set to `hidden` to guard against letting any content that happens to be too wide cause problems when the content is placed within the layout. Setting `display` to `inline` for floated elements with margins avoids the infamous "double margin" bug in earlier versions of Internet Explorer that doubled the margins for floated elements.

Example 4-17. HTML for the Results layout

```
<div id="layres">
   <div class="layreshdr">

      ...

   </div>
   <div class="layresmaj">
      <div class="layrespri">

         ...

      </div>
      <div class="layressec">

         ...

      </div>
```

```
    <div class="layrester">

        ...

    </div>
</div>
<div class="layresftr1">

    ...

</div>
<div class="layresftr2">

    ...

</div>
</div>
```

Example 4-18. CSS for the Results layout

```
#layres
{
    float: left;
    background: #e3e4e8;
}
#layres .layreshdr
{
    float: left;
    width: 950px;
    overflow: hidden;
    border-left: 1px solid #d1d6dc;
    border-right: 1px solid #d1d6dc;
    border-top: 1px solid #fff;
    padding: 10px 9px 0;
}
#layres .layresmaj
{
    float: left;
    width: 968px;
    border-left: 1px solid #d1d6dc;
    border-right: 1px solid #d1d6dc;
    background: #e3e4e6;
}
#layres .layrespri
{
    float: left;
    display: inline;
    width: 750px;
    overflow: hidden;
    margin: 10px 10px 0 9px;
}
#layres .layressec
{
    float: left;
    display: inline;
    width: 190px;
```

```
      overflow: hidden;
      margin: 10px 9px 0 0;
}
#layres .layrester
{
      clear: both;
      float: left;
      display: inline;
      width: 950px;
      overflow: hidden;
      margin: 10px 9px;
}
#layres .layresftr1
{
      clear: both;
      float: left;
      width: 968px;
      overflow: hidden;
      border-left: 1px solid #d1d6dc;
      border-right: 1px solid #d1d6dc;
}
#layres .layresftr2
{
      clear: both;
      float: left;
      width: 970px;
      overflow: hidden;
      border-bottom: 1px solid #fff;
}
```

Figure 4-4 presents an example layout that is well suited to pages containing details about a search result or listing; we'll call it the Details layout.

Let's look at some examples of the types of content that might appear within each section of the layout:

laydtl *(outer wrapper)*
: Contains no content directly, but provides overarching structure for the other sections in the layout.

laydtlhdr *(header)*
: Extends across the top of the page and might contain branding, banner advertising, primary navigation, and header information.

laydtlmaj *(major)*
: Contains no content directly, but provides overarching structure for the major part of the page containing the laydtlpri, laydtlsec, and laydtlter sections.

laydtlpri *(primary)*
: Contains no content directly, but provides overarching structure for the leader and latter sections.

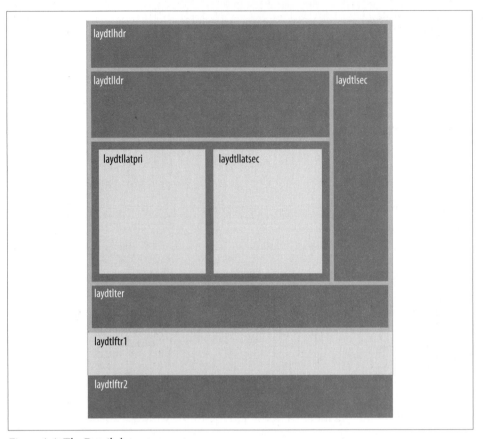

Figure 4-4. The Details layout

`laydtlldr` *(leader)*
 Contains no content directly, but provides overarching structure for the leader content.

`laydtllat` *(latter)*
 Provides overarching structure for the latter section containing the `laydtllatpri` and `laydtllatsec` sections.

`laydtllatpri` *and* `laydtllatsec` *(latter primary and secondary)*
 Holds the latter content, which is important content just beneath the leader section. In our example, the latter content will always be in a two-column format, which the layout reflects.

`laydtlsec` *(secondary)*
 Placed to the right to hold secondary content, such as business partner callouts and additional advertising.

`laydtlter` *(tertiarty)*

Holds tertiary content, which, because of its position well down the page, is intended for less frequently used modules.

`laydtlftr1` *and* `laydtlftr2` *(footers)*

Sections for footers. These serve the same purpose as in the Results layout presented earlier.

Examples 4-19 and 4-20 present the implementation for the Details layout. For the same reasons discussed earlier, this layout sets `overflow` to `hidden` and `display` to `inline` in certain places.

Example 4-19. HTML for the Details layout

```
<div id="laydtl">
   <div class="laydtlhdr">

      ...

   </div>
   <div class="laydtlmaj">
      <div class="laydtlpri">
         <div class="laydtlldr">

            ...

         </div>
         <div class="laydtllat">
            <div class="laydtllatpri">

               ...

            </div>
            <div class="laydtllatsec">

               ...

            </div>
         </div>
      </div>
      <div class="laydtlsec">

         ...

      </div>
      <div class="laydtlter">

         ...

      </div>
   </div>
   <div class="laydtlftr1">
```

```
        ...

    </div>
    <div class="layresftr2">

        ...

    </div>
</div>
```

Example 4-20. CSS for the Details layout

```css
#laydtl
{
    float: left;
    background: #e3e4e8;
}
#laydtl .laydtlhdr
{
    float: left;
    width: 950px;
    overflow: hidden;
    border-left: 1px solid #d1d6dc;
    border-right: 1px solid #d1d6dc;
    border-top: 1px solid #fff;
    padding: 10px 9px 0;
}
#laydtl .laydtlmaj
{
    float: left;
    width: 950px;
    border-left: 1px solid #d1d6dc;
    border-right: 1px solid #d1d6dc;
    padding: 10px 9px 0;
}
#laydtl .laydtlpri
{
    float: left;
    display: inline;
    width: 750px;
    overflow: hidden;
    margin-right: 10px;
}
#laydtl .laydtlldr
{
    float: left;
    display: inline;
    width: 750px;
    overflow: hidden;
}
#laydtl .laydtllat
{
    float: left;
    display: inline;
    width: 710px;
    overflow: hidden;
```

```
    padding: 20px;
    background: #ccc;
    margin-top: 10px;
}
#laydtl .laydtllatpri
{
    float: left;
    display: inline;
    width: 310px;
    overflow: hidden;
    margin-right: 30px;
}
#laydtl .laydtllatsec
{
    float: left;
    display: inline;
    width: 370px;
    overflow: hidden;
}
#laydtl .laydtlsec
{
    float: left;
    display: inline;
    width: 190px;
    overflow: hidden;
}
#laydtl .laydtlter
{
    clear: both;
    float: left;
    display: inline;
    width: 950px;
    overflow: hidden;
    background: #fff;
    margin-top: 10px;
}
#laydtl .laydtlftr1
{
    clear: both;
    float: left;
    width: 968px;
    overflow: hidden;
    border-left: 1px solid #d1d6dc;
    border-right: 1px solid #d1d6dc;
    margin-top: 10px;
}
#laydtl .laydtlftr2
{
    clear: both;
    float: left;
    width: 970px;
    overflow: hidden;
    border-bottom: 1px solid #fff;
}
```

Example Containers

Figure 4-5 shows two presentations for an example container. This container holds two modules placed side by side in a single row. Examples 4-21 and 4-22 present an implementation for a 2×1 container using the techniques discussed in "Floating" on page 70. The examples also use the techniques discussed previously for presentation switching to achieve different versions of the container that fit within different sections of various layouts.

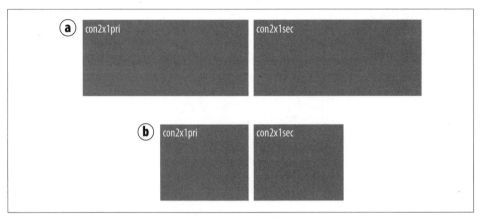

Figure 4-5. The 2×1 container: a) default version, and b) minimum version

The presentation selected with the class `default` consists of two sections with room for 370 pixels of content each. The presentation selected with the class `minimum` consists of two sections with room for 150 pixels of content each. In Chapter 7, we will explore techniques for managing various aspects of containers in a dynamic fashion. This way, containers can be reused on any page that needs the same arrangement of modules. Other containers might arrange three or four sections of modules.

Example 4-21. HTML for the 2×1 container

```
<div id="con2x1" class="default">
   <div class="con2x1pri">

   ...

   </div>
   <div class="con2x1sec">

   ...

   </div>
</div>
```

Example 4-22. CSS for the 2x1 container

```
#con2x1.default
{
    float: left;
    width: 750px;
    overflow: hidden;
}
#con2x1.default .con2x1pri
{
    float: left;
    display: inline;
    width: 370px;
    overflow: hidden;
    margin-right: 10px;
}
#con2x1.default .con2x1sec
{
    float: left;
    width: 370px;
    overflow: hidden;
}
#con2x1.minimum
{
    float: left;
    width: 310px;
    overflow: hidden;
}
#con2x1.minimum .con2x1pri
{
    float: left;
    display: inline;
    width: 150px;
    overflow: hidden;
    margin-right: 10px;
}
#con2x1.minimum .con2x1sec
{
    float: left;
    width: 150px;
    overflow: hidden;
}
```

Example 4-23 shows how you could use the default version of the 2x1 container within the primary content section of the Results layout presented earlier. From this example, coupled with what we observed in Chapter 3 about constructing an information architecture to create reusable modules, you can begin to see how a page built from a layout, with containers inserted as needed, and modules inserted into the layout and various containers, helps build modular web applications in which components are reusable, maintainable, and reliable.

Example 4-23. The default version of the 2x1 container within the Results layout

```
<div id="layres">
   <div class="layreshdr">

      ...

   </div>
   <div class="layresmaj">
      <div class="layrespri">
         <div id="con2x1" class="default">
            <div class="con2x1pri">

               ...

            </div>
            <div class="con2x1sec">

               ...

            </div>
         </div>
      </div>
      <div class="layressec">

         ...

      </div>
      <div class="layrester">

         ...

      </div>
   </div>
   <div class="layresftr1">

      ...

   </div>
   <div class="layresftr2">

      ...

   </div>
</div>
</div>
```

Other Practices

To ensure browsers render your presentations in a pixel-perfect manner, use the following practices to help write reliable CSS as you develop large web applications. The goals of these practices are to establish a consistent platform on which to apply your styles and to address inconsistencies with the way browsers render fonts.

Browser Reset CSS

All browsers provide a default set of styles on which your own styles will be layered. Unfortunately, default styles are inconsistent across various browsers. Without a common starting point on which to layer the application's own presentation, you end up making many more adjustments in CSS for particular browsers to maintain consistency. Fortunately, Yahoo! makes some CSS rules available in its YUI (Yahoo! User Interface) library to reset modern browsers to a consistent set of neutral styles. You can download the library and read its complete documentation at *http://developer.yahoo.com/yui*. To apply this CSS, simply add the following link before any CSS of your own:

```
<link href="http://yui.yahooapis.com/2.7.0/build/reset/reset-min.css"
    rel="stylesheet" type="text/css" media="all" />
```

Because it is helpful to see which properties must be reset, Example 4-24 lists the CSS. Alternatively, you can place this CSS directly in your own CSS file to avoid the additional server request with the previous link.

Example 4-24. Browser reset CSS from the YUI library

```
/*
Copyright (c) 2009, Yahoo! Inc. All rights reserved.
Code licensed under the BSD License:
http://developer.yahoo.net/yui/license.txt
version: 2.7.0
*/

html
{
    color: #000;
    background: #FFF;
}
body, div, dl, dt, dd, ul, ol, li, h1, h2, h3, h4, h5, h6, pre, code,
form, fieldset, legend, input, button, textarea, p, blockquote, th, td
{
    margin: 0;
    padding: 0;
}
table
{
    border-collapse: collapse;
    border-spacing: 0;
}
fieldset, img
{
    border: 0;
}
address, caption, cite, code, dfn, em, strong, th, var, optgroup
{
    font-style: inherit;
    font-weight: inherit;
}
del, ins
```

```
{
    text-decoration: none;
}
li
{
    list-style: none;
}
caption, th
{
    text-align: left;
}
h1, h2, h3, h4, h5, h6
{
    font-size: 100%;
    font-weight: normal;
}
q:before, q:after
{
    content: '';
}
abbr, acronym
{
    border: 0;
    font-variant: normal;
}
sup
{
    vertical-align: baseline;
}
sub
{
    vertical-align: baseline;
}
legend
{
    color: #000;
}
input, button, textarea, select, optgroup, option
{
    font-family: inherit;
    font-size: inherit;
    font-style: inherit;
    font-weight: inherit;
}
input, button, textarea, select
{
    *font-size: 100%;
}
```

Font Normalization

The ways in which browsers render fonts, especially when it comes to font size, are not consistent. Fortunately, Yahoo! makes CSS available in its YUI library to normalize fonts within the modern browsers. To apply this CSS, add the following link before any CSS of your own:

```
<link href="http://yui.yahooapis.com/2.7.0/build/fonts/fonts-min.css"
    rel="stylesheet" type="text/css" media="all" />
```

Example 4-25 lists the CSS for font normalization. As with the browser reset CSS shown earlier, you can place this CSS directly in your own CSS file to avoid the additional server request with the previous link.

Example 4-25. Font normalization CSS from the YUI library

```
/*
Copyright (c) 2009, Yahoo! Inc. All rights reserved.
Code licensed under the BSD License:
http://developer.yahoo.net/yui/license.txt
version: 2.7.0
*/

body
{
    font: 13px/1.231 arial, helvetica, clean, sans-serif;
    *font-size: small;
    *font: x-small;
}
select, input, button, textarea, button
{
    font: 99% arial, helvetica, clean, sans-serif;
}
table
{
    font-size: inherit;
    font: 100%;
}
pre, code, kbd, samp, tt
{
    font-family: monospace;
    *font-size: 108%;
    line-height: 100%;
}
```

Assuming you use the CSS from Example 4-25, Table 4-1 specifies the percentage to specify in your CSS to render a font in the number of pixels listed for today's browsers. Research conducted at Yahoo! across many versions of the most popular browsers has shown that fonts render the most consistently across browsers when you specify font sizes using percentages as opposed to points or ems. This is the reason that we use percentages for fonts throughout this book.

Table 4-1. Font sizing in modern browsers, assuming normalization from the YUI library

To render in pixels	Use this percentage
10	77%
11	85%
12	93%
13	100%
14	108%
15	116%
16	123.1%
17	131%
18	138.5%
19	146.5%
20	153.9%
21	161.6%
22	167%
23	174%
24	182%
25	189%
26	197%

CHAPTER 5

Large-Scale JavaScript

The behaviors supported by JavaScript in a web application form a distinct layer beyond the information architecture defined by HTML and the presentation defined by CSS. Although in many web applications it's important to consider how the application would operate without the behavior layer (for reasons of accessibility, printing, and search engine optimization, for example), the widespread use of Ajax has made the behavior layer in many large web applications more important than ever. In many cases, the designs for large web applications have advanced to the point that user experience designers, product managers, and engineers will agree that certain parts of an application, or even the entire application, will only make sense with a fully functioning behavior layer. Think of Google Maps, in which tiles are requested from the server as you interact with the map. This application only makes sense with a strong layer dedicated to behavior using JavaScript.

JavaScript has been around for a long time, of course, but early web applications rarely made much use of its powerful object-oriented features. Most developers simply wrote functions to accomplish various tasks, paying little attention to JavaScript's capabilities for developing systems of loosely coupled, highly encapsulated objects using prototype-based inheritance (see Chapter 2). A more advanced use of object-oriented JavaScript is an important aspect of achieving Tenet 5 from Chapter 1:

> Tenet 5: Large-scale JavaScript forms a layer of behavior applied in a modular and object-oriented fashion that prevents side effects as we reuse modules in various contexts.

We begin this chapter by exploring some fundamental techniques for writing modular JavaScript. We'll look at ways to include JavaScript in an HTML file and establish a scope in which the JavaScript for a module can operate without conflicting with other JavaScript in use within the application. Next, we'll explore some important methods for working with the DOM, which JavaScript applications have to manipulate in order to handle web pages in the structured manner we need. This includes a discussion of several important methods that all major browsers support as well as a look at methods in some popular JavaScript libraries that standardize other helpful DOM operations. We'll follow this with a look at techniques for improving event handling in large web applications and some examples of JavaScript animation. Finally, we'll explore an example of modular JavaScript for implementing chained selection lists.

Modular JavaScript

Once we have divided the components of a web page into reusable modules that reflect the information architecture (see Chapter 3) and have added a layer of presentation with CSS (see Chapter 4), we can focus on writing an additional layer to implement dynamic behaviors with JavaScript. As mentioned in Tenet 5, the JavaScript for a module, like the CSS for a module, should:

- Have distinct modules of its own that apply to specific parts of the architecture (in other words, it should be well targeted), and
- Not produce unexpected consequences as a module is reused in various contexts (in other words, it should be free of side effects).

Once you separate most of your JavaScript methods into modules, you'll find that it takes only a small amount of JavaScript unique to each page to stitch them together.

Including JavaScript

Let's look at three ways to include JavaScript in a web application: *linking*, *embedding*, and *inlining*. Although linking is generally the most desirable of these options, it is common to find some combination of these methods in use across a large web application, even within a single page, since each method has some benefit depending on the specific situation.

Linking

Linking allows you to place JavaScript in a file, which you then include by placing a `script` tag with a `src` attribute in an HTML file. As with CSS files, this has desirable effects: architecturally, multiple pages can share the same JavaScript, while in terms of performance, the browser can cache the file after downloading it the first time. Although it's common to place a linked JavaScript file in the `head` section at the top of an HTML file, Chapter 9 presents some very good reasons related to performance for placing linked JavaScript at the end of the `body` tag (i.e., at the bottom of the page). The following example links a JavaScript file:

```
<script src="http://.../sitewide.js" type="text/javascript">
</script>
```

Once you modify a file that browsers may have already cached, you need to make sure browsers know when to bust the cache and download the new copy. Version numbers help you manage this situation. Incorporating a date stamp into the JavaScript file's name works well, and you can add a sequence number when updating the JavaScript file more than once a day (or you could use the version number from your source control system instead of the date stamp). For each new copy, simply bump up the version number as shown here:

```
<script src="http://.../sitewide_20090422.js" type="text/javascript">
</script>
```

Of course, each page that includes a link to the JavaScript file must also be updated to refer to the new version. Chapter 7 presents information on managing this in a centralized way.

Embedding

Embedding places JavaScript directly within a page. One benefit of this approach is that you can conveniently generate and include JavaScript programmatically as you build the page. While it's common to place embedded JavaScript in the head section at the top of an HTML file, Chapter 9 presents some very good reasons related to performance for placing embedded JavaScript at the end of the body tag (i.e., at the bottom of the page). Example 5-1 illustrates some embedded JavaScript.

Example 5-1. Embedding JavaScript

```
<head>

...

</head>
<body>

...

<script type="text/javascript">
// Embedded JavaScript is JavaScript contained within script tags.
var GreenSearchResultsModel.MReg = new Array();
var GreenSearchResultsModel.VReg = new Array();

...

</script>
</body>
```

Inlining

Inlining JavaScript lets you add small amounts of JavaScript for event handlers to HTML elements within the HTML itself. These stubs of JavaScript usually call upon other JavaScript that has been included using linking or embedding. The following illustrates the inlining of some JavaScript for an onclick handler:

```
<img class="btnl" src="http://.../slide_arrow_l.gif" width="14"
    onclick="picsld.slideL();" />
```

Rather than using inline JavaScript, it is almost always preferable to register for events using methods within JavaScript that is linked or embedded (see the discussion later in this chapter about `YAHOO.util.Event.addListener`).

Scoping with JavaScript

In Chapter 7, we'll examine techniques for creating modules as self-contained components of the user interface. These modules will encompass everything needed (e.g., HTML, CSS, and JavaScript) to make an independently functioning and cohesive unit that you can use in a variety of contexts across various pages. To accomplish this, the JavaScript for a module needs to form a nicely encapsulated bundle as well. In this section, we'll look at how the use of objects in JavaScript makes this possible.

Namespaces with JavaScript

JavaScript objects provide a natural way to create namespaces in which to place the data and methods for specific modules. Once you have defined a method for an object, you invoke it directly through the object itself. For example, the following invokes the `slideL` method on the `picsld` instance of `PictureSlider`, an object that implements the behavior layer for a module that displays images in a slideshow or carousel-type filmstrip:

```
picsld = new PictureSlider();

...

picsld.slideL();
```

You should notice two important things here:

- Because `slideL` is a member of `picsld` (as opposed to the global `window` object), you can be sure that this use of `slideL` will not conflict with any other use in your web application.

- The `slideL` method will have access to data members within `PictureSlider`, which provides better encapsulation and abstraction for the event handler than a global one does.

A good convention for naming JavaScript objects that correspond to modules is to name them the same as the class used to manage the module on the server. For example, in Chapter 7 we'll look at an example of a slideshow module called `PictureSlider`, which encapsulates the HTML, CSS, and JavaScript for the module neatly within a PHP class. The PHP class is called `PictureSlider`, so we've created a JavaScript object called `PictureSlider` to address the behavior layer for the module. This convention works well, but the exact convention is not what is important here; establishing a system of unique qualification that clearly preserves modularity is the key.

The use of objects also gives you a way to group prototype objects into libraries. You can see examples of this in the YUI library, which we'll present later. When you call YAHOO.util.Dom.getStyle, for example, you're calling a method that is actually a member of the Dom object, which is a member of the util object, which, in turn, is a member of the YAHOO object. At the end of this chapter, we'll explore a prototype object called MultiSelect that we've placed in the MVC namespace. Whenever you do this, you need to check whether the namespace object already exists so that if it doesn't exist, you can create it, as shown here:

```
// Place the component within the MVC namespace; create it if needed.
if (!window.MVC)
{
    MVC = {};
}

...

MVC.MultiSelect = function(text, url, id, name, prev)
{
    ...
}
```

Accessing a module by ID

Once you have an object that encapsulates the data and methods for a module, that object typically spends most of its time working in just the part of the DOM that contains the elements for that module. Therefore, it's useful in the constructor for the module object to set data members to whatever parts of the DOM you'll need access to rather than retrieving them over and over again within various parts of the object. This improves performance and acts somewhat as a means of "binding" a JavaScript object to the HTML elements for which the object is adding a behavior layer.

One of the most important DOM methods for this is document.getElementById. This method returns a reference to the element with the ID you specify. As we saw in Chapter 4, a good way to scope a module for CSS (and JavaScript, too) is to give its outermost div an id attribute. Once you have a reference to this div, you can target all other DOM operations within the proper scope for the module. Thus, Example 5-2 illustrates accessing the DOM for a PictureSlider instance in the constructor for the object. The example also uses other DOM methods to get various elements within the module, which we'll explore further in the next section.

Example 5-2. The constructor for the PictureSlider object

```
PictureSlider = function()
{
    // Set up references to the elements needed for the slider and viewer.
    this.slider = document.getElementById("picsld");

    if (this.slider)
    {
```

```
        this.tab = this.slider.getElementsByTagName("table");
        this.tab = (this.tab && this.tab.length > 0) ? this.tab[0] : null;
    }

    if (this.slider)
    {
        this.lb = YAHOO.util.Dom.getElementsByClassName
        (
            "btnl",
            "img",
            this.slider
        );

        this.lb = (this.lb && this.lb.length > 0) ? this.lb[0] : null;

        this.rb = YAHOO.util.Dom.getElementsByClassName
        (
            "btnr",
            "img",
            this.slider
        );

        this.rb = (this.rb && this.rb.length > 0) ? this.rb[0] : null;
    }

    this.viewer = document.getElementById("picvwr");



    ...
};
```

Working with the DOM

The previous section illustrates how important it is for JavaScript to be capable of
referencing an element by ID. There are several other methods for performing DOM
operations in large web applications that you can expect to use frequently. This section
presents some of the most common methods that are supported across the major
browsers. Then we'll look at a few methods in popular JavaScript libraries that provide
additional capabilities with the DOM.

Common DOM Methods

Some of the most important DOM methods supported intrinsically across the major
browsers allow you to access elements by tag name, create new elements, insert nodes
into the DOM, remove nodes, and change text.

Accessing elements by tag name

The following method returns an array of HTML elements that are `img` tags enclosed by the invoking element (`element`):

```
elements = element.getElementsByTagName("img");
```

Creating an element

The following method creates an HTML `img` element. The method returns a reference to the element that was created.

```
element = document.createElement("img");
```

The following method creates a text node containing the string `"Welcome"`. The method returns a reference to the node.

```
textNode = document.createTextNode("Welcome");
```

Inserting or removing an element

The following method inserts `newNode` into the DOM at the end of the list of children of `parentNode`. HTML elements are derived from DOM nodes, so you can use this method to insert an HTML element (e.g., created by `document.createElement`) wherever you would like it to appear; or use this method to insert a text node (e.g., created by `document.createTextNode`).

```
parentNode.appendChild(newNode);
```

The following method removes `oldNode` from the children of `parentNode`. HTML elements are derived from DOM nodes, so you can use this method to remove an HTML element or use this method to remove a text node.

```
parentNode.removeChild(oldNode);
```

Changing the text in an element

To change the text for an element that doesn't contain any other nodes as its children, you can use the `innerHTML` property, as shown here:

```
element.innerHTML = "Goodbye";
```

Popular DOM Libraries

Several JavaScript libraries provide excellent support for working with the DOM. These include Dojo, jQuery, Prototype, and the YUI library. Of course, the methods provided here are just a tiny sampling of what these libraries offer for working with the DOM, as well as support for event handling, animation, drag and drop, browser history management, user interface components, and Ajax (see Chapter 8). As you'll see, there are only minor differences in how these libraries support the most common DOM operations.

DOM methods in Dojo

Dojo is a JavaScript library built on several contributed code bases. You can download the library and get complete documentation at *http://www.dojotoolkit.org*.

Accessing the DOM

The following method returns all `img` elements contained by the element with the ID `picsld` as a Dojo `NodeList` object. The first parameter for `dojo.query` is almost any CSS selector (see Chapter 4). You can also provide an optional second parameter for the root node at which to start the query. `NodeList` implements an interface that allows you to call the other methods in this section directly on a `NodeList` object, too. Omit the first parameter (`element`) of the other methods in this section in that case:

```
nodelist = dojo.query
(
    "#picsld img"
);
```

Working with attributes

The following method provides a uniform way to get the value of an attribute for `result` (the `src` attribute in this case) across the major browsers:

```
value = dojo.attr
(
    element,
    "src"
);
```

The following method provides a uniform way to set attributes for `result` (the `src` and `class` attributes in this case) across the major browsers:

```
dojo.attr
(
    element,
    {
        src: "http://...slide_arrow_1.gif",
        class: "btn1"
    }
);
```

Working with styles

The following method gets the value of a style for `result` (the `color` property in this case):

```
value = dojo.style
(
    element,
    "color"
);
```

The following method sets a collection of styles for `result` (the `color` and `backgroundColor` properties in this case). Use CamelCase for properties that are hyphenated, as illustrated by the string `backgroundColor`:

```
dojo.style
(
    element,
    {
        color: "#0f0f0f",
        backgroundColor: "#f0f0f0"
    }
);
```

DOM methods in jQuery

The jQuery JavaScript library has especially good documentation. You can download the library and read its complete documentation at *http://www.jquery.com*.

Accessing the DOM

The following method returns all `img` elements contained by the element with the ID `picsld` as a `jQuery` instance. The first parameter for `jQuery` is almost any CSS selector (see Chapter 4). You can also provide an optional second parameter for the root node at which to start the query. The jQuery library also defines `$`, a legal identifier in JavaScript, to do the same thing as the `jQuery` object:

```
result = jQuery
(
    "#picsld img"
);
```

Working with attributes

The following method provides a uniform way to get the value of an attribute for `element` (the `src` attribute in this case) across the major browsers:

```
value = result.attr
(
    "src"
);
```

The following method provides a uniform way to set attributes for the first element in `elements` (the `src` and `class` attributes in this case) across the major browsers:

```
result.attr
(
    {
        src:    "http://.../slide_arrow_l.gif",
        class: "btnl"
    }
);
```

Working with styles

The following method gets the value of a style for `element` (the `color` property in this case):

```
value = result.css
(
    "color"
);
```

The following method sets a collection of styles for `element` (the `color` and `backgroundColor` properties in this case). Use CamelCase for properties that are hyphenated:

```
result.css
(
    {
        color: "#0f0f0f",
        backgroundColor: "#f0f0f0"
    }
);
```

DOM methods in Prototype

Prototype is one of the earliest of the popular JavaScript libraries. You can download the library and read its complete documentation at *http://www.prototypejs.org*.

Accessing the DOM

The following method returns all `img` elements contained by the element with the ID `picsld` as an array. `$$` is a special method in Prototype that returns an array of elements that match a CSS selector. Its parameter is almost any CSS selector (see Chapter 4):

```
elements = $$
(
    "#picsld img"
);
```

Working with attributes

The following method provides a uniform way to get the value of an attribute for the first element in `elements` (the `src` attribute in this case) across the major browsers:

```
value = elements[0].readAttribute
(
    "src"
);
```

The following method provides a uniform way to set attributes for `element` (the `src` and `class` attributes in this case) across the major browsers:

```
elements[0].writeAttribute
(
    {
```

```
        src: "http://...slide_arrow_l.gif",
        class: "btnl"
    }
);
```

Working with styles

The following method gets the value of a style for the first element in `elements` (the `color` property in this case):

```
value = elements[0].getStyle
(
    "color"
);
```

The following method sets a collection of styles for the first element in `elements` (the `color` and `backgroundColor` properties in this case). Use CamelCase for properties that are hyphenated:

```
elements[0].setStyle
(
    {
        color: "#0f0f0f",
        backgroundColor: "#f0f0f0"
    }
);
```

DOM methods in YUI

The YUI library was developed at Yahoo! for use both within Yahoo! and by the world's web development community. You can download the library and read its complete documentation at *http://developer.yahoo.com/yui*.

 As this book was being completed, YUI 3 was in beta development. The information below pertains to versions prior to this. One of the big differences between YUI 2 and YUI 3 is the `YUI` object, which places YUI 3 features in their own namespace. This lets you transition from YUI 2 to YUI 3 without having to change all your code at once.

Accessing the DOM

The following method returns an array of `img` elements that pass a test implemented by `method`. You can provide an optional third parameter for the root node at which to start the query. `YAHOO.util.Dom.getElementsByClassName` lets you specify a class name as the first parameter instead of a method:

```
elements = YAHOO.util.Dom.getElementsBy
(
    method,
    "img",
);
```

Working with attributes

The following method provides a uniform way to get the value of an attribute for the first element of elements (the src attribute in this case) across the major browsers:

```
value = YAHOO.util.Dom.getAttribute
(
    elements[0],
    "src"
);
```

The following method provides a uniform way to set the value of an attribute for the first element in elements (the src attribute in this case) across the major browsers:

```
YAHOO.util.Dom.setAttribute
(
    elements[0],
    "src",
    "http://.../slide_arrow_l.gif"
);
```

Working with styles

The following method gets the value of a style for the first element in elements (the color property in this case):

```
value = YAHOO.util.Dom.getStyle
(
    elements[0],
    "color"
);
```

The following method sets a style for the first element in elements (the background Color property in this case). Use CamelCase for properties that are hyphenated:

```
YAHOO.util.Dom.setStyle
(
    elements[0],
    "backgroundColor",
    "#f0f0f0"
);
```

Working with Events

Much of the behavior layer in large web applications is dedicated to handling events. Unfortunately, event handling in web browsers can be a source of inconsistency and trouble. In addition, event handlers that perform more than just simple actions tend to be hard to maintain. Event handlers often use too much global data, and many applications would have better modularity if they used custom events to become even more event-driven.

Event Handling Normalization

To address the inconsistencies in the way that web browsers handle events, the YUI library (as well as the other libraries introduced earlier) provides an interface that offers uniform event handling across the different browsers. The following YUI method lets you register an event handler:

```
YAHOO.util.Event.addListener
(
    element,
    type,
    handler,
    object,
    overrideContext
);
```

The method accepts up to five parameters. The final two parameters are optional, but we will see in a moment that they provide some very important capabilities for large web applications. Here is a description of each parameter:

element
: The element for which the event handler is being registered. This can be an ID, an element reference, or an array of IDs and elements to which to assign the event handler.

type
: The type of the event. Specify the event type as the same string as you would use in an HTML element but without the `on` prefix (i.e., use `"click"` instead of `"onclick"`).

handler
: The method that the event invokes.

object
: An object to pass as the second parameter to the handler (the first parameter passed to the handler is always the event object itself).

overrideContext
: If set to true, `object` becomes the execution context for the handler (referenced by `this` in the handler). If you specify an object for this parameter, this object becomes the execution context for the handler.

A Bad Example: Global Data in Event Handlers

To address the issue of too much global data in event handlers, let's first look at why this is often the case. Essentially, web developers tend to write event handlers that use a lot of global data because the vast majority of event handlers are *defined globally themselves*. That is, they are members of the `window` object instead of an object that is more specific to what they really need to do. This tendency is understandable, because an event handler may be called upon to handle an event at any time as an application runs and its data needs to be in a scope that's accessible; however, such a broad scope leads to unwieldy code over time. As a starting point, Example 5-3 illustrates the common approach for event handling with global data found in many web applications.

Example 5-3. Global data in an event handler

```
var State1;
var State2;

...

YAHOO.util.Event.addListener
(
    element,
    "click",
    slideL,
);

...

function slideL()
{
    // Since an event handler can be called at any moment, the tendency
    // is to use global data since it's always in scope.
    alert(State1);
    alert(State2);
}
```

A Good Example: Object Data in Event Handlers

Now let's look at a better approach for event handlers, which uses object data. This involves defining an event handler as a method of the object that it affects and defining the data required by that event handler within the object. This is especially beneficial if you consider that many objects in the modular JavaScript we're presenting in this chapter are created to provide a layer of behavior for a specific module in the user interface. Therefore, modularity is enhanced by implementing the event handlers for that module as part of the object itself. (For JavaScript that affects multiple modules on a page, define an object for the page, which implements its own handlers for that level of event handling.)

Example 5-4 implements an event handler as a method of the `PictureSlider` object. During event registration with YUI, the code sets up the object itself as the execution context for the event handler so that the event handler has access to all the module's data members.

Example 5-4. Object data in an event handler

```
PictureSlider = function()
{
    this.state1 = ...;
    this.state2 = ...;
```

```
...

if (this.slider)
{
    // Create placeholders for left and right buttons, but only if
    // there are more slides than can fit the width given for them.
    this.lb = YAHOO.util.Dom.getElementsByClassName
    (
        "btnl",
        "img",
        this.slider
    );

    this.lb = (this.lb && this.lb.length > 0) ? this.lb[0] : null;

    ...

}

YAHOO.util.Event.addListener
(
    this.lb,
    "click",
    this.slideL,
    this,
    true
);

...
};

PictureSlider.prototype = new Object();

PictureSlider.prototype.slideL = function()
{
    // Because when we registered this event handler we specified that
    // PictureSlider should be the execution context, we have access here
    // to everything encapsulated in the object using the this pointer.
    alert(this.state1);
    alert(this.state2);
};
```

Event-Driven Applications

A good way to achieve further modularity within the JavaScript of a large web application is to design your application to be more event-driven. This means using events instead of method calls directly to communicate between modules. Event-driven applications define custom events to describe what modules are doing and trigger the proper events at various points to communicate what has happened. Other parts of the application listen for those events and respond by doing whatever they need to do.

The reason that event-driven applications tend to be more modular than applications tied together by method calls directly is that firing events and handling events are independent actions. That is, you can fire a new event or add or remove a handler without directly affecting other parts of the system. In addition, JavaScript and its libraries' support for event handling, presented earlier, give you everything you need to abstract the tracking of custom events and their delivery to the correct recipients. You just have to define which events you need and write the code to trigger or handle the events at the right places.

Suppose you wanted to use a custom event to indicate that there was a change of location (e.g., a postal code) associated with a web page after it was loaded. This could occur after a visitor types a new location into an input somewhere, or for any number of other reasons. Whatever the case, various modules on the page may want to know about the change so that they can update themselves for the new location (e.g., a list of new cars might need to update itself via Ajax with different listings).

Custom events usually provide a way to pass data (sometimes called a *payload*) along with the event to provide additional details. For example, in the case of a location change, you would likely want a handler to know what the location was changed to, and possibly what the location was previously. You can learn more about custom events from the YUI library at *http://developer.yahoo.com/yui*.

Working with Animation

Many web developers think that you need to use Flash to achieve animation effects in web browsers. In actuality, you can accomplish a great number of animated effects using JavaScript. This section presents a few examples of some common types of animations that may be helpful in large web applications.

Motion Animation

A motion animation changes the position of an element over the course of time. You can perform a motion animation with the YUI library using `YAHOO.util.Motion`. Example 5-5 sets up a motion animation that moves an element specified by `element` over a span of one second, with easing that starts quickly and decelerates toward the end (`YAHOO.util.Easing.easeOut`). The example illustrates a few ways to move an element using the parameter for attributes:

`attr1`

> Move the element from its current position to position 450,0 on the page. You can also specify `from` to use a starting point that is different from the current position.

attr2

> Move the element from its current position 450 pixels to the right relative to its current position. You can also specify `from` to use a starting point that is different from the current position.

attr3

> Move the element from its current position to position 450,0 on the page and move via a smooth curve through point 200,200. You can also use `from` as usual.

Once you have set up the animation using `YAHOO.util.Motion`, start the animation by calling `animate` on the object that was returned.

Example 5-5. Setting up a motion animation

```
attr1 =
{
    points: {to: [450, 0]}
};

attr2 =
{
    points: {by: [450, 0]}
};

attr3 =
{
    points: {to: [450, 0], control: [[200, 200]]}
};

animation = new YAHOO.util.Motion
(
    element,
    attr1,
    1,
    YAHOO.util.Easing.easeOut
);

...

animation.animate();
```

Sizing Animation

A sizing animation changes the width and height of an element over the course of time. You can perform a sizing animation with the YUI library using `YAHOO.util.Anim`. Example 5-6 sets up a sizing animation that resizes an element specified by `element` over a span of one second, with easing that starts slowly, speeds up, and decelerates again toward the end (`YAHOO.util.Easing.easeBoth`). The example illustrates a few ways to resize an element using the parameter for attributes:

attr1

> Resize the element from its current width to 100 pixels. You can also specify from to use a starting size that is different from the current size.

attr2

> Resize the element from its current width up by 100 pixels. You can also specify from to use a starting size that is different from the current size.

Once you have set up the animation using YAHOO.util.Anim, start the animation by calling animate on the object that was returned.

Example 5-6. Setting up a sizing animation

```
attr1 =
{
    width: {to: 100}
};

attr2 =
{
    width: {by: 100)
};

animation = new YAHOO.util.Anim
(
    element,
    attr1,
    1,
    YAHOO.util.Easing.easeBoth
);

...

animation.animate();
```

Color Transition

A color transition changes various color properties of an element over the course of time. You can perform a color transition using YAHOO.util.ColorAnim. Example 5-7 sets up a color transition that colors an element specified by element over a span of one second, with easing that starts slowly and accelerates toward the end (YAHOO.util.Easing.easeIn). The example illustrates a few ways to transition the color of an element using the attributes parameter:

attr1

> Transition the background color for the element from its current color to #fff. You can also specify from to use a starting color that is different from the current color.

attr2

> Transition the foreground color for the element from #fff to #000. This setup demonstrates how to use the from property.

Once you have set up the animation using `YAHOO.util.ColorAnim`, start the animation by calling `animate` on the object that was returned.

Example 5-7. Setting up a color transition

```
attr1 =
{
    backgroundColor: {to: "#fff"}
}

attr2 =
{
    color: {from: "#fff", to: "#000"}
}

animation = new YAHOO.util.ColorAnim
(
    element,
    attr1,
    1,
    YAHOO.util.Easing.easeIn
);

...

animation.animate();
```

An Example: Chained Selection Lists

One example of highly modular JavaScript is an implementation for *chained selection lists*. These provide a dynamic way to organize selection lists in which a selection in one list causes a new set of options to be loaded in subsequent lists. For example, imagine selecting a make-model-trim 3-tuple for a car (e.g., BMW, 09 3-Series, 335i) from a set of selection lists. Rather than having a huge list of all make-model-trim combinations, a better user experience is to have three selection lists: one for the makes, one for the models, and one for the trims. Once you select a make, the model selection list is populated with models for just that make. Once you select a model, the trim selection list is populated with trims available for that make-model combination. Figure 5-1 shows three states of chained selection lists for cars: a) the initial state, b) after selecting a make, and c) after selecting a model.

One way to implement chained selection lists is to create multiple instances of the same selection object, which we'll call `MultiSelect`, and link them together so that each can respond to changes in the others based on their positions in the chain. Example 5-8 shows the HTML for the chained selection lists in Figure 5-1. It also shows the JavaScript for setting up the chain of selection lists.

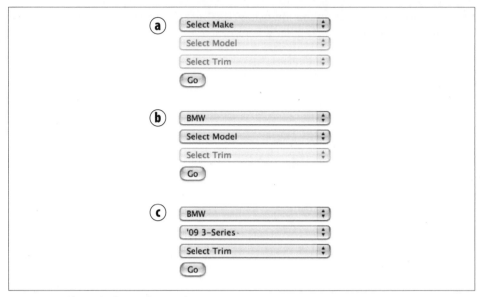

Figure 5-1. Chained selection lists in three states

Example 5-8. HTML for chained selection lists

```
<body>

...

<div id="nwcsel">
   <form action="..." method="GET">
      <div id="makesel">
      </div>
      <div id="modelsel">
      </div>
      <div id="trimsel">
      </div>
      <input class="nwcbtnsub" type="submit" value="Go" />
   </form>
</div>

...

<!--
   Before the JavaScript for MultiSelect, you need to link files required
   by the MultiSelect implementation. Chapter 7 presents techniques for
   ensuring that everything a module requires (the HTML, CSS, JavaScript,
   etc.) is able to travel with the module wherever the module is used.
-->
<script src="http://..." type="text/javascript"></script>
...

<script type="text/javascript">
// Set up the name of the service for populating the chained selections.
```

```
var proc = "...";

// Create the make selection list.
var makeSelect = new MVC.MultiSelect
(
    "Select Make",
    proc + "?req=mk",
    "makesel",
    "mk"
);

// Chain the model selection list.
var modelSelect = new MVC.MultiSelect
(
    "Select Model",
    proc + "?req=md",
    "modelsel",
    "md",
    makeSelect
);

// Chain the trim selection list.
var trimSelect = new MVC.MultiSelect
(
    "Select Trim",
    proc + "?req=tr",
    "trimsel",
    "tr",
    modelSelect
);

// Once selection lists in the chain have been created, initialize them.
makeSelect.init();
modelSelect.init();
trimSelect.init();
</script>
</body>
```

The JavaScript for the `MultiSelect` component uses Ajax and the MVC (Model-View-Controller) design pattern, which are presented in more detail in Chapter 8. MVC and Ajax work together to let us make a new request for data each time a selection list should be updated. This is far better than loading all combinations when the page first loads, since all the combinations require a lot of data and most go unused. Because the `MultiSelect` component is a generic component that uses MVC, a logical place to include it might be in the MVC library. Therefore, Example 5-9 shows that we have placed the component within the MVC namespace.

Example 5-9. JavaScript for the MultiSelect object

```
// Place the component within the MVC namespace; create it if needed.
if (!window.MVC)
{
    MVC = {};
}
```

```
MVC.MultiSelect = function(text, url, id, name, prev)
{
    // Pass a string for the selection list in text, or pass null for a
    // default label; url is the URL to fetch options, id is the ID of
    // the container in which to place the selection list, name is the
    // select name attribute, and prev is the predecessor list, or null.
    t = (text) ? text : null;
    p = (prev) ? prev.view : null;

    this.model = new MVC.MultiSelectModel(t, url);
    this.view  = new MVC.MultiSelectView(name, p);
    this.view.attach(this.model, id);
}

MVC.MultiSelect.prototype.init = function()
{
    // Call this method once the chain of selections has been set up.
    this.model.init();
}

MVC.MultiSelect.prototype.getSelect = function()
{
    // Return the select element currently in use by the selection list
    // so that you can make whatever customizations are needed (e.g., you
    // can append your own handlers or perform various DOM operations).
    return this.view.getSelect();
}
```

One of the most important features of the implementation for the MultiSelect component is that it is implemented in a generic and modular fashion. You can chain any
number of them together and they work with any type of data, provided the data is
returned from the server in a data structure like that shown in Example 5-10. This is
an example of JSON (JavaScript Object Notation), presented in Chapter 6. This data
structure is simply an array of objects with two members: value and text. Each pair
represents one option in the list: value is the hidden value for each option, and text is
the displayable string.

Example 5-10. The data structure for loading chained selection lists

```
{
    "options" :
    [
        {
            "value": "bmw",
            "text":  "BMW"
        },
        {
            "value": "honda",
            "text":  "Honda"
        },
        {
            "value": "toyota",
            "text":  "Toyota"
```

```
        }
    ]
}
```

Examples 5-11 and 5-12 present the implementation details for chained selection lists using JavaScript. Together, the examples illustrate many of the ideas presented in this chapter: the use of objects for namespacing, methods for accessing and modifying the DOM, and event handling using object data instead of global data, among others. Fundamentally, the implementation works by maintaining a model and a view for each selection list in the chain.

Example 5-11 shows the implementation for `MultiSelectModel`. This is the model responsible for storing the current set of options for one selection list in the chain. Whenever the model changes, it notifies the view attached to the model automatically so that the view can update itself with the new options.

You'll see in Chapter 8 that in MVC, a model tells a view to update itself by calling the view's `update` method. For now, you just need to know that this happens as follows: `setState` sets the data in the model; it then calls `notify` in the model; `notify` then calls `update` for each view attached to the model. The `setState` and `notify` methods are defined by the `Model` prototype object, so you will not see them defined in the examples here.

Example 5-11. MultiSelectModel object for the chained selection list implementation

```
MVC.MultiSelectModel = function(text, url)
{
    MVC.Model.call(this);

    // All selection lists use an empty string as the marker for the
    // label appearing in the selection list before an option is chosen.
    this.labelValue = "";

    if (text)
        this.labelText = text;
    else
        this.labelText = "Select";

    // This is the URL to contact for loading options.
    this.proc = url;

    // If the model ends up being the model for the first selection list
    // in the chain, the view with this model will set this member.
    this.firstModel = false;
}

MVC.MultiSelectModel.prototype = new MVC.Model();

MVC.MultiSelectModel.prototype.init = function()
{
    if (this.firstModel)
    {
```

```
    // Initialize options for the first selection list in the chain.
    this.setState("GET", this.proc);
}
else
{
    // Initialize other selection lists to an empty array of options.
    // Do the view notification explicitly since we're not using the
    // setState method here (which would do the notification itself).
    this.state.options = new Array();
    this.notify();
}
}


MVC.MultiSelectModel.prototype.abandon = function()
{
    alert("Timeout occurred while trying to load selection options.");
}

MVC.MultiSelectModel.prototype.recover = function()
{
    alert("Problem occurred while trying to load selection options.");
}
```

Example 5-12 shows the implementation for `MultiSelectView`. This is the view object for one selection list in the chain. `MultiSelectView` defines the `update` method invoked by a model whenever there is a new set of options to render. It also defines `changeHandler`, an event handler for whenever the selected value in the selection list changes. When the selection changes, the view sets the next model in the chain to a new set of selection list options. It does this in `changeHandler` by calling `setState` for the next model. This, in turn, produces a call to the `update` method of the view attached to that model. `MultiSelectView` creates a `select` element if the view doesn't already have one in the HTML.

Example 5-12. MultiSelectView object for the chained selection implementation

```
MVC.MultiSelectView = function(n, p)
{
    MVC.View.call(this);

    this.name = n;

    if (p)
    {
        // The selection list is not first in the chained selections.
        this.prev = p;
        p.next = this;
        this.disabled = true;
    }
    else
    {
        // This selection list has no predecessor, so it's the first one.
        this.prev = null;
        this.next = null;
```

```
            this.disabled = false;
    }
}

MVC.MultiSelectView.prototype = new MVC.View();

MVC.MultiSelectView.prototype.attach = function(m, i)
{
    // This method hooks up a view to its data source, which is a model.
    MVC.View.prototype.attach.call(this, m, i);

    // If the view has no predecessor view, it must be first in the chain.
    if (!this.prev)
        this.model.firstModel = true;

    this.container = document.getElementById(this.id);
}

MVC.MultiSelectView.prototype.update = function()
{
    // Called when a change in the model takes place. Render new options.
    var select = this.getSelect();

    // Remove any existing select element not created by the view.
    if (select && !YAHOO.util.Dom.hasClass(select, "mltsel"))
    {
        select.parentNode.removeChild(select);
        select = null;
    }

    // Insert a new select only the first time the view is being managed.
    if (!select)
    {
        select = document.createElement("select");
        YAHOO.util.Dom.addClass(select, "mltsel");
        select.setAttribute("name", this.name);

        YAHOO.util.Event.addListener
        (
            select,
            "change",
            this.changeHandler,
            this,
            true
        );

        // Insert the select element for the selection list into the DOM.
        if (this.container)
            this.container.appendChild(select);
    }

    if (this.disabled)
        select.disabled = true;
    else
        select.disabled = false;
```

```javascript
    var o;
    var options;
    var count;

    // Start the options with the model's label for the selection list.
    select.options.length = 0;
    o = new Option(this.model.labelText, this.model.labelValue);
    select.options[select.options.length] = o;

    options = this.model.state.options;
    count = options.length;

    // Load the rest of the selection list remaining with the options.
    for (var i = 0; i < count; i++)
    {
        o = new Option(options[i].text, options[i].value);
        select.options[select.options.length] = o;
    }
}

MVC.MultiSelectView.prototype.changeHandler = function(e)
{
    // Handle changes in one of the selection lists by adjusting others.
    var select = this.getSelect();
    var option = select.options[select.selectedIndex].value;

    if (option == "")
    {
        // The selection list has been set back to its initial state;
        // selection lists beyond it in the chain must be reset as well.
        this.reset(this.next);
    }
    else
    {
        if (this.next)
        {
            // Use Ajax to get options for the next selection in the chain.
            if (this.next.model.proc.indexOf("?") == -1)
                option = "?value=" + option;
            else
                option = "&value=" + option;

            this.next.model.setState("GET", this.next.model.proc + option);
            this.next.enable();

            // Move to the next selection list in the chain and reset all
            // views beyond it (when a choice has been made out of order).
            var iter = this.next;

            if (iter)
                this.reset(iter.next);
        }
    }
}
```

```
MVC.MultiSelectView.prototype.reset = function(view)
{
   // Initialize all selection lists after the given one in the chain.
   var iter = view;

   while (iter)
   {
      iter.model.init();
      iter.disable();
      iter = iter.next;
   }
}

MVC.MultiSelectView.prototype.enable = function()
{
   var select = this.getSelect();

   this.disabled = false;

   if (select)
      select.disabled = this.disabled;
}

MVC.MultiSelectView.prototype.disable = function()
{
   var select = this.getSelect();

   this.disabled = true;

   if (select)
      select.disabled = this.disabled;
}

MVC.MultiSelectView.prototype.getSelect = function()
{

   var elements;

   // Retrieve the current select element used by the selection list.
   if (this.container)
      elements = this.container.getElementsByTagName("select");
   else
      return null;

   if (elements.length > 0)
      return elements[0];
   else
      return null;
}
```

A logical extension of this implementation for chained selection lists is to use it to build highly reusable modules for different types of chained selection lists you might need to support around a large web application. For example, you could build a New Cars Selection module for anywhere you need a make-model-trim 3-tuple for new cars. This module would bundle the generic chaining behavior presented in the preceding examples with the HTML and CSS to make it a fully reusable component. We'll learn more about this encapsulation for modules in Chapter 7.

CHAPTER 6

Data Management

As you examine the design for a web page, it's important to distinguish between data on the page that is *dynamic* and data that is *static*. Dynamic data, such as a list of search results, changes each time the page is loaded (based on the query); static data, such as a label for the query box, does not. The distinction between static and dynamic data is important because each requires its own management strategy. On the one hand, static data is easy—you simply specify it directly within the HTML of the page. With dynamic data, however, you must enlist the help of a server-side scripting language, such as PHP, so that you can interact with backend systems to store and retrieve the data. In this chapter, we look at techniques for managing dynamic data.

One of the most important goals for managing dynamic data in a large web application is to establish a clearly defined data interface through which to interact with the backend. A clearly defined data interface allows modules in the user interface (see Chapter 7) to remain loosely coupled with the backend, allows details of the backend (e.g., data dependencies) to be abstracted from modules, and gives modules the flexibility to work with any set of data that contains what the data interface requires. In teams where web developers and backend engineers are separate roles, these qualities let each role work independently, knowing that both are working toward a common point where the user interface and backend will meet. This goal for managing dynamic data is captured in the following tenet from Chapter 1:

> Tenet 6: Dynamic data exchanged between the user interface and the backend is managed through a clearly defined data interface. Pages define a single point for loading data and a single point for saving it.

We begin this chapter by looking at what we mean by a dynamic module. We then discuss the concept of a data manager, look at important techniques for using data managers to store and retrieve dynamic data, and examine methods for making data managers extensible using inheritance and aggregation. Next, we look at some examples of data managers using SQL and XML, and explore some techniques for working with database connections, accessing time-consuming web services in parallel, and working with JSON, which is particularly useful for Ajax applications. Finally, we look at a few things to keep in mind when working with dynamic data in cookies and forms.

Dynamic Modules

Let's reconsider the New Car Reviews module from Example 3-3, which contains a list of three new car reviews. That example illustrates well-constructed HTML for the module, but it doesn't address how the HTML was generated on the server or which parts of that module are dynamic versus static. Exploring that module again, it's reasonable to expect that the list of reviews should be generated dynamically so that we can insert whichever reviews are relevant wherever the module is used. An associative array is a good data structure for organizing dynamic data. The list of reviews might be structured as shown in the PHP code in Example 6-1.

Example 6-1. An associative array for dynamically generated new car reviews

```
array
(
    "0" => array
    (
        "name"  => "2009 Honda Accord",
        "price" => "21905",
        "link"  => "http://.../reviews/00001/"
    ),

    "1" => array
    (
        "name"  => "2009 Toyota Prius",
        "price" => "22000",
        "link"  => "http://.../reviews/00002/"
    ),

    "2" => array
    (
        "name"  => "2009 Nissan Altima",
        "price" => "19900",
        "link"  => "http://.../reviews/00003/"
    )
)
```

Example 6-2 shows a method that uses the data structure of Example 6-1 to generate the HTML for the list items in the New Car Reviews module (Chapter 7 presents a complete class for implementing a module in PHP, which might employ a method like this). This method takes the array of new car reviews as an argument.

Example 6-2. A method for generating list items for new car reviews dynamically

```
protected function get_reviews($reviews)
{
    $count = count($reviews);
    $items = "";
```

```
    for ($i = 0; $i < $count; $i++)
    {
        $pos = ($i == 0) ? "beg" : (($i == $count - 1) ? "end" : "mid");

        $price = "&#36;".number_format($reviews[$i]["price"]);

        $items .= <<<EOD
<li class="$pos">
    <p>
        <strong>{$reviews[$i]["name"]}</strong>
        <em>(from $price)</em>.
    </p>
    <a href="{$reviews[$i]["link"]}">Read the review</a>
</li>

EOD;
    }

    return $items;
}
```

The point in Example 6-2 is how members of the data structure for the list of reviews
have been used in the dynamic generation of HTML markup for the list items of the
module. To get dynamic data like this into a data structure that you can use within the
PHP for a module, you need a standard, systematic way to access the data. A good way
to handle this is to encapsulate access to the data within an object. That leads to our
next section.

Data Managers

A data manager is an object that abstracts and encapsulates access to a specific set of
data. Its purpose is to provide a well-defined, consistent interface by which you can get
and set data in the backend, and to create a clear structure for the data itself. In Chapter 7, we will look at some techniques for invoking data managers during the generation
of a complete page. Data managers are also useful for managing the data exchanged in
Ajax requests. For now, let's look at how data managers simplify access to dynamic
data.

Because a data manager is an object, you simply instantiate the data manager and call
its get_data method anywhere you need to get the data it manages. Example 6-3 illustrates the use of a couple of data managers to get data from the backend within the
kind of PHP class for pages that we'll develop in Chapter 7. In Chapter 7, you'll also
see that a page's load_data method defines a single point at which to load its data.

Example 6-3. Loading data for a page using a data manager

```
class NewCarSearchResultsPage extends SitePage
{
    ...
```

```
public function load_data()
{
    // Set up load_args for each of the data managers called below.
    ...

    $dm = new NewCarListingsDataManager();

    $dm->get_data
    (
        $this->load_args["new_car_listings"],
        $this->load_data["new_car_listings"],
        $this->load_stat["new_car_listings"]
    );

    $dm = new NewCarReviewsDataManager();

    $dm->get_data
    (
        $this->load_args["new_car_reviews"],
        $this->load_data["new_car_reviews"],
        $this->load_stat["new_car_reviews"]
    );

    ...

}

...
}
```

Notice the use of new_car_listings and new_car_reviews members (named after the data managers themselves) for each argument of the get_data calls. These ensure that the arguments, data, and status for each data manager are uniquely identifiable. All you need to know right now about get_data is that the $load_args argument is the input (allowing you to control the method's operation), the $load_data argument is the main output, and the $load_stat argument is additional output that you can use in case something goes wrong. After get_data returns, the $load_data member of the page class contains the data retrieved by each data manager, with the data for each module placed within its own area of the data structure. Example 6-4 shows an example of this data structure.

Example 6-4. The $load_data member of the page class after calling load_data

```
array
(
    "new_car_listings" => array
    (
        // Data retrieved by the New Car Listings data manager is here.
        ...
    ),
    "new_car_reviews" => array
    (
        // Data retrieved by the New Car Reviews data manager is here.
```

```
"0" => array
(
    "name"  => "2009 Honda Accord",
    "price" => "21905",
    "link"  => "http://.../reviews/00001/"
),

"1" => array
(
    "name"  => "2009 Toyota Prius",
    "price" => "22000",
    "link"  => "http://.../reviews/00002/"
),
"2" => array
(
    "name"  => "2009 Nissan Altima",
    "price" => "19900",
    "link"  => "http://.../reviews/00003/"
)
)
)
```

Anytime you need to set some data in the backend managed by a data manager, you simply instantiate the data manager and call its **set_data** method. Example 6-5 illustrates the use of a data manager to set data in the backend within the kind of PHP class for pages that we'll develop in Chapter 7. The **save_data** method defines a single point at which to save data for a page. As in Example 6-3, notice the use of the new_car_queries member for each argument of **set_data** to ensure the arguments, data, and status for this data manager are uniquely identifiable.

Example 6-5. Saving data for a page using a data manager

```
class NewCarSearchResultsPage extends SitePage
{
  ...

  public function save_data()
  {
    // Set up save_args and save_data for each data manager called below.
    ...

    $dm = new NewCarQueriesDataManager();

    $dm->set_data
    (
      $this->save_args["new_car_queries"],
      $this->save_data["new_car_queries"],
      $this->save_stat["new_car_queries"]
    );

    ...

  }
```

```
    ...
}
```

To allow a data manager to be configured before accessing the data that it manages, you can define parameters for its constructor or define various setter methods. For example, to tell the data manager whether you'd like abbreviated or full information for the listings that are retrieved, you can define a method such as set_full_listings, which can be called anytime before calling get_data.

Creating Data Managers

A good approach for creating data managers is to define them for fairly granular sets of data grouped logically *from the backend perspective*. Backend developers may be in the best position to do this since they have good visibility into details about backend systems. Ideally, these details should be abstracted from the user interface. Once data managers are defined, the user interface can instantiate whichever of them are needed to load and save data for the page.

It's important to realize that data managers don't necessarily correspond one-to-one to modules on the page. In fact, this is a key design attribute that makes it easy for multiple modules to access the same data, which is common in large web applications. For example, imagine a postal code stored by the backend for the current visitor. You may need to use this within multiple modules on a page, but ideally there should be a single data manager that defines the interface for getting and setting it.

Because all data managers fundamentally do the same thing (i.e., get and set data), it's useful to define a DataManager base class (see Example 6-6). This base class defines a standard interface that all data managers implement. For each data manager that you derive from this base class, implement either or both of the methods in the interface as needed, and provide whatever supporting methods are helpful for these methods to manage the data efficiently. The default implementations do nothing.

Example 6-6. The DataManager base class

```
class DataManager
{
    public function __construct()
    {
    }

    public function get_data($load_args, &$load_data, &$load_stat)
    {
    }

    public function set_data($save_args, &$save_data, &$save_stat)
    {
    }
}
```

Defining get_data

The `get_data` method of a data manager abstracts the process of getting data from the backend. A key part of implementing a clearly defined data interface for getting data is to define well-organized data structures for each of the parameters that `get_data` accepts or returns:

```
public function get_data($load_args, &$load_data, &$load_stat)
```

`$load_args`
> Input arguments needed for getting the data—for example, configuration settings, a database connection, or the maximum number of items in a list of data to retrieve. Since more than one input argument is frequently required, an associative array works well for this data structure.

`$load_data`
> A reference for where to place the retrieved data. Since more than one data member is frequently retrieved, an associative array works well for this data structure.

`$load_stat`
> A reference for where to return the status of the operation. A status indication may be a numeric code or a string in the simplest situations, or it could be an associative array that provides more details.

Defining set_data

The `set_data` method of a data manager abstracts the process of setting data in the backend.

```
public function set_data($save_args, &$save_data, &$save_stat)
```

The `set_data` method of a data manager uses the same arguments and internal structures as `get_data`, except `$save_data` is the data to save. This argument is a reference so that a data manager has the option to pass back some data after saving.

Extending Data Managers

Often, it makes sense to build on existing data managers when creating new ones. For example, you might create a data manager that relies on common methods for working with web services from another data manager or combine access to multiple, finer-granularity data managers within a single data manager that a page can instantiate on its own. The extension of data managers offers more than just a convenience—it also provides the opportunity for certain optimizations. For example, you might encapsulate how you share database connections or file handles. Because data managers are objects, you can extend them easily using either *inheritance* or *aggregation*.

Extending via inheritance

Inheritance establishes an "is-a" relationship between data managers. To extend a data manager using inheritance, derive your new data manager class from the data manager class with the characteristics that you desire. The extension of a data manager via inheritance is a good approach when you need a data manager that is a more specific type of an existing one.

Example 6-7 derives the New Car Listings data manager from the Web Service data manager, which provides common capabilities for any data manager that accesses web services. When you extend a data manager using inheritance, the derived data manager has access to all the public and protected members of its parent. You can then add new methods or override methods from the parent to augment functionality.

Example 6-7. Extending a data manager using inheritance

```
class NewCarListingsDataManager extends WebServiceDataManager
{
    // This class has access to all the WebServiceDataManager protected
    // and public members to support managing the New Car Listings data.
}
```

Extending via aggregation

Aggregation establishes a "has-a" relationship between data managers. To extend a data manager using aggregation, create an instance of the data manager class with the capabilities that you desire as a member of the new data manager. The extension of a data manager via aggregation is a good approach to let a single data manager provide access to the data of multiple data managers.

Example 6-8 aggregates several data managers into a New Car Listings data manager so we can retrieve new car reviews as a part of retrieving other data related to new car listings. When you extend a data manager using aggregation, your data manager has access only to the public members of the data manager that has been aggregated.

Example 6-8. Extending a data manager using aggregation

```
class NewCarListingsDataManager
{
    protected $new_car_reviews_dm;

    ...

    public function __construct()
    {
        parent::__construct();

        $this->new_car_reviews_dm = new NewCarReviewsDataManager();
    }

    public function get_data($load_args, &$load_data, &$load_stat)
    {
```

```
    $this->new_car_reviews_dm->get_data
    (
        $load_args["new_car_reviews"],
        $load_data["new_car_reviews"],
        $load_stat["new_car_reviews"]
    );

    // Get other data needed for the New Car Listings data manager.
    ...
  }
}
```

Just as we saw in Example 6-3, the use of the `new_car_reviews` member (named after the data manager itself) for each argument of `get_data` ensures that the arguments, data, and status for the New Car Reviews data manager are uniquely identifiable. Assuming the `get_data` method of `NewCarListingsDataManager` is passed an associative array member called `new_car_listings` for its `$load_data` argument (per the same convention), the data structure returned by the New Car Listings data manager will be similar to the one shown in Example 6-9. This structure reflects nicely that the New Car Listings data aggregates some New Car Reviews data.

Example 6-9. Data from a data manager extended via aggregation

```
array
(
    "new_car_listings" => array
    (
        // Data from the New Car Reviews data manager, by which the
        // New Car Listings data manager was extended via aggregation.
        "new_car_reviews" => array
        (
            "0" => array
            (
                "name"  => "2009 Honda Accord",
                "price" => "21905",
                "link"  => "http://.../reviews/00001/"
            ),

            ...
        ),

        // Other data retrieved by the New Car Listings data manager.
        ...
    )
)
```

Data Using SQL As a Source

Databases using SQL are some of the most common sources for data from the backend that a data manager may need to manage. In this section, we look at a canonical data manager that manages access to a simple database.

An SQL Example

Example 6-10 shows an implementation for the NewCarDetailsDataManager class, which uses SQL to access a database. The purpose of this data manager is to get detailed data about a new car. The example also shows DatabaseDataManager, a sample base class to provide common capabilities needed by most data managers that access databases, such as opening the database, looking up a user and password from a secure location, closing the database, and handling database errors, among other things.

Because the New Car Details data manager is a specific type of database data manager, we've extended its class from the DatabaseDataManager class using inheritance. It's important to notice a few key points about the data managers in Example 6-10:

- DatabaseDataManager does not implement either get_data or set_data, because this class is not intended to be instantiated directly.

- One of the useful features that DatabaseDataManager implements is a check of whether or not a database is already open and whether to close it when finished. This allows multiple data managers to share the same database connection when they are aggregated within other data managers.

- Defining another data manager (e.g., NewCarDatabaseDataManager) would let you keep the details for accessing this specific database (e.g., building queries with SQL, etc.) out of NewCarDetailsDataManager, in practice.

- The database support required by most large web applications can be abstracted into other database data managers as well. These can handle things that backend systems typically deal with, such as implementing a caching layer.

Example 6-10. Data managers using SQL to get data from a database

```
class DatabaseDataManager extends DataManager
{
    protected $host;
    protected $name;
    protected $file;
    protected $user;
    protected $pass;

    protected $connection;
    protected $close_flag;

    public function __construct($connection, $close_flag)
    {
        parent::__construct();

        $this->connection = $connection;
        $this->close_flag = $close_flag;
    }

    protected function db_open()
    {
        // If there is not already an open connection, open the database.
```

```php
        if (empty($this->connection))
        {
            $this->db_access();

            $this->connection = mysql_connect
            (
                $this->host,
                $this->user,
                $this->pass
            );

            if (!$this->connection)
            {
                $this->db_handle_error();
                return false;
            }

            if (!mysql_select_db($this->name))
            {
                $this->db_handle_error();
                return false;
            }
        }

        return true;
    }

    protected function db_access()
    {
        list($user, $pass) = explode(":", file_get_contents($this->file));

        $this->user = trim($user);
        $this->pass = trim($pass);
    }

    protected function db_close()
    {
        if ($this->connection)
            mysql_close($this->connection);
    }

    protected function db_handle_error()
    {
        ...
    }

    ...
}

...

class NewCarDetailsDataManager extends DatabaseDataManager
{
    public function __construct($connection = "", $close_flag = true)
    {
```

```php
        parent::__construct($connection, $close_flag);

        // Provide the host and name for the database as well as the
        // path of the secure file containing the user and password.
        $this->host = ...
        $this->name = ...
        $this->file = ...

        $this->db_open();
    }

    public function get_data($load_args, &$load_data, &$load_stat)
    {
        $load_stat = $this->get_details
        (
            $load_args["id"],
            $load_data
        );

        // Close the database after getting the data if set up for this.
        if ($this->close_flag)
            $this->db_close();
    }

    protected function get_details($id, &$details)
    {
        $query = "SELECT * FROM new_cars WHERE id='$id'";
        $result = mysql_query($query);

        if (!$result)
        {
            $details = array();
            $this->db_handle_error();
            return false;
        }

        $details = $this->get_details_result($result);
        mysql_free_result($result);

        return true;
    }

    protected function get_details_result($result)
    {
        $data = mysql_fetch_array($result, MYSQL_ASSOC);

        if (!empty($data))
        {
            // Massage the data structure as needed before returning it.
            ...
        }

        return $data;
    }
}
```

Data Using XML As a Source

XML data is another common source for data from the backend that a data manager may need to manage. In this section, we look at a canonical data manager that manages access to data defined by XML.

An XML Example

Example 6-11 presents an implementation for the `NewCarArticlesDataManager` class, which accesses short articles about new cars stored in XML. The example also illustrates the `XMLDataManager` base class, which provides common capabilities needed by most data managers that process XML. In this example, a single method is shown that performs postprocessing on extracted data, but you can imagine many others to assist in various operations for XML parsing. Because the New Car Articles data manager is a specific type of XML data manager, we've extended its class from `XMLDataManager` using inheritance. Example 6-12 presents a sample of the XML (from two XML files) that the data manager processes. This XML might be from a feed produced by a content management system.

 For most XML data, which is accessed frequently but doesn't change very often, it would be a good idea to use the APC cache facilities provided by PHP to improve performance.

Example 6-11. Data managers for accessing data stored using XML

```
class XMLDataManager extends DataManager
{
    public function __construct()
    {
        parent::__construct();
    }

    protected static function clean($text, $lower = false)
    {
        $clean = trim($text);
        $clean = ($lower) ? strtolower($clean) : $clean;

        return $clean;
    }

    ...
}

...

class NewCarArticlesDataManager extends XMLDataManager
{
    public function __construct()
```

```php
{
    parent::__construct();
}

public function get_data($load_args, &$load_data, &$load_stat)
{
    // Populate this with the path of the file containing XML data.
    $file = ...

    $data = array();

    if (file_exists($file))
    {
        $xml = simplexml_load_file
        (
            $file,
            "SimpleXMLElement",
            LIBXML_NOCDATA
        );

        foreach ($xml->article as $article)
        {
            $article_id = XMLDataManager::clean($article->article_id);

            if ($article_id == $load_args["article_id"])
            {
                $article_id = XMLDataManager::clean($article->article_id);
                $title = XMLDataManager::clean($article->title);
                $content = XMLDataManager::clean($article->content);

                // Populate the array with info about related new cars.
                if (empty($article->new_car_ids))
                    $new_cars = array();
                else
                    $new_cars = self::get_new_cars($article->new_car_ids);

                $data = array
                (
                    "article_id" => $article_id,
                    "title"      => $title,
                    "content"    => $content,
                    "new_cars"   => $new_cars
                );

                break;
            }
        }
    }

    $load_data = $data;
}

protected static function get_new_cars($new_car_ids)
{
    // Populate this with the path of the file containing XML data.
```

```
$file = ...

$data = array();

if (file_exists($file))
{
   $xml = simplexml_load_file
   (
      $file,
      "SimpleXMLElement",
      LIBXML_NOCDATA
   );

   foreach ($new_car_ids->new_car_id as $new_car_id)
   {
      $new_car_id = XMLDataManager::clean($new_car_id);

      foreach ($xml->new_car as $new_car)
      {
         $comp_id = XMLDataManager::clean($new_car->new_car_id);

         if ($comp_id == $new_car_id)
         {
            $name = XMLDataManager::clean($new_car->name);
            $price = XMLDataManager::clean($new_car->price);
            $preview = XMLDataManager::clean($new_car->preview);
            $details = XMLDataManager::clean($new_car->details);

            $data[$new_car_id] = array
            (
               "new_car_id" => $new_car_id,
               "name"       => $name,
               "price"      => $price,
               "preview"    => $preview,
               "details"    => $details,
               ...
            );

            break;
         }
      }
   }
}

return $data;
   }
}
```

Example 6-12. Sample XML data for the articles processed in Example 6-11

```
<?xml version="1.0"?>
<articles>
   <article>
      <article_id>
         2009_may
      </article_id>
```

```
        <title>
            Featured New Cars for May 2009
        </title>
        <content>
            <![CDATA[
                ...
            ]]>
        </content>
        <new_car_ids>
            <new_car_id>
                new_car_00001
            </new_car_id>
            <new_car_id>
                new_car_00002
            </new_car_id>
            ...
        </new_car_ids>
    </article>
    ...
</articles>

...

<?xml version="1.0"?>
<new_cars>
    <new_car>
        <new_car_id>
            new_car_00001
        </new_car_id>
        <name>
            New_car 1
        </name>
        <cost>
            20.95
        </cost>
        <preview>
            <![CDATA[
                ...
            ]]>
        </preview>
        <details>
            <![CDATA[
                ...
            ]]>
        </details>
    </new_car>
    ...
</new_cars>
```

Data from Web Services

A web service is a system that defines an API for accessing information over a network. Data often is returned as XML, but JSON (see "Data in the JSON Format" on page 132) is very popular as well. The simple interface, natural abstraction, and ubiquity of web services makes them very desirable for interfacing with backend systems.

To access a web service from a data manager, you can use the PHP Client URL (cURL) library. This library provides a simple way to communicate with many different servers using various protocols. Example 6-13 provides a basic example of a data manager to access a web service using cURL.

Example 6-13. Using cURL inside of a data manager to access a web service

```
class NewCarListingsDataManager
{
    public function __construct()
    {
        parent::__construct();
    }

    public function get_data($load_args, &$load_data, &$load_stat)
    {
        $ch = curl_init();

        // Set the URL to the web service required by the data manager.
        $url = ...

        curl_setopt($ch, CURLOPT_URL, $url);
        curl_setopt($ch, CURLOPT_HEADER, false);

        curl_setopt($ch, CURLOPT_RETURNTRANSFER, true);

        header("Content-Type: application/xml");
        $results = curl_exec($ch);

        curl_close($ch);

        // Do whatever processing is needed to the data that was returned.
        ...
    }
}
```

Because web services involve establishing connections over a network, they can take time to generate a response. To address this, it's a good idea to run multiple data managers for web services in parallel. You can do this using the cURL functions for making parallel requests (e.g., `curl_multi_init`, `curl_multi_add_handle`, `curl_multi_exec`, etc.).

Data in the JSON Format

When we explore large-scale Ajax in Chapter 8, you'll see that often it's useful to exchange data between the server and browser using JSON. This is because JSON is just the normal JavaScript syntax for object literals. Once you evaluate the data in the browser using eval, or more safely, json_parse (downloadable from *http://json.org/json _parse.js*), you can use the data like any other JavaScript object. It's also very lightweight. Considering its simplicity and conciseness, JSON is increasingly being recognized as a great format for exchanging data in other types of applications as well.

To convert a data structure (typically an associative array or object) in PHP to JSON, use the following:

```
$json = json_encode($data);
```

It's just as easy to get data in the JSON format back into a format that's easy to work with in PHP:

```
$data = json_decode($json, true);
```

The second parameter of json_decode, when set to true, causes the function to return the data as an associative array as opposed to an object. Example 6-14 illustrates what the new car reviews data from Example 6-1 would look like encoded as JSON data.

Example 6-14. The array of new car reviews from Example 6-1 in JSON

```
[
    {
        "name"  : "2009 Honda Accord",
        "price" : "21905",
        "link"  : "http://.../reviews/00001/"
    },

    {
        "name"  : "2009 Toyota Prius",
        "price" : "22000",
        "link"  : "http://.../reviews/00002/"
    },

    {
        "name"  : "2009 Nissan Altima",
        "price" : "19900",
        "link"  : "http://.../reviews/00003/"
    }
]
```

Assuming this data is in the variable json, you can get the name of the first new car in the array using JavaScript as follows:

```
var reviews = json_parse(json);
var name = reviews[0].name;
```

To get data into the JSON format, you can either pass flags to data managers to transform the data themselves or let the PHP scripts that handle Ajax requests transform the data from the associative arrays that the data managers normally return. Whatever the case, all it takes is a call to `json_encode`.

Cookies and Forms

Cookies and forms present their own considerations for the data they manage. Cookies provide a mechanism for browsers to store a small amount of persistent data on a visitor's computer. Some common uses for cookies are saving visitor preferences and managing shopping carts. Forms allow visitors to enter data for transmission back to the server. Some common places where forms are used include order processing and queries for product listings.

Managing Data in Cookies

A cookie consists of one or more name-value pairs. You can read and write them using JavaScript as well as server-side scripting languages like PHP. The following JavaScript writes two cookies that expire in one month (using the `max-age` cookie attribute) to save a postal code and a range in miles for new car search results:

```
var m = 60 * 60 * 24 * 30;
document.cookie = "nwcsrspos=94089;max-age=" + m;
document.cookie = "nwcsrsdst=50;max-age=" + m;
```

To write a cookie in PHP, you must send the cookie before echoing any output for the page (just as with the `header` function). The following PHP code writes a cookie that expires in one week to save a postal code for new car search results:

```
$t = time() + (60 * 60 * 24 * 7);
setcookie("nwcsrspos", "94089", $t);
```

In JavaScript, you retrieve the value of a cookie on a page by parsing the name-value pair that you are interested in from `document.cookie`. In PHP, you retrieve the value of a cookie by accessing the appropriate member of the associative array in `$_COOKIE` or `$_REQUEST`. For example, the following uses PHP to get the `nwcsrspos` cookie:

```
$pos = $_COOKIE["nwcsrspos"];
```

One of the concerns with cookies in large web applications is how to preserve modularity so that cookies written by one module do not conflict with those of another. To prevent conflicts, make sure to name each cookie within its own namespace. If you create unique identifiers for your modules (see Chapter 3), a simple solution is to prefix each cookie with the identifier of the module to which it belongs. For example, the `nwcsrspos` cookie contains name segments indicating it was the postal code cookie for the New Car Search Results module. For cookies that you need to share across multiple modules (e.g., suppose you want the cookie for a postal code to have the same identifier anywhere you use it), you can establish a naming convention that reflects the wider scope in which the cookies will be used.

Managing Data from Forms

A form typically utilizes a number of named input elements whose names and values are passed to another page for processing when the form is submitted. The values are available to the target page as members of associative arrays within the following variables. Since these variables often contain the data that you need to save to the backend, you often pass their values as arguments to the `set_data` method of data managers:

`$_GET`

> An associative array of values passed to the current page via URL parameters (e.g., via the GET method of a form).

`$_POST`

> An associative array of values passed to the current page via the HTTP POST method (e.g., via the POST method of a form).

`$_REQUEST`

> An associative array that contains all the values available in the `$_GET`, `$_POST`, and `$_COOKIE` variables.

One of the concerns with form data in a large web application, as it is with cookies, is to preserve modularity across forms within different modules. Specifically, you need to ensure that modules containing forms do not conflict with one another as their values are passed in tandem to other pages. Otherwise, it would be impossible for those pages to know which of the modules actually sent the similarly named data.

Fortunately, the same solution given for cookies works well here, too. If you create unique identifiers for your modules (see Chapter 3), you can use the module identifiers as a prefix for each form parameter to indicate the module to which it belongs. In addition, for common parameters that may be entered from multiple modules (e.g., suppose multiple modules let you set your postal code as a location), you can establish other naming conventions that reflect the scope in which the parameters will be used.

CHAPTER 7

Large-Scale PHP

In previous chapters, we explored techniques for writing highly maintainable, reusable, and reliable HTML, CSS, and JavaScript. In this chapter, we explore techniques for binding together these disparate technologies to assemble complete pages. To do this, we'll look at a large web application in terms of two deceptively simple yet powerful abstractions: *modules* and *pages*. A module is a self-contained component of the user interface that encompasses everything needed (e.g., the HTML, CSS, and JavaScript) to make an independently functioning and cohesive unit that you can use in a variety of contexts across various pages. A page, from the point of view of this chapter, is the canvas responsible for assembling a collection of modules so that they work together within a single context.

This chapter presents PHP as the implementation language for classes to represent pages and modules in large web applications. However, as mentioned in Chapter 1, all of the concepts presented here are relatively easy to transfer to other object-oriented, server-side scripting languages as well. Object orientation provides a more structured, extensible alternative to building pages than using a purely procedural approach. Fortunately, PHP 5 (and to a lesser extent PHP 4) offers a rich set of object-oriented features. Object orientation is an important part of achieving Tenet 7, as well as Tenet 6, from Chapter 1:

> Tenet 7: Pages are constructed from highly reusable modules that encapsulate everything required (e.g., HTML, CSS, JavaScript, and anything else) to make each module an independently functioning and cohesive unit that can be used in a variety of contexts across various pages.

> Tenet 6: Dynamic data exchanged between the user interface and the backend is managed through a clearly defined data interface. Pages define a single point for loading data and a single point for saving it.

We begin this chapter by introducing a skeleton implementation of a modular web page using a PHP class. It includes loading and saving data and creating content as a set of modules. Next, we explore the interfaces and implementations for some classes that represent various types of pages and modules. We then examine some real examples of modules, including modules for a slideshow and special modules that act as

reusable layouts and containers for other modules. Finally, we look at special considerations for working with modules and pages, including handling variations of the same
module, placing multiple instances of a module on a single page, generating dynamic
CSS and JavaScript, and implementing nested modules.

Modular Web Pages

A modular web page contains many potentially reusable pieces that interact in predictable ways when used together. Our goal is also to make it as simple as possible to
create a page. When you implement a page as a nicely encapsulated class, you don't
need much in your *index.php* file (or your *index.html* file if your server is configured to
run *.html* files as PHP), as Example 7-1 shows. The class for the page is included from
a file called *index_main.inc*, which resides at the same point in the directory structure
as *index.html* or *index.php*.

Example 7-1. Creating a modular web page

```php
<?php
require_once(".../index_main.inc");

$page = new NewCarSearchResultsPage();
$body = $page->create();

print($page->get_page());
?>
```

As you can see, the **create** method, a *factory method* in design pattern parlance, does
most of the work. The **create** method assembles the content that goes in the **body** tag
for the page and stores it in the page object (it also returns it). The **get_page** method is
then responsible for doing the final assembly of the page by marrying its body content
with everything else a page requires to be complete. Since the steps executed by
create and **get_page** are the same for most pages, both methods are good candidates
to implement in a base class for all pages. Later, we'll define a base class for all pages
called **Page**.

Although the steps performed by **create** and **get_page** are the same for each page, the
specific items that go into each step differ, of course. To define how to carry out each
of these steps for a specific page, such as a page for new car search results, you derive
your own page class from **Page** and implement several methods that **create** and
get_page call at the appropriate moments.

Generating Pages in PHP

The PHP that you'll see in a moment to generate a page looks very different from the
PHP code that most web developers are used to. When web developers build a page in
a brute force manner, loading each element in order, they tend to just print strings and

variables that contain the desired HTML. This chapter presents one approach to generating more structured pages using object orientation.

The `Page` base class performs the main tasks that all pages require: aggregating the HTML, CSS, and JavaScript from modules on the page and wrapping the page with the usual other tags (`title`, `head`, etc.). Each specific page class that you derive from `Page` creates the modules needed to build a page piece by piece. For each module in your application, you derive a module class from `Module` and implement methods that return the HTML, CSS, and JavaScript for just that module. Each module knows what it needs to function, such as the CSS to set the font and the JavaScript to animate a unique element on the page.

The `create` method for the page sets the process of generating the page in motion. Although we won't explore the complete code for `create` until later, some of the key tasks that `create` performs are:

- Calling `save_data`, which you define in your own page class, if needed, as the single point at which to save data to the backend.

- Calling `load_data`, which you define in your own page class, if needed, as the single point at which to load data from the backend.

- Calling `get_content`, which you define in your own page class as the single point at which to return the main content for the page.

You create the modules for a page in its `get_content` method. To create a module, call its `create` method, just as for creating pages. To use data from the backend in your modules, pass data retrieved via `load_data` into the module's constructor.

The `create` method for a module performs two very important tasks: it returns the HTML markup for the module, which you insert into the appropriate place within the overall layout for the page, and it adds to the page any CSS and JavaScript that the module requires. Modules are able to add CSS and JavaScript to a page because they store a reference to the page on which they reside. The reference is passed to the module when it is constructed by the application and stored in its `$page` member.

Using the `$page` member that every module contains, modules add CSS files to the page by doing the following:

```
$this->page->add_to_css_linked($this->get_css_linked());
```

Using a similar approach via the `$page` member, modules add JavaScript files to the page by doing the following:

```
$this->page->add_to_js_linked($this->get_js_linked());
```

Here, we've explained just enough of the mechanics of these object-oriented structures to let you see past them to the main goal. The key idea is that *all* parts of a module's implementation, including its CSS and JavaScript, need to travel as a neatly encapsulated bundle wherever the module is used.

In the rest of this chapter, we'll explore more of the details about how this object-oriented approach works. For now, Example 7-2 shows the implementation of a simple web page using the concepts just described.

Example 7-2. Implementing a modular web page

```php
<?php
require_once("../common/sitepage.inc");
require_once("../common/navbar.inc");
require_once("../common/subnav.inc");
require_once("../common/nwcresults.inc");
...

require_once("../layout/resultslayout.inc");
...

require_once("../datamgr/nwcqueries.inc");
require_once("../datamgr/nwclistings.inc");
...

class NewCarSearchResultsPage extends SitePage
{
    ...

    public function __construct()
    {
        parent::__construct();

        // Do whatever is needed to set up the page class at the start.
        // This often includes calling methods to process URL arguments.
        ...
    }

    public function save_data()
    {
        // If your page needs to save data to the backend, instantiate
        // the data managers you need (see Chapter 6) and call set_data.
        $dm = new NewCarQueriesDataManager();

        // The class members for saving are provided by the Page class.
        // Set them as needed to use the data manager and call set_data.
        ...

        $dm->set_data
        (
            $this->save_args["new_car_queries"],
            $this->save_data["new_car_queries"],
            $this->save_stat["new_car_queries"]
        );

        // Check the status member and handle any errors. Errors often
        // require a redirect to another page using the header function.
        if ($this->save_stat != 0)
            header("Location: ...");
```

```
        ...
    }

    public function load_data()
    {
        // If your page needs to load data from the backend, instantiate
        // the data managers you need (see Chapter 6) and call get_data.
        $dm = new NewCarListingsDataManager();

        // The class members for loading are provided by the Page class.
        // Populate them as needed by the data manager and call get_data.
        ...

        $dm->get_data
        (
            $this->load_args["new_car_listings"],
            $this->load_data["new_car_listings"],
            $this->load_stat["new_car_listings"]
        );

        // Check the status member and handle any errors. Errors often
        // require a redirect to another page using the header function.
        if ($this->load_stat != 0)
            header("Location: ...");

        ...
    }

    public function get_content()
    {
        // Create a module for the navigation bar to place on the page.
        $mod = new NavBar
        (
            $this,
            ...
        );

        $navbar = $mod->create();

        // Create a module for the sub navigation to place on the page.
        $mod = new SubNav
        (
            $this,
            ...
        );

        $subnav = $mod->create();

        // Create a module for showing new car search results. This module
        // uses the dynamic data loaded earlier by the load_data method.
        $mod = new NewCarSearchResults
        (
            $this,
            $this->load_data["new_car_listings"]
        );
```

```
$search = $mod->create();

// There would typically be several other modules to create here.
...

// Place the HTML markup for each module within the page layout.
$mod = new ResultsLayout
(
    $this,
    array($navbar, $subnav, ...),
    array($search),
    array(...),
    array(...),
    array(...),
    array(...)
);

// Return the content, which the create method for the page uses.
return $mod->create();
}

...

}
?>
```

Example 7-2 also illustrates the goal that using a module on a page should be easy. To this end, only a single include file is required for each module, the data for each module flows through a clearly defined interface in the constructor, and the creation of each module follows a clear and consistent pattern.

The first point about Example 7-2 requiring only a single include file for each module is key for encapsulation. Just as the implementation of `NewCarSearchResultsPage` includes only the files it needs for its components (e.g., specific data managers, specific modules, etc.), the files required for the implementation of a module should be included by that module itself. This way, its implementation details are hidden from users of the module. Using `require_once` is important so that a file included by multiple, nicely encapsulated implementations is included wherever necessary, but never more than once.

Research conducted with real pages at Yahoo! showed no significant change in overall performance when pages redeveloped using object-oriented PHP were compared against original versions of the same pages implemented without it. Even should you experience a slight increase on the server, be sure to consider the benefits you'll achieve from better software engineering, and remember that most of the overall latency for a page comes from downloading components in the browser (see Chapter 9).

Working with Pages

As mentioned earlier, a page, from the point of view of this chapter, is the canvas responsible for assembling a collection of modules so that they work well together within a single context. Because most pages perform a similar set of tasks, it's useful to define a base class that provides a minimum set of capabilities for all pages. For example, all pages fundamentally need a way to save and load data, define content, and assemble the page's components, among other things.

In this section, we'll take a closer look at Page, the base class that performs tasks that are common for all pages. Although it's not hard to imagine features beyond those presented here for such a class, the example provides a good starting point for many large web applications. We'll explore the class by examining its public interface, abstract interface, and implementation details.

Public Interface for the Page Class

The public interface for Page consists of methods for which most pages can benefit from a default implementation. For example, the public interface for Page provides methods for assembling a page as well as managing the CSS and JavaScript for the page overall. It's worthwhile to take a moment to observe carefully how the methods in this class are implemented because these provide a high-level definition of the steps that allow pages to be assembled in a modular fashion.

Structure and assembly

The methods for working with the structure and assembly of a page let you generate the body of the page, assemble the final page, and get some individual tags for the document type, title, and various metadata about the page:

create()

> Creates the body for the page and returns the HTML markup for the body tag. The body is returned so that pages that would prefer to assemble themselves rather than calling get_page have that option. In the process, create performs several important tasks. These include, in order, registering links (see register_links), saving and loading dynamic data, setting various parameters for the page, setting up the CSS and JavaScript common to the entire site, and getting the site header, content, and footer. Saving data, if needed, is performed before loading, because a problem encountered when saving often means the page should redirect itself or load different data. If your application differs from this model, you can always override create. The create method performs most of its tasks by calling methods from the abstract interface (see "Abstract Interface for the Page Class" on page 144).

get_page()

A convenience method for assembling the final page. Call get_page anytime after create has been called. To display the page, simply print what get_page returns. This method calls the next three methods to get the critical elements at the start of a page—the document type, meta tags, and title, respectively. Because they are public methods, developers who are assembling the final page without the help of get_page can call them directly.

get_doctype()

Gets the document type for the page. The default implementation returns the HTML 4.01 Strict DTD document type, but you can override this however you wish.

get_meta()

Gets the meta tags for the page. The default implementation returns several meta tags, but you can override this method to return whichever tags you desire.

get_title()

Gets the title for the page. The default implementation returns the title that you've set for the page wrapped in a title tag.

CSS management

These methods in the public interface let modules add the CSS that each requires to the page as links to CSS files or embedded CSS. There is also a method to get the entire block of CSS assembled for the page, which includes all CSS links and embedded CSS. If PHP supported C++'s concept of friends of classes, the two methods for adding CSS would not be necessary because the Module base class could provide an implementation for adding CSS itself:

add_to_css_linked($keys)

Adds links for CSS files to the set of CSS links for the page. $keys must contain an array of keys defined in register_links (described later). Each link is added when the first module requests it; subsequent requests are ignored to prevent duplicates.

add_to_css($css)

Adds the text in $css to the string of embedded CSS for the page.

get_all_css()

Gets the entire block of CSS for the page. The various forms of CSS are given the following order:

1. CSS links specified by get_css_common (for the global CSS files)

2. CSS links specified by the page class (see get_css_linked)

3. Embedded CSS specified by the page class (see get_css)

4. CSS links added by modules (see get_css_linked in "Public Interface for the Module Class" on page 162)

5. Embedded CSS added by modules (see `get_css` in "Public Interface for the Module Class" on page 162)

The CSS for modules appears in the order in which each module was created. This ordering works well and is deterministic; however, you can always override it by providing an alternate implementation for `get_all_css` in a derived page class.

JavaScript management

These methods in the public interface let modules add the JavaScript that each requires to the page as links to JavaScript files or embedded JavaScript. There are also methods to get the entire block of JavaScript assembled for the page, which includes all JavaScript links and embedded JavaScript, and to set a flag that causes the JavaScript to be placed at the top of the page instead of the bottom. As we mentioned for CSS, if PHP supported C++'s concept of friends of classes, the two methods for adding JavaScript would not be necessary because the `Module` base class could provide an implementation for adding JavaScript itself:

`add_to_js_linked($keys)`
Adds links for JavaScript files to the set of JavaScript links for the page. `$keys` must contain an array of keys defined in `register_links` (described later). Each link is added when the first module requests it; subsequent requests are ignored to prevent duplicates.

`add_to_js($js)`
Adds the text in `$js` to the string of embedded JavaScript for the page.

`get_all_js()`
Gets the entire block of JavaScript for the page. The various forms of JavaScript are given the following order:

1. JavaScript links specified by `get_js_common` (for the global JavaScript files)

2. JavaScript links specified by the page class (see `get_js_linked`)

3. Embedded JavaScript specified by the page class (see `get_js`)

4. JavaScript links added by modules (see `get_js_linked` in "Public Interface for the Module Class" on page 162)

5. Embedded JavaScript added by modules (see `get_js` in "Public Interface for the Module Class" on page 162)

The JavaScript for modules appears in the order in which each module was created. This ordering works well and is deterministic; however, you can always override it by providing an alternate implementation for `get_all_js` in a derived page class.

`set_js_top()`
Sets a flag to indicate that `get_page` should place all JavaScript at the top of the page. The `get_page` method normally places JavaScript at the bottom for better performance; however, for some pages, you may want an easy way to change this

placement (for example, where JavaScript is needed for the primary call to action on the page).

Abstract Interface for the Page Class

The abstract interface for Page consists of methods that we expect various types of pages to need and that each subclass of Page can implement as needed. The Page class calls upon these methods at the appropriate moments, primarily via the **create** method. Because Page provides empty implementations for each of the methods, a class derived from Page is not required to implement all of the methods in the abstract interface; it implements only the methods that it requires. For example, if a page doesn't have any data to save, it doesn't have to provide an implementation for save_data. The simplest pages may implement little more than just the get_content method.

CSS management

The methods in the abstract interface for managing CSS let you link CSS files that most pages have in common across an entire web application, as well as CSS files or embedded CSS to use in specific pages:

get_css_common()
> Implement this method to return an array of keys registered in register_links (see register_links) for the common CSS files to link across all pages in your entire web application. You normally define this method in the base class from which you will derive all the pages in your entire application (see "Defining a sitewide page class" on page 157). This is a good place to include the CSS for browser resets (see Chapter 4), font normalization (see Chapter 4), and certain highly standardized elements (e.g., links), for example.

get_css_linked()
> Implement this method to return an array of keys registered in register_links (see register_links) for additional CSS files to link, beyond what the modules on the page specify. Define this method for specific pages or in the base class from which pages within a certain section of your entire web application will be derived (see "Defining sectional page classes" on page 161).

get_css()
> Implement this method to return a string of CSS to embed on the page. This method generally is useful for embedding a small amount of CSS on a specific page in order to affect the styling of a module outside its borders (see "Scoping at the page level" on page 59 in Chapter 4), or to apply other very minimal stylistic changes to one instance of a module within the context of a specific page.

JavaScript management

The methods in the abstract interface for managing JavaScript let you link JavaScript files that most pages have in common across an entire web application, as well as JavaScript files or embedded JavaScript to use in specific pages:

get_js_common()
> Implement this method to return an array of keys registered in `register_links` (see `register_links`) for the common JavaScript files to link across all pages in your entire web application. You normally define this method in the base class from which you will derive all the pages in your entire application (see "Defining a sitewide page class" on page 157). This is a good place to include the JavaScript required for site analytics on all pages, for example.

get_js_linked()
> Implement this method to return an array of keys registered in `register_links` (see `register_links`) for additional JavaScript files to link, beyond what the modules on the page specify. Define this method for specific pages or in the base class from which pages within a certain section of your entire web application will be derived (see "Defining sectional page classes" on page 161).

get_js()
> Implement this method to return a string of JavaScript to embed on the page. This method generally is useful to embed a small amount of dynamically generated JavaScript in a specific page. This JavaScript is often needed to initialize or stitch together the layer of behavior for modules.

Dynamic data management

The methods for dynamic data management provide a single interface in your program for loading data from the backend and a single interface for saving data that the backend needs to store:

load_data()
> Implement this method to instantiate data managers to load data for the page from the backend (see Chapter 6). Call `get_data` for each data manager. You typically implement `load_data` only in the page class for a specific page. The class `Page` defines the following data members:
>
> $load_args
> > The arguments passed to data managers when loading data
>
> $load_data
> > Where data managers store data
>
> $load_stat
> > Where data managers record their status when loading data

Your `load_data` method should be capable of handling errors based on the value passed back in `$load_stat`. On return, the `$load_data` data member contains all data loaded from the backend.

`save_data()`

Implement this method to instantiate the data managers to save data for the page within the backend (see Chapter 6). The behavior for saving mirrors the behavior just described for loading. Call `set_data` for each data manager. You typically implement `save_data` only in the page class for a specific page. The class `Page` defines the following data members:

`$save_args`

The arguments passed to data managers when saving data

`$save_data`

Where data managers read the data to be stored

`$save_stat`

Where data managers record their status when saving data

Your `save_data` method should be capable of handling errors based on the value passed back in `$save_stat`.

Headers, footers, and content

The focus of any web page, of course, is its content. Since most large web applications have a standard header and footer across the top and bottom of all pages, respectively, our `Page` class provides methods for managing the header and footer separately from the main content:

`get_header()`

Implement this method to return the HTML markup for the header of a page. The `create` method places the header immediately before the content. You typically implement this method in the sitewide page class (see "Defining a sitewide page class" on page 157) for all pages across the site and override it in derived classes for just the pages on which you need a different header.

`get_footer()`

Implement this method to return the HTML markup for the footer of a page. The `create` method places the footer immediately after the content. You typically implement this method in the sitewide page class (see "Defining a sitewide page class" on page 157) for all pages across the site and override it in derived classes for just the pages on which you need a different footer.

`get_content()`

Implement this method to return the HTML markup for the content of a page. You typically implement this method in just the page classes for specific pages since the content for every page is different. This is the method in which you normally create most modules. You place the HTML markup that each module returns into a layout whose markup is ultimately returned by this method.

General page information

The remaining methods defined by `Page` manage general information about a page. These methods set the title and meta information for a page, set a CSS ID for the body, and register keys for links to CSS and JavaScript files. The CSS ID is useful for creating individual namespaces for pages (see "Scoping at the page level" on page 59 in Chapter 4). The use of keys for links to CSS and JavaScript files in a large web application centralizes the management of filenames, versioning of CSS and JavaScript for caching (see Chapter 9), and switching between local and also-known-as paths to support different locations for different environments (e.g., production versus development):

`set_title()`
> Implement this method to set the `$title` data member. This member is used to construct a `title` tag when `get_title` is called.

`set_meta()`
> Implement this method to set the `$equiv`, `$desc`, and `$keywd` data members. These members are used to construct several `meta` tags when `get_meta` is called. You can also use this method to set additional members in your derived class and have your own implementation of `get_meta` build appropriate tags for them to be placed at the top of the page.

`set_css_id()`
> Implement this method to set the `$css_id` data member. This member is used in `get_page` when adding the CSS ID to the `body` tag.

`register_links()`
> Implement this to set up the `$css_linked_info` and `$js_linked_info` data members. These members are used to resolve keys for CSS and JavaScript files into paths to files that can be linked. You typically implement this method in your sitewide page class and augment the data structures (as opposed to overriding the method) in classes for certain sections of pages on the site. "Extending the Page Class" on page 157 contains an example of the data structures for `$css_linked_info` and `$js_linked_info`.

Implementation of the Page Class

This section presents some of the implementation details for the `Page` class. Many of the implementation details are managed through private methods and therefore are accessible only to the `Page` class itself. All of the private methods focus on the aggregation of CSS and JavaScript for the page. This aggregation takes place as pages and modules are created, each incrementally specifying the CSS and JavaScript that it requires:

`manage_css_linked($keys)`
> Looks up and returns the corresponding CSS links for an array of keys in `$keys`. The method keeps track of all CSS links already included and skips the addition

of any CSS link that was added previously. This ensures that a CSS link is included at the first point it is required, but never more than once.

create_css_linked($k)

Converts a single key, $k, for a CSS file registered in register_links to a CSS link. The resulting link is returned.

create_css($css)

Creates a complete block of CSS by wrapping the CSS specified in $css within the proper style tags. The method returns the resulting block of CSS.

set_css_common

Sets the $css_common member of the class so that CSS links common to the entire web application are stored and can be included at the proper time.

set_css_page

Sets the $css_page member of the class so that CSS links included at the page level are stored and can be included at the proper time.

manage_js_linked($keys)

Looks up and returns the corresponding JavaScript links for an array of keys in $keys. The method keeps track of all JavaScript links already included and skips the addition of any JavaScript link added previously. This ensures that a JavaScript link is included at the first point it is required, but never more than once.

create_js_linked($k)

Converts a single key, in $k, for a JavaScript file registered in register_links to a JavaScript link. The resulting link is returned.

create_js($js)

Creates a complete block of JavaScript by wrapping the JavaScript specified in $js within the proper script tags. The method returns the block of JavaScript.

set_js_common

Sets the $js_common member of the class so that JavaScript links common to the entire web application are stored and can be included at the proper time.

set_js_page

Sets the $js_page member of the class so that JavaScript links included at the page level are stored and can be included at the proper time.

Example 7-3 presents the code for the Page class, including implementations for many of the methods presented earlier.

Example 7-3. Implementation of the Page class

```
class Page
{
    // Members for aggregating CSS styles from modules as they are added
    // to the page, storing information about how and when to link files,
    // and keeping track of various sections of CSS styles on the page.
    protected $css;
    protected $css_linked;
```

```php
protected $css_linked_info;
protected $css_linked_used;
protected $css_is_local;

protected $css_common;
protected $css_page;
protected $css_module;

protected $css_id;

// Members for aggregating JavaScript from modules as they are added
// to the page, storing information about how and when to link files,
// and keeping track of various sections of JavaScript on the page.
protected $js;
protected $js_linked;

protected $js_linked_info;
protected $js_linked_used;
protected $js_is_local;

protected $js_common;
protected $js_page;
protected $js_module;

protected $js_is_top;

// Members to manage loading and saving data stored by the backend.
protected $load_args;
protected $load_data;
protected $load_stat;
protected $save_args;
protected $save_data;
protected $save_stat;
protected $save_data_flag;

// Members to manage meta information about the page and its body.
protected $title;
protected $equiv;
protected $desc;
protected $keywd;
protected $body;

/*
 * The following methods comprise the public interface for the class.
 */

public function __construct()
{
    $this->css = "";
    $this->css_linked = "";
    $this->css_linked_info = array();
    $this->css_linked_used = array();
    $this->css_is_local = true;
    $this->css_common = "";
```

```php
        $this->css_page = "";
        $this->css_module = "";
        $this->css_id = "";

        $this->js = "";
        $this->js_linked = "";
        $this->js_linked_info = array();
        $this->js_linked_used = array();
        $this->js_is_local = true;
        $this->js_common = "";
        $this->js_page = "";
        $this->js_module = "";
        $this->js_is_top = false;

        $this->load_args = array();
        $this->load_data = array();
        $this->load_stat = "";
        $this->save_args = array();
        $this->save_data = array();
        $this->sava_stat = "";
        $this->save_data_flag = false;

        $this->title = "";
        $this->equiv = "";
        $this->desc = "";
        $this->keywd = "";
    }

    public function create()
    {
        $this->register_links();

        if ($this->save_data_flag)
            $this->save_data();

        $this->load_data();

        // Do these steps now to give the page the opportunity to execute
        // them based on data from the backend that may have been loaded.
        $this->set_title();
        $this->set_meta();
        $this->set_css_id();

        // This needs to be done before the modules add JavaScript and CSS
        // so that files from multiple sources appear in the order linked.
        $this->set_js_common();
        $this->set_js_page();
        $this->set_css_common();
        $this->set_css_page();

        $header = $this->get_header();
        $content = $this->get_content();
        $footer = $this->get_footer();

        // We wrap the body of the page in a canvas division with its own
```

```
        // body, which provides some additional hooks useful for styling.
        $this->body = <<<EOD
<div id="sitecvs">
    <div class="sitecvsbd">
$header
$content
$footer
    <!-- sitecvsbd -->
    </div>
<!-- sitecvs -->
</div>

EOD;

        return $this->body;
    }

    public function get_page()
    {
        if (empty($this->css_id))
            $css_id = "";
        else
            $css_id = " id=\"".$this->css_id."\"";

        $doctype = $this->get_doctype();
        $meta = $this->get_meta();
        $title = $this->get_title();

        // Generally, it's a good idea for performance to place JavaScript
        // at the bottom of the page; however, a flag lets us alter this.
        if ($this->js_is_top)
        {
            $js_top = $this->get_all_js();
            $js_btm = "";
        }
        else
        {
            $js_top = "";
            $js_btm = $this->get_all_js();
        }

        $css = $this->get_all_css();

        // Return the entire page suitable for echoing back to the browser.
        return <<<EOD
$doctype
<html>
<head>
$meta
$title
$css
$js_top
</head>
<body{$css_id}>
$this->body
```

```php
$js_btm
</body>
</html>

EOD;
    }

    public function get_doctype()
    {
        return <<<EOD
<!DOCTYPE HTML PUBLIC "-//W3C//DTD HTML 4.01//EN"
"http://www.w3.org/TR/html4/strict.dtd">

EOD;
    }

    public function get_meta()
    {
        $meta = <<<EOD
<meta http-equiv="Content-Type" content="text/html; charset=UTF-8" />

EOD;

        if (!empty($this->equiv))
        {
            $meta .= <<<EOD
<meta name="http-equiv" content="{$this->equiv}" />

EOD;
        }

        if (!empty($this->desc))
        {
            $meta .= <<<EOD
<meta name="description" content="{$this->desc}" />

EOD;
        }

        if (!empty($this->keywd))
        {
            $meta .= <<<EOD
<meta name="keywords" content="{$this->keywd}" />

EOD;
        }

        return $meta;
    }

    public function get_title()
    {
        return <<<EOD
<title>{$this->title}</title>
```

```php
EOD;
    }

    public function add_to_css_linked($keys)
    {
        $this->css_linked .= $this->manage_css_linked($keys);
    }

    public function add_to_css($css)
    {
        $this->css .= $css;
    }

    public function get_all_css()
    {
        // First, we get all the styles that were appended by modules.
        $this->css_module = $this->css_linked;
        $this->css_module .= $this->create_css($this->css);

        // Then we assemble all the CSS styles for the page in one block.
        return <<<EOD
<!-- Common CSS -->
$this->css_common
<!-- Page CSS -->
$this->css_page
<!-- Module CSS -->
$this->css_module

EOD;
    }

    public function add_to_js_linked($keys)
    {
        $this->js_linked .= $this->manage_js_linked($keys);
    }

    public function add_to_js($js)
    {
        $this->js .= $js;
    }

    public function get_all_js()
    {
        // First, we get all JavaScript that was appended by modules.
        $this->js_module = $this->js_linked;
        $this->js_module .= $this->create_js($this->js);

        // Then we assemble all the JavaScript for the page in one block.
        return <<<EOD
<!-- Common JS -->
$this->js_common
<!-- Page JS -->
$this->js_page
<!-- Module JS -->
$this->js_module
```

```
EOD;
    }

    public function set_js_top()
    {
        $this->js_is_top = true;
    }

    /*
     * The following methods comprise the abstract interface for the
     * class. These are methods with empty implementations by default,
     * many of which specific page classes override for their needs.
     */

    public function get_css_common()
    {
    }

    public function get_css_linked()
    {
    }

    public function get_css()
    {
    }

    // See the section on the abstract interface for the complete list
    // of methods for which empty implementations would be given here.
    ...

    /*
     * The following methods are for implementation details in the class.
     */

    private function manage_css_linked($keys)
    {
        $css = "";

        if (empty($keys))
            return "";

        // Normalize so that we can pass keys individually or as an array.
        if (!is_array($keys))
            $keys = array($keys);

        foreach ($keys as $k)
        {
            // Log an error for unknown keys when there is no link to add.
            if (!array_key_exists($k, $this->css_linked_info))
            {
                error_log("Page::manage_css_linked: Key \"".$k."\" missing");
                continue;
            }

            // Add the link only if it hasn't been added to the page before.
```

```php
            if (array_search($k, $this->css_linked_used) === false)
            {
                $this->css_linked_used[] = $k;
                $css .= $this->create_css_linked($k);
            }
        }

        return $css;
    }

    private function create_css_linked($k)
    {
        // Links can be fetched locally or from an also-known-as location.
        if ($this->css_is_local)
            $path = $this->css_linked_info[$k]["loc_path"];
        else
            $path = $this->css_linked_info[$k]["aka_path"];

        // Links have an optional media type (with a default type "all").
        if (empty($this->css_linked_info[$k]["media"]))
            $media = "all";
        else
            $media = $this->css_linked_info[$k]["media"];

        return <<<EOD
<link href="$path" type="text/css" rel="stylesheet" media="$media" />

EOD;
    }

    private function create_css($css)
    {
        if (!empty($css))
        {
            return <<<EOD
<style type="text/css" media="all" >
$css</style>

EOD;
        }
        else
        {
            return "";
        }
    }

    private function set_css_common()
    {
        $this->css_common = $this->manage_css_linked($this->get_css_common());
    }

    private function set_css_page()
    {
        $this->css_page = $this->manage_css_linked($this->get_css_linked());
        $this->css_page .= $this->create_css($this->get_css());
    }
```

```php
    }

    private function manage_js_linked($keys)
    {
        $js = "";

        if (empty($keys))
            return "";

        // Normalize so that we can pass keys individually or as an array.
        if (!is_array($keys))
            $keys = array($keys);

        foreach ($keys as $k)
        {
            // Log an error for unknown keys when there is no link to add.
            if (!array_key_exists($k, $this->js_linked_info))
            {
                error_log("Page::manage_js_linked: Key \"".$k."\" missing");
                continue;
            }

            // Add the link only if it hasn't been added to the page before.
            if (array_search($k, $this->js_linked_used) === false)
            {
                $this->js_linked_used[] = $k;
                $js .= $this->create_js_linked($k);
            }
        }

        return $js;
    }

    private function create_js_linked($k)
    {
        // Links can be fetched locally or from an also-known-as location.
        if ($this->js_is_local)
            $path = $this->js_linked_info[$k]["loc_path"];
        else
            $path = $this->js_linked_info[$k]["aka_path"];

        return <<<EOD
<script src="$path" type="text/javascript"></script>

EOD;
    }

    private function create_js($js)
    {
        if (!empty($js))
        {
            return <<<EOD
<script type="text/javascript">
$js</script>
```

```
EOD;
    }
    else
    {
        return "";
    }
}

private function set_js_common()
{
    $this->js_common = $this->manage_js_linked($this->get_js_common());
}

private function set_js_page()
{
    $this->js_page = $this->manage_js_linked($this->get_js_linked());
    $this->js_page .= $this->create_js($this->get_js());
}
}
```

Extending the Page Class

One of the most important benefits of an object-oriented approach to defining pages for a large web application is the ease with which you can derive classes for new types of pages from classes that you have already created. In the previous section, we focused on one example of a class, Page, with features generally useful to all types of pages across all types of web applications. In this section, we look at some common derivations of Page. These include a page class to handle the specifics of a single web application, page classes for certain sections of a web application, and page classes for specific pages. As we explore these types of classes, we'll look at the role that each is likely to play in a large web application, especially in terms of which parts of Page's abstract interface each class is likely to implement.

Such a systematic hierarchy of page classes helps us create large web applications that are ultimately more maintainable because each class is highly modular and has a great potential for reuse. In addition to maintainability and reusability, page classes create a nice division of responsibility. One group of engineers can focus on extending the Page base class to build a framework that makes sense for an entire web application while another group can work on the classes that support various sections of it. Other teams can then focus on specific pages. As common needs arise across certain scopes of the site, appropriate teams can perform those implementations within the right level of the class hierarchy.

Defining a sitewide page class

A sitewide page class is derived from Page and customizes Page for the unique characteristics that apply to your entire web application. This type of page class typically implements the following methods from Page's abstract interface: get_css_common, get_js_common, register_links, get_header, and get_footer. In addition, you often use the sitewide page class to define other methods and data members of your own that you expect to be relevant across the entire web application. Data members used for paths are a good example. The placement of members in a sitewide page class is a nice alternative to using global variables. Some examples are listed below:

$path_root
> The path to the starting point in your directory structure at which to find PHP include files and other source code. This is commonly called a *prefix path*. This path often has the form */home/userid/docroot*.

$path_common
> The path where you plan to place components that are common to most parts of your web application. This member is typically derived from $path_root.

$path_layout
> The path where you plan to place components related to layout and containers, which are typically common across an entire application. This member is typically derived from $path_root.

$path_datamgr
> The path for all data managers (see Chapter 6). This member is typically derived from $path_root.

$path_base
> The prefix address and path for all URLs in your web application (e.g., links to CSS files, links to JavaScript files, sources for images, etc.). This path has the form *http://hostname.com/path*.

$path_css
> The prefix address and path for all URLs related to CSS files. This member is typically derived from $path_base.

$path_js
> The prefix address and path for all URLs related to JavaScript files. This member is typically derived from $path_base.

$path_img
> The prefix address and path for all URLs used for image sources. This member is typically derived from $path_base.

Example 7-4 presents an example of a sitewide page class, SitePage, which illustrates implementations for the methods mentioned previously. The example also shows the ease with which you can override default implementations provided by Page. For example, SitePage overrides Page's implementation of get_all_js to add Google analytics to the site (see Chapter 9). It does this by delegating most of the work back to the implementation of get_all_js in Page. However, it then appends the analytics code to the JavaScript previously assembled. It makes sense to implement this in the sitewide page class because analytics are run for the entire site.

Example 7-4 shows a common way to add capabilities in object-oriented systems, which may be unfamiliar to PHP programmers who are new to objects. To differentiate between a method in the base class that has also been implemented in the derived class, you use the scope (::) operator. For instance, __construct starts with:

```
parent::__construct();
```

Derived classes typically do this as the first line in the constructor to set up the parts of the object inherited from the base class. More statements can then be added to the derived class constructor to carry out tasks specific to the derived class.

Example 7-4. Implementing a sitewide page class

```
class SitePage extends Page
{
    const path_css = "...";
    const path_js  = "...";
    const path_img = "...";

    ...

    public function __construct()
    {
        parent::__construct();

        ...
    }

    public function get_all_js()
    {
        // First, get all the JavaScript that was assembled for modules,
        // etc. on the page.
        $js = parent::get_all_js();

        $analytics = <<<EOD
<!-- Google Analytics -->
<script type="text/javascript">
var gaJsHost = (("https:" == document.location.protocol)
    ? "https://ssl."
    : "http://www.");

document.write(unescape("%3Cscript src='" +
    gaJsHost + "google-analytics.com/ga.js'
    type='text/javascript'%3E%3C/script%3E"));

var pageTracker = _gat._getTracker("...");
pageTracker._setDomainName("...");
pageTracker._trackPageview();
</script>
EOD;
    }

        // Append Google Analytics to the JavaScript that was assembled
        // otherwise for the page.
        return <<<EOD
```

```php
$js
$analytics

EOD;
    }

    public function get_js_common()
    {
        // Specify an array of JavaScript files to link for every page.
        return array
        (
            "yahoo-dom-event.js",
            "sitewide.js"
        );
    }

    public function get_css_common()
    {
        // Specify an array of stylesheet files to link for every page.
        return array
        (
            "sitewide.css"
        );
    }

    public function get_header()
    {
        // Return the HTML markup for the header across the entire site.
        return <<<EOD
<div id="sitehdr">
    ...
</div>

EOD;
    }

    public function get_footer()
    {
        // Return the HTML markup for the footer across the entire site.
        return <<<EOD
<div id="siteftr">
    ...
</div>

EOD;
    }

    public function register_links()
    {
        // Build the data structure for resolving stylesheet filenames.
        $this->css_linked_info = array
        (
            "sitewide.css" => array
            (
                "aka_path" => "...",
```

```
            "loc_path" => "...",
            "media"    => "all"
        ),

        ...
    );


    // When this member is set to true, stylesheet keys resolve to
    // the loc_path paths; otherwise, the aka_path paths are used.
    $this->css_is_local = false;

    // Build the data structure for resolving JavaScript filenames.
    $this->js_linked_info = array
    (
        "sitewide.js" => array
        (
            "aka_path" => "...",
            "loc_path" => "..."
        ),
        "yahoo-dom-event.js" => array
        (
            "aka_path" => "...",
            "loc_path" => "..."
        ),

        ...
    );


    // When this member is set to true, JavaScript keys resolve to
    // the loc_path paths; otherwise, the aka_path paths are used.
    $this->js_is_local = false;
}

// You would likely define a number of other methods here for tasks
// specific to your web application and that apply to all parts of it.
...
}
```

Defining sectional page classes

A sectional page class is a class derived from your sitewide page class that customizes the sitewide page class for a section of your application (e.g., `NewCarsPage` for a section of the site containing multiple pages related to new cars). Some methods that a sectional page class might define are `get_header` and `get_footer` to display a different header and footer for a section, or `get_css_linked` and `get_js_linked` to link additional CSS and JavaScript files for just that section.

In addition, a sectional page class may want to register its own set of links for CSS and JavaScript files. It does this by implementing its own `register_links` method, which calls the parent's `register_links` method first to let the parent add links for the entire web application, then appends its own entries for CSS and JavaScript files to the `$css_linked_info` and `$js_linked_info` members.

Defining page-specific classes

Page-specific classes are the most common pages that you'll implement. These are classes like `NewCarSearchResultsPage`, presented earlier in Example 7-1. In page-specific classes, you typically implement the following from `Page`'s abstract interface: `save_data`, `load_data`, `get_content`, `set_title`, `set_meta`, and `set_css_id`. You might also implement `get_css` and `get_js` to provide small amounts of CSS and JavaScript to embed on the page beyond what the modules already provide; however, the modules normally should have already specified everything they are able to encapsulate themselves. Of course, object orientation lets you override any method in a page's specific class to do something different from the base class.

Working with Modules

As mentioned at the start of the chapter, a module is a self-contained component of the user interface that encompasses everything needed (e.g., the HTML, CSS, and JavaScript) to make an independently functioning and cohesive unit that can be used in a variety of contexts across various pages. Considering that a page is the canvas responsible for assembling a collection of modules so that they work together within a single context, modules must provide a page with everything that the page requires to assemble itself. This common requirement among modules suggests that we should have a base class from which to derive all modules.

In this section, we'll look at one example of a base class for modules called `Module`. Although it's not hard to imagine features beyond those presented here for such a class, the example provides a good starting point by which to implement modules in many large web applications.

A module specifies what it needs loaded for HTML, CSS, and JavaScript, but these pieces are actually assembled later by the page, because only the page can put everything together in the proper order. Therefore, when you create an instance of the `Module` class, you pass in a reference to the page on which the module will reside. The module then places references to all the pieces it needs in data structures within that page, and the page uses them later.

Just as we did for `Page`, let's explore the `Module` class by examining its public interface, abstract interface, and implementation details.

Public Interface for the Module Class

The public interface for `Module` consists of a single method named `create`, which has an implementation in the base class that is sufficient for most modules. This interface is nicely parallel to the interface for creating pages:

`create()`

> Creates a module and returns its HTML markup. In the process, `create` performs several important tasks. These include, in order, adding CSS links and embedded CSS for the module to the page, adding JavaScript links and embedded JavaScript for the module to the page, and getting the content for the module. The `create` method performs each of these tasks by calling methods from the abstract interface, discussed next.

Abstract Interface for the Module Class

The abstract interface for `Module` consists of methods that specific modules are expected to implement as needed. The `Module` class calls upon these methods at the appropriate moments from its `create` method. Because `Module` provides empty implementations for each of the methods, a class derived from `Module` is not required to implement all of the methods in the abstract interface; it implements only the methods that it requires. For example, if a module doesn't need to link any JavaScript files, it doesn't have to provide an implementation for `get_js_linked`. The simplest modules may implement just the `get_content` and `get_css_linked` methods.

CSS management

The methods in the abstract interface for managing CSS let you specify the CSS files to link and the CSS to embed for a module. These are aggregated by the page on which the module resides when the module is created so that the page can insert them at the appropriate point when the page is assembled:

`get_css_linked()`

> Implement this method to return an array of keys registered in `register_links` (see `register_links`) for the CSS files to link for the module. If you follow the convention that the `get_css_common` method of the page class will include a sitewide file, you don't have to specify it here; however, specifying it will cause no harm because the page will check and make sure not to include it twice.

`get_css()`

> Implement this method to return a string of CSS to embed for the module. This method is useful when you need to specify dynamically generated CSS for a module.

JavaScript management

The methods in the abstract interface for managing JavaScript let you specify the JavaScript files to link and the JavaScript to embed for a module. As with CSS, the links and embedded JavaScript are passed to the page to assemble later:

get_js_linked()

Implement this method to return an array of keys registered in `register_links` (see `register_links`) for the JavaScript files to link for the module. Modules that require JavaScript often link several JavaScript libraries to ensure that all dependencies between the libraries are addressed.

get_js()

Implement this method to return a string of JavaScript to embed for the module. This method is useful when you need to specify dynamically generated JavaScript for a module.

Content for the module

Modules define a single method for working with content. This method generates the HTML that appears in the module:

get_content

Implement this method to return the HTML markup for the content of the module. If needed, you can also create other modules within the `get_content` method for a module in the same way as you do for pages (see "Implementing Nested Modules" on page 182).

Implementation of the Module Class

Because modules perform just a few tasks, our implementation of `Module` does not need any private or protected methods. Example 7-5 presents the code for the `Module` class.

Example 7-5. Implementation of the Module class

```php
class Module
{
    // Used to store a reference to the page on which the module resides.
    protected $page;

    /*
    *  The following methods comprise the public interface for the class.
    */

    public function __construct($page)
    {
        // All modules store a reference to the page on which they reside.
        // In PHP 5, objects are passed by reference. In PHP 4, we would
        // have had to specify we wanted a reference explicitly (using &).
        $this->page = $page;
    }

    public function create()
    {
        // Add module CSS styles to the page on which the module resides.
        $this->page->add_to_css_linked($this->get_css_linked());
        $this->page->add_to_css($this->get_css());
```

```
    // Add module JavaScript to the page on which the module resides.
    $this->page->add_to_js_linked($this->get_js_linked());
    $this->page->add_to_js($this->get_js());

    return $this->get_content();
}

/*
 * The following methods comprise the abstract interface for the
 * class. These are methods with empty implementations by default,
 * many of which specific module classes override for their needs.
 */

public function get_css_linked()
{
}

public function get_css()
{
}

public function get_js_linked()
{
}

public function get_js()
{
}

public function get_content()
{
}
}
```

Extending the Module Class

Just as we extended the Page class for new types of pages, we can derive new types of modules from Module. Generally, you will find that most modules can be derived directly from Module. However, our object-oriented approach to developing modules provides the same opportunities for good maintainability and reusability as we saw with page classes earlier. One example of a specific type of module that provides a good opportunity for reuse is the Layout base class for all layouts and containers (see "Layouts and Containers" on page 177). Layouts require the same capabilities as other modular-type entities, while adding some of their own.

An Example Module: Slideshow

Modules can be many things in a large web application: a list of search results, a form for entering search queries, a menu bar, a wrapper for standard advertising units, or a highly reusable user interface component like a selection list, paginator, or stylized button, to name a few. In this section, we explore a popular component in many large web applications: a slideshow, which presents a series of slides along with some navigation (right, left, or an arbitrarily chosen slide).

One way to implement a slideshow is to define two modules that work together. One module, which we'll call the Picture Slider module, provides a slider of thumbnail images from which the visitor makes selections. The other module, which we'll call the Picture Viewer module, provides a larger view of the image selected in the picture slider (see Figure 7-1). This slideshow isn't fancy; it doesn't change slides automatically at fixed time intervals, but it keeps the current slide as well as the position of the slider in sync with the movements specified by the visitor.

Figure 7-1. The Picture Slider and Picture Viewer modules in a slideshow

Example 7-6 presents implementations for `PictureSlider` and `PictureViewer`, the two classes that define the Picture Slider and Picture Viewer modules, respectively. Because these classes are normally used together, you might decide to place them both in a single include file called *slideshow.inc*. You'll notice with a closer look that even though the classes for the two modules are often used together, they are not tightly coupled; each works completely independently. One benefit of defining two separate classes is that you can arrange the slider and viewer on the page however you desire. For example, you can place the slider above or below the viewer, or you can place a small module of some other type between them.

The Picture Slider and Picture Viewer modules are easy to configure. When you instantiate `PictureSlider`, for example, you simply pass it a gallery of images to display as an array of image data. Each member in the array is an associative array consisting of the URL for a thumbnail of the image (`img_t`), a URL for the large version of the image (`img_l`), the text for the caption (`text`), and text for the attribution (`attr`). When you instantiate `PictureViewer`, you pass it one member of the gallery for it to display.

Notice that both `PictureSlider` and `PictureViewer` define the methods outlined for `Module` earlier that let you specify the CSS and JavaScript for a module and get its content. These effectively allow the CSS and JavaScript to travel with the module wherever it is used. Furthermore, they document exactly where to find the CSS and JavaScript for the module, should you decide to refactor the code for the module in the future.

Example 7-6. PictureSlider and PictureViewer classes for the slideshow

```php
<?php
require_once("../../common/module.inc");

class PictureSlider extends Module
{
    var $gallery;
    var $type;
    var $picture_width;
    var $slider_frames;

    public function __construct($page, $gallery)
    {
        parent::__construct($page);

        $this->gallery = $gallery;
        $this->type = "default";
        $this->picture_width = 65;
        $this->slider_frames = 8;
    }

    public function get_css_linked()
    {
        // Specify the file in which the CSS for the module is provided.
        return array("sitewide.css");
    }

    public function get_js_linked()
    {
        // Specify the JavaScript files that must be included on the page
        // where this module is created. The JavaScript for this module
```

```php
        // needs YUI libraries for managing the DOM and doing animation.
        // Presumably, the module's own JavaScript resides in sitewide.js.
        return array
        (
            "yahoo-dom-event.js",
            "animation.js",
            "sitewide.js"
        );
    }

    public function get_js()
    {
        // The JavaScript here is dynamically generated. We're using PHP
        // to create some JavaScript that is parameterized by the module.
        // For instance, the total width depends on the number of slides,
        // calculated from the slides passed to the module's constructor.
        $strip_width = $this->picture_width * $this->slider_frames;
        $count = count($this->gallery);
        $total_width = $this->picture_width * $count;

        return <<<EOD
var picsld = new PictureSlider();

picsld.init = function()
{
    this.stripWidth = $strip_width;
    this.totalCount = $count;
    this.totalWidth = $total_width;

    this.update();

    // Show the slider only after the JavaScript it needs is loaded. If
    // we're placing JavaScript at the bottom of the page for performance
    // reasons, we must ensure that no interactions take place before the
    // JavaScript has been loaded to handle them.
    this.loaded();
}

picsld.init();

EOD;
    }

    public function get_content()
    {
        $strip = $this->get_strip();
        $count = count($this->gallery);

        if ($count > 0)
        {
            $showing = <<<EOD
Showing picture <strong>1</strong> of $count

EOD;
    }
```

```
        else
            $showing = "";

        return <<<EOD
<div id="picsld" class="{$this->type}">
    <div class="sldpos">
$showing
    </div>
    <div class="sldtab">
        <img class="btnl" src="..../slide_arrow_l.gif" width="14" onclick=
            "picsld.slideL();" />
        <div class="vwpt">
$strip
        </div>
        <img class="btnr" src="..../slide_arrow_r.gif" width="14" onclick=
            "picsld.slideR();" />
    </div>
</div>

EOD;
    }

    protected function get_strip()
    {
        // Initialize the HTML that lays out the pictures and the number
        // to assign each picture.
        $items = "";
        $i = 0;

        foreach ($this->gallery as $picture)
        {
            $item_id = "picslditm".$i;

            // Prepare the strings for insertion later between the single
            // quotes in the picsld.select method.
            $img = str_replace("'", "\'", $picture["img_l"]);
            $text = str_replace("'", "\'", $picture["text"]);
            $attr = str_replace("'", "\'", $picture["attr"]);
            $n = $i + 1;

            // At the start, the leftmost slide is selected; therefore, it
            // is shown in the picture viewer.
            if ($i == 0)
                $sel = " selected";
            else
                $sel = "";

            // Create the HTML for one picture. The HTML will be added to
            // the module's HTML after all the pictures have been created.
            $items .= <<<EOD
                <td>
                    <div id="$item_id" class="item{$sel}">
                        <img src="{$picture["img_t"]}" alt="{$picture["text"]}"
                            width="55" height="55" onmousedown="picsld.select
                            ('$item_id', $n, '$img', '$text','$attr');" />
```

```php
                    </div>
                </td>

EOD;

            $i++;
        }

        // Add blank slides to fill frames when the number of pictures is
        // not evenly divisible by the frames that appear in the slider.
        while ($i % $this->slider_frames != 0)
        {
            $items .= <<<EOD
                <td>
                    <div class="item">
                        <img src=".../slide_blank_bg.gif" width="55"
                            height="55" />
                    </div>
                </td>

EOD;

            $i++;
        }

        return <<<EOD
<table cellspacing="0" cellpadding="0" border="0">
    <tr>
$items
    </tr>
</table>

EOD;
    }
}

class PictureViewer extends Module
{
    var $picture;
    var $type;

    public function __construct($page, $picture)
    {
        parent::__construct($page);

        $this->picture = $picture;
        $this->type = "default";
    }

    public function get_css_linked()
    {
        // Specify the file in which the CSS for the module is provided.
        return array("sitewide.css");
    }

    public function get_content()
```

```
    {
        // The content for this module consists of a single image, along
        // with text for the caption and the attribution.
        $attr = "";

        if (!empty($this->picture["attr"]))
        {
            $attr = <<<EOD
<cite>
    courtesy of {$this->picture["attr"]}
</cite>

EOD;
        }

        if (empty($this->picture["img_l"]))
            $img = "";
        else
        {
            $img = <<<EOD
<img src="{$this->picture["img_l"]}" alt="{$this->picture["text"]}"
    width="600" />

EOD;
        }

        return <<<EOD
<div id="picvwr" class="{$this->type}">
    <div class="vwrimg">
$img
    </div>
$attr
    <div class="vwrcap">
        {$this->picture["text"]}
    </div>
</div>

EOD;
    }
}
?>
```

Example 7-7 presents the JavaScript that implements behaviors for the Picture Slider module. In a manner consistent with what we discussed for large-scale JavaScript in Chapter 5, the module has a JavaScript object that neatly encapsulates the functionality that the component requires, and the object is named `PictureSlider` to reflect the module's name. In Example 7-6, the `get_js_linked` method of `PictureSlider` specifies that this object is defined in the file identified by the key *sitewide.js*. The JavaScript for the module needs two YUI libraries (which you can download from *http://developer .yahoo.com/yui*) to support it. Therefore, `get_js_linked` specifies keys for these files before *sitewide.js*.

Example 7-7. PictureSlider JavaScript object for the slideshow

```javascript
PictureSlider = function()
{
    // Set up references to the elements needed for the slider and viewer.
    this.slider = document.getElementById("picsld");

    if (this.slider)
    {
        this.tab = this.slider.getElementsByTagName("table");
        this.tab = (this.tab && this.tab.length > 0) ? this.tab[0] : null;
    }

    if (this.slider)
    {
        this.lb = YAHOO.util.Dom.getElementsByClassName
        (
            "btnl",
            "img",
            this.slider
        );

        this.lb = (this.lb && this.lb.length > 0) ? this.lb[0] : null;

        this.rb = YAHOO.util.Dom.getElementsByClassName
        (
            "btnr",
            "img",
            this.slider
        );

        this.rb = (this.rb && this.rb.length > 0) ? this.rb[0] : null;
    }

    this.viewer = document.getElementById("picvwr");

    // You pass values for the following parameters to the module's
    // constructor in PHP. The module's get_js method in PHP dynamically
    // generates the JavaScript to set these members from those values.
    this.stripWidth = 0;
    this.totalCount = 0;
    this.totalWidth = 0;

    // This lock is needed to ensure that one left or right move of the
    // slider runs to completion; otherwise, misalignment could happen.
    this.lock = false;
};

PictureSlider.prototype = new Object();

PictureSlider.prototype.slideL = function()
{
    // Moving to the left adjusts the slider in a positive direction.
    this.adjust(+(this.stripWidth));
};
```

```
PictureSlider.prototype.slideR = function()
{
    // Moving to the right adjusts the slider in a negative direction.
    this.adjust(-(this.stripWidth));
};

PictureSlider.prototype.adjust = function(amt)
{
    // If already locked, do nothing; otherwise, get the lock and go.
    if (this.lock)
        return;
    else
        this.lock = true;

    var anim;
    var ease = YAHOO.util.Easing.easeOut;
    var pos = parseInt(YAHOO.util.Dom.getStyle(this.tab, "left"));

    // Prevent moving past either end of the slider during an adjustment.
    if (amt > 0)
    {
        if (pos + amt > 0)
        amt = 0;
    }

    if (amt < 0)
    {
        if (pos + amt <= -(this.totalWidth))
        amt = 0;
    }

    // The following creates a closure that ensures access to members
    // of the PictureSlider instance from inside the update method.
    var obj = this;

    function handleComplete()
    {
        obj.update();
        obj.lock = false;
    }

    // Do the sliding animation if there is any amount to move; otherwise,
    // just call update directly to ensure the arrow buttons are updated.
    if (amt != 0)
    {
        anim = new YAHOO.util.Anim(this.tab, {left: {by: amt}}, 0.5, ease);
        anim.onComplete.subscribe(handleComplete);
        anim.animate();
    }
    else
    {
        this.update();
        this.lock = false;
    }
};
```

```javascript
PictureSlider.prototype.update = function()
{
    var pos;

    pos = parseInt(YAHOO.util.Dom.getStyle(this.tab, "left"));

    // Switch images to indicate which buttons are enabled or disabled.
    if (pos >= 0)
        this.lb.src = ".../slide_arrow_off_l.gif";
    else
        this.lb.src = ".../slide_arrow_l.gif";

    if (pos <= -this.totalWidth + this.stripWidth)
        this.rb.src = ".../slide_arrow_off_r.gif";
    else
        this.rb.src = ".../slide_arrow_r.gif";
};

PictureSlider.prototype.select = function(targ, n, img, text, attr)
{
    var sld;
    var el;

    // Switch the selection by changing the frame with the selected class.
    el = YAHOO.util.Dom.getElementsByClassName
    (
        "selected",
        "div",
        this.slider
    );

    if (el && el.length > 0)
        YAHOO.util.Dom.removeClass(el[0], "selected");

    if (targ)
        YAHOO.util.Dom.addClass(targ, "selected");

    // Reload the picture viewer with the current selection in the slider.
    this.reload(img, text, attr);

    // Update the text indicating the position of the selected picture.
    el = YAHOO.util.Dom.getElementsByClassName
    (
        "sldpos",
        "div",
        this.slider
    );

    if (el && el.length > 0)
    {
        el[0].innerHTML = "Showing picture <strong>" + n + "</strong> of "
            + this.totalCount;
    }
};
```

```
PictureSlider.prototype.reload = function(img, text, attr)
{
   // Handle the case of no viewer associated with the picture slider.
   if (!this.viewer) return;

   var el;

   // Get the image viewer and change the image currently being shown.
   el = YAHOO.util.Dom.getElementsByClassName
   (
      "vwrimg",
      "div",
      this.viewer
   );

   if (el && el.length > 0)
   {
      el = el[0].getElementsByTagName("img");

      if (el && el.length > 0)
      {
         el[0].src = img;
         el[0].alt = text;
      }
   }

   // Change the attribution in the picture viewer for the selection.
   el = this.viewer.getElementsByTagName("cite");

   if (el && el.length > 0)
      el[0].childNodes[0].nodeValue = "courtesy of" + attr;

   // Change the caption in the picture viewer based on the selection.
   el = YAHOO.util.Dom.getElementsByClassName
   (
      "vwrcap",
      "div",
      this.viewer
   );

   if (el && el.length > 0)
      el[0].childNodes[0].nodeValue = text;
};

PictureSlider.prototype.loaded = function()
{
   // Fire this from your initialization method for the picture slider.
   var el;

   el = YAHOO.util.Dom.getElementsByClassName
   (
      "sldtab",
      "div",
      this.slider
```

```
    );

    YAHOO.util.Dom.setStyle
    (
        el[0],
        "visibility",
        "visible"
    );
};
```

As you can see, a slideshow contains enough interrelated pieces that defining it using nicely encapsulated modules is critical to making it highly reusable, maintainable, and ultimately reliable in the long life cycle of a large web application. Example 7-8 demonstrates how easy this module is to use despite all the interconnected pieces of its implementation. Just as we saw for the simple modules at the start of the chapter, you need only instantiate the modules with the necessary arguments to configure them, call their **create** methods, and place them within the proper section of the layout for the page. Furthermore, you need only include a single include file, *slideshow.inc*, to use the slideshow. The necessary HTML, CSS, and JavaScript for its modules travel with the slideshow wherever you use it.

Example 7-8. Creating the modules for a slideshow

```
<?php
require_once(".../common/sitepage.inc");
require_once(".../common/slideshow.inc");

...

class NewCarDetailsPage extends SitePage
{
    ...

    public function get_content()
    {
        ...

        // Create the picture slider and picture viewer for the slideshow.
        // The backend data will have been loaded earlier during a call to
        // load_data.
        $mod = new PictureSlider
        (
            $this,
            $this->load_data["new_car_info"]["gallery"]
        );

        $slider = $mod->create();

        $mod = new PictureViewer
        (
            $this,
            $this->load_data["new_car_info"]["gallery"][0]
        );
```

```
$viewer = $mod->create();

...

// Place the HTML markup for each module within the page layout.
$mod = new DetailsLayout
(
    $this,
    array(...),
    array($slider, $viewer),
    array(...),
    array(...),
    array(...),
    array(...)
);

// Return the content, which the create method for the page uses.
return $mod->create();
}

...
}
?>
```

Layouts and Containers

In Chapter 4, we discussed layouts as highly reusable, generic templates that define the overarching structure of pages. You saw that containers are even finer groupings of modules typically placed within layouts. Together, layouts and containers play a vital role in fostering reusability, maintainability, and reliability in large web applications by defining a number of standard *sections* in which to place modules on a page. A section is simply a region in which we can insert one or more modules.

As we explore implementations for layouts and containers, you'll see that layouts and containers are just specialized types of modules. That is, they require many of the same things that other modules do. The main distinction is that aside from the additional structural elements that a layout or container defines, the content for a layout or container is actually just the content of other modules.

Because the operations you need to perform to generate the individual sections of a layout or container are generally the same for most layouts and containers, it's useful to define a base class, Layout, for this purpose. Example 7-9 presents the Layout class, which is derived from Module. This class defines get_section, which places a set of modules within a div and assigns the div a specified class so that styles for positioning and formatting the section can be applied.

Example 7-9. Implementation of the Layout class

```php
class Layout extends Module
{
    public function __construct($page)
    {
        parent::__construct($page);
    }

    public function get_section($class, $modules)
    {
        if (count($modules) == 0)
            return "";

        foreach ($modules as $content)
            $section .= empty($content) ? "" : $content;

        if (empty($section))
            return "";

        return <<<EOD
<div class="$class">
$section
<!-- $class -->
</div>

EOD;
    }
}
```

Example 7-10 presents a layout class intended for laying out any page related to search results, be they search results for new cars, used cars, reviews, or articles in our web application. This layout has sections for a header at the top, three content sections in the middle, and two footers across the bottom (this is the same layout from Figure 4-3 in Chapter 4). Because any HTML for modules that you pass through the layout's interface for each section simply gets inserted into the proper locations in the overall structure of the layout, it is highly reusable for any page whose design observes this same structure; you simply insert different modules. As a result, layouts and containers provide a good opportunity for engineers and designers to work together to establish standard guidelines under which pages can be designed and built. Classes for containers are defined in much the same way as for layouts, but they typically organize smaller groups of modules for use within sections of a layout.

Example 7-10. Implementing a layout class

```php
class ResultsLayout extends Layout
{
    protected $layreshdr;
    protected $layrespri;
    protected $layressec;
    protected $layrester;
    protected $layresftr1;
    protected $layresftr2;
```

```php
    public function __construct
    (
        $page,
        $layreshdr,
        $layrespri,
        $layressec,
        $layrester,
        $layresftr1,
        $layresftr2
    )
    {
        parent::__construct($page);

        $this->layreshdr = $layreshdr;
        $this->layrespri = $layrespri;
        $this->layressec = $layressec;
        $this->layrester = $layrester;
        $this->layresftr1 = $layresftr1;
        $this->layresftr2 = $layresftr2;
    }

    public function get_css_linked()
    {
        return array("sidewide.css");
    }

    public function get_content()
    {
        $layreshdr = $this->get_section("layreshdr", $this->layreshdr);
        $layrespri = $this->get_section("layrespri", $this->layrespri);
        $layressec = $this->get_section("layressec", $this->layressec);
        $layrester = $this->get_section("layrester", $this->layrester);
        $layresftr1 = $this->get_section("layresftr1", $this->layresftr1);
        $layresftr2 = $this->get_section("layresftr2", $this->layresftr2);

        // The content for the layout is just the content of the modules
        // passed into the layout and inserted into the layout sections.
        return <<<EOD
<div id="layres">
$layreshdr
    <div class="layresmaj">
$layrespri
$layressec
$layrester
    <-- layresmaj -->
    </div>
$layresftr1
$layresftr2
<!-- layres -->
</div>

EOD;
    }
}
```

Special Considerations

The more you work with any large web application, the more you'll turn up special considerations that you didn't originally think about. Fortunately, it's relatively easy to adapt the techniques with large-scale PHP introduced in this chapter for many different situations. Indeed, this is one of the most important tests of a good architecture: can it adapt to new situations without undue contortions? This section presents some examples of special situations in large web applications with solutions using the techniques from this chapter.

Handling Module Variations

In large web applications, modules frequently need to function or appear in a different manner on different pages. For example, suppose you would like a module to support default, compact, and mid-size presentations, as illustrated in Chapter 4. Example 7-11 demonstrates a solution wherein the class of the module's containing `div` becomes parameterized. To do this, you specify a data member for the module named `$class` and define setter methods that change its value. The module picks up the proper CSS when the `class` attribute of its containing `div` is set to the value stored in the `$class` data member.

For more extensive variations requiring more significant changes to the HTML markup or JavaScript for a module, you can manage those variations in a similar manner using data members to control how the HTML markup or JavaScript is generated. It helps to have a nicely encapsulated class for the module and a well-defined interface for selecting the variations.

Example 7-11. Handling variations of the Popular New Cars module

```
class PopularNewCars extends Module
{
    protected $class;

    ...

    public function __construct($page, ...)
    {
        parent::__construct($page);

        $this->class = "default";

        // Set up the module using other arguments from the constructor.
        ...
    }

    public function set_mode_default()
    {
        $this->class = "default";
    }
```

```
    public function set_mode_compact()
    {
        $this->class = "compact";
    {

    public function set_mode_midsize()
    {
        $this->class = "midsize";
    }

    public function get_content()
    {
        return <<<EOD
<div id="nwcpop" class="$this->class">

    ...

</div>

EOD;
    }
}
```

Multiple Instances of a Module

In large web applications, multiple instances of the same module often need to appear on the same page. For example, suppose you have a paginator (containing links for paginating lists across multiple pages) that you would like to place at both the top and bottom of a list of search results. Example 7-12 presents one solution using the method set_instance that lets you supply a unique identifier by which to identify each instance of the module. The module appends this unique ID to a base ID for the module to keep all IDs on the page unique.

Now, because there may be multiple instances of the module on the same page, you should also scope the CSS for the module by class name instead of ID (see Chapter 4, "Scoping within a module" on page 58). To target a specific instance of the module on a page for smaller amounts of additional CSS (e.g., different margins for different instances), you can use the get_css method for the page to specify the CSS based on the module's ID, or you can add CSS scoped to the specific page in your sitewide or sectional CSS file (see Chapter 4, "Scoping at the page level" on page 59).

Example 7-12. Handling multiple instances of the Paginator module

```
class Paginator extends Module
{
    protected $class;
    protected $ident;

    ...

    public function __construct($page, ...)
```

```
    {
        parent::__construct($page);

        $this->class = "pagint";
        $this->ident = $this->class."def";

        // Set up other members for configuring the paginator state based
        // on other arguments passed into the constructor for the module.
        ...
    {

    public function set_instance($instance)
    {
        $this->ident = $this->class.$instance;
    }

    public function get_content()
    {
        return <<<EOD
<div id="$this->ident" class="$this->class">

    ...

</div>

EOD;
    }
}
```

Dynamic JavaScript and CSS

Earlier, in the `PictureSlider` class in Example 7-6, you saw an example that used PHP to generate dynamic JavaScript for the Picture Slider module based on several member variables set within the class. The `get_css` and `get_js` methods defined by the base classes for pages and modules provide a consistent interface for the generation of dynamic CSS and JavaScript, respectively, at either the page or module level, as needed.

Implementing Nested Modules

One of the reasons that the page and module classes we've discussed in this chapter work well for large web applications is that they are very extensible. We've seen that this is true when defining hierarchies of classes—once you have a class for one type of page or module, it's relatively easy to extend it for another. Another example of extensibility is the ability to create modules within other modules, which is especially useful for user interface components. The paginator mentioned previously in "Multiple Instances of a Module" on page 181 is a good example.

Example 7-13 illustrates the creation of two instances of the Paginator module within the New Car Search Results module. The creation of a module within another module proceeds exactly as within a page. Just remember that the first parameter passed to each module is the $page member of the enclosing module (as opposed to $this, which for pages is the page itself, but for modules is the module instance).

Example 7-13. Creating nested paginators in the New Car Search Results module

```
class NewCarSearchResults extends Module
{
    ...

    public function get_content()
    {
        // Create a paginator to appear at the top of the search results.
        $mod = new Paginator($this->page, ...);

        $mod->set_instance("pri");
        $pgnpri = $mod->create();

        // Create an additional paginator module to appear at the bottom.
        $mod = new Paginator($this->page, ...);

        $mod->set_instance("sec");
        $pgnsec = $mod->create();

        // Call upon a private method to build the actual list of results.
        $results = $this->get_results();

        return <<<EOD
<div id="nwcsrs">
$pgnpri
$results
$pgnsec
</div>

EOD;
    }
}
```

CHAPTER 8

Large-Scale Ajax

Ajax (Asynchronous JavaScript and XML) is not so much a new technology as a set of existing technologies used together in a new way, bound together by a mechanism that lets you communicate between the browser and server without reloading the entire page. In its most fundamental form, Ajax requires that you understand only one new piece: the `XMLHttpRequest` object in JavaScript (or its equivalent depending on the browser). This is the object that allows you to make a connection back to the originating server to request additional data. Once you receive the data, you can use it to adjust only the portion of the page that you need to update.

Although the object's name and the term "Ajax" itself imply that XML is the only format for exchanging data, there are others. JSON is especially good because it lets you pass a string of JavaScript on which you call `json_parse` (which you can download from *http://json.org/json_parse.js*), to yield a JavaScript object.

Certain practices simplify working with Ajax. Usually, it's helpful to load a library that abstracts the `XMLHttpRequest` object. Fortunately, there are several libraries that help with this. In addition, within the browser, the MVC design pattern is a good model for maintaining a clear separation between data changes and updates to a presentation. On the server, the same principles discussed in Chapter 6 for managing data for complete pages can also provide a good structure for data in Ajax requests. These ideas are captured in the following tenet from Chapter 1:

> Tenet 8: Large-scale Ajax is portable and modular, and it maintains a clear separation between data changes and updates to a presentation. Data exchange between the browser and server is managed through a clearly defined interface.

This chapter is divided broadly into three sections: the first explores Ajax within the browser, the second explores Ajax on the server, and the third illustrates Ajax with MVC. We'll begin by discussing the fundamentals of a simple Ajax transaction and look at comparisons between basic Ajax requests in some popular libraries. The libraries we'll examine are Dojo, jQuery, Prototype, and YUI. On the server, we'll explore common formats for data exchange, server proxies, and techniques for handling Ajax requests in a modular fashion. Finally, we'll look at a set of prototype objects in

JavaScript to support MVC and explore two examples of Ajax with MVC. One is a simple control panel that has multiple views; the other is an illustration of accordion lists.

In the Browser

Like most transactions that take place on the Web, Ajax transactions consist of two coordinated sets of operations: one in the browser and the other on the server. In this section, we look at some of the fundamentals for working with Ajax in the browser.

Managing Connections

Ajax employs JavaScript to establish a connection to the server from a web page and load additional data into the page. Example 8-1 demonstrates the JavaScript to establish the simplest of Ajax requests. The libraries that virtually all developers use hide most of these logistics, but you should understand them in order to use Ajax effectively.

In the example, handleConnect is a method that you can call, perhaps triggered by an event handler, to initiate an Ajax request. As the "A" in Ajax signifies, requests are normally asynchronous (you do have the option to make them synchronous, but this is ill-advised), leaving your code with the job of determining when the response has arrived from the server. JavaScript offers this information as a state change in the request. The handleConnect method creates an instance of the XMLHttpRequest object, specifies a method that JavaScript will call as the request's state changes, configures the request, and, finally, sends the request.

The handleRequest method in Example 8-1 is the method called whenever the state of the request changes. To make sure its operations take place when the request is in the right state—when data has arrived from the server—the method checks whether the readyState member is set to 4 and the status member is set to 200 (there are other states with other meanings, but we won't explore those here). When the state is 4, the status is 200, and there is data from the server in XML format, the responseXML member will have been populated with a complete DOM constructed from the XML. In this case, you can use JavaScript DOM methods to access the data you need. For example, to get all elements that have a specific tag, you can invoke responseXML.getElementsByTagName. If the server sends plain text or text to be interpreted as JSON, the responseText member is populated with a string. If you expect a response in JSON format, pass the text to eval, or more safely, json_parse to get a valid JavaScript object. Example 8-1 illustrates working with JSON data in responseText.

Although eval is fast, it's important to recognize that it will execute any piece of JavaScript, even those that could contain malicious code. If you have complete trust and control of the JSON data you're evaluating, eval may be acceptable; however, json_parse is more secure because it recognizes only JSON text.

Example 8-1. A simple Ajax request

```
function handleRequest()
{
    // The request is in the proper state for us to handle it only when
    // is readyState member has been set to 4 and its status shows 200.
    if (this.readyState == 4 && this.status == 200)
    {
        if (this.responseXML != null)
        {
            // This is the response member to read for XML; it holds a DOM.
            ...
        }
        else if (this.responseText != null)
        {
            var data;

            // This is the response member to read for JSON data (or text).
            data = json_parse(this.responseText);

            // For illustration, just show the message in an alert dialog.
            // The response is an object containing one member: a message.
            alert(data.message);
        }
    }
}

function handleConnect()
{
    var req;

    // Create the request object and set up the handler for state changes.
    req = new XMLHttpRequest();
    req.onreadystatechange = handleRequest;

    // Set up the type of request, where it should go, and do the request.
    req.open("GET", "service.php...");
    req.send();
}
```

For the sake of viewing what this example looks like end to end, Example 8-2 shows the PHP server code for *service.php*, the script used to handle the Ajax request from Example 8-1. It returns a JSON object with one member called message.

Example 8-2. A simple JSON response

```php
<?php
// Create a PHP hash containing the string to return as the response.
$data = array
(
    "message" => "Hello"
);

// Encode the PHP data structure so that it becomes a JSON structure.
$json = json_encode($data);

// Set the content type to inform that we're sending a JSON response.
header("Content-Type: application/json");

// Send the JSON response.
print($json);
?>
```

As you can see, carrying out a simple Ajax transaction is not very difficult. That said, Ajax becomes more complicated when you consider that prior to Internet Explorer 7.0, there were serious interoperability issues among the major browsers. These included inconsistent or missing XMLHttpRequest objects, memory leaks, and other implementation details. In addition, a real Ajax application typically requires a lot more management than the simple steps illustrated in Examples 8-1 and 8-2. Fortunately, there are a number of libraries today that help with this and that standardize support for Ajax across the major browsers. Other techniques for fetching data asynchronously besides using the XmlHttpRequest object include using iframe elements and script nodes as the transport mechanism.

In the approach using iframe elements, you hide an iframe on your original page. Then, whenever you need additional data, you use JavaScript to alter the location to which the iframe element points. The request returns whatever data you need in its own DOM, which your original page can access. The use of iframe elements is one of the original ways in which web developers implemented Ajax, so you may see it when working with Ajax applications that have been around for a while.

In the script node approach, whenever you need additional data, you use JavaScript to add a script node with a src attribute that points to a page that fetches whatever data you need as a set of JavaScript objects. The objects returned in that request are accessible by the original page.

Although clever, iframe and script approaches can be difficult to manage in large web applications because both approaches require that you write some custom code to abstract and coordinate the transport layer itself between the HTML and JavaScript. Now that other support for Ajax is so widely available, there is little need for these approaches, except in some very specific applications.

Using Ajax Libraries

In this section, we explore several Ajax libraries that can help manage the complexities of large Ajax applications while standardizing how Ajax works across the major browsers. These include Dojo, jQuery, Prototype, and the YUI library. Specifically, we'll look at how each library supports fundamental GET and POST requests for comparison purposes. Of course, this is far from a complete depiction of what the libraries can do. For example, they all offer various options for carrying out requests, support flexible data formats, and define numerous events for which you can provide handlers, which we only touch on here.

Ajax with Dojo

Dojo is a JavaScript library built on several contributed code bases. You can download the library and read its complete documentation at *http://www.dojotoolkit.org*:

GET

The following method executes an Ajax GET request with Dojo. The method accepts one object as a parameter; the most commonly used members of the object are shown below. The `handleAs` member can be `text`, `xml`, or `json`, indicating that the `data` argument passed to the function specified for `load` is a string, DOM, or JSON object, respectively. The `url` member is the destination for the request. The `timeout` member is measured in milliseconds:

```
dojo.xhrGet
(
    {
        url:       "service.php?key1=val1&key2=val2&...",
        timeout:   5000,
        handleAs:  "json",
        load:      function(data, args)
        {
            // Do what is needed when the Ajax call returns successfully.
        },
        error:     function(error, args)
        {
            // Do what is needed when the Ajax call returns on a failure.
        }
    }
);
```

POST

The following method executes an Ajax POST request with Dojo. The parameters for the method are the same as described for GET except that you set the data to post as an object in the `content` member:

```
dojo.xhrPost
(
    {
        url:       "service.php",
        timeout:   5000,
```

```
            handleAs:  "json",
            content:
            {
                "key1": "val1",
                "key2": "val2",
                ...
            },
            load:      function(data, args)
            {
                // Do what is needed when the Ajax call returns successfully.
            },
            error:     function(error, args)
            {
                // Do what is needed when the Ajax call returns on a failure.
            }
        }
    );
```

Ajax with jQuery

The jQuery library is another JavaScript library with especially good documentation for its Ajax support. You can download the library and read its complete documentation at *http://www.jquery.com*:

GET

The following method executes an Ajax GET request with jQuery. The method accepts one object as a parameter whose most common members are shown below. The `dataType` member can take a number of values, of which the most common are `text`, `xml`, or `json`, indicating that the `data` argument passed to the function specified for `success` is a string, DOM, or JSON object, respectively. The `url` member is the destination for the request. You can specify the query parameters for the GET as an object in the `data` member. The `timeout` member is measured in milliseconds:

```
    jQuery.ajax
    (
        {
            url:        "service.php",
            type:       "GET",
            timeout:    5000,
            data:
            {
                "key1": "val1",
                "key2": "val2",
                ...
            },
            dataType: "json",
            success:  function(data)
            {
                // Do what is needed when the Ajax call returns successfully.
            },
            error:    function(xhr, text, error)
            {
```

```
        // Do what is needed when the Ajax call returns on a failure.
      }
    }
  );
```

POST

The following method executes an Ajax POST request with jQuery. The parameters for the method are the same as described for GET except you set the `type` member to `POST`:

```
jQuery.ajax
(
  {
    url:       "service.php",
    type:      "POST",
    timeout:   5000,
    data:
    {
      "key1": "val1",
      "key2": "val2",
      ...
    },
    dataType:  "json",
    success:   function(data)
    {
      // Do what is needed when the Ajax call returns successfully.
    },
    error:     function(xhr, text, error)
    {
      // Do what is needed when the Ajax call returns on a failure.
    }
  }
);
```

Ajax with Prototype

Prototype is one of the earliest of the JavaScript libraries to support Ajax. You can download the library and read its complete documentation at *http://www.prototypejs.org*:

GET

The following method executes an Ajax GET request with Prototype. The method accepts two parameters: the destination for the request and an object whose most common members are shown below. In the handler specified by `onSuccess`, you access `transport.responseText` for responses using plain text. For XML responses, `transport.responseXML` will have been populated with a DOM that you can access with JavaScript DOM methods. For JSON responses, the `transport.responseJSON` member will have been populated with the JavaScript object that is the result of the evaluated response text. You specify the query parameters for the GET as an object in the `parameters` member:

```
Ajax.Request
(
    "service.php",
    {
        method:     "get",
        parameters:
        {
            "key1": "val1",
            "key2": "val2",
            ...
        },
        onSuccess:  function(transport)
        {
            // Do what is needed when the Ajax call returns successfully.
        },
        onFailure:  function(transport)
        {
            // Do what is needed when the Ajax call returns on a failure.
        }
    }
);
```

POST

The following method executes an Ajax POST request with Prototype. The parameters for the method are the same as described for GET except you set the method member to post:

```
Ajax.Request
(
    "service.php",
    {
        method:     "post",
        parameters:
        {
            "key1": "val1",
            "key2": "val2",
            ...
        },
        onSuccess:  function(transport)
        {
            // Do what is needed when the Ajax call returns successfully.
        },
        onFailure:  function(transport)
        {
            // Do what is needed when the Ajax call returns on a failure.
        }
    }
);
```

Ajax with YUI

The YUI library was developed at Yahoo! for use both within Yahoo! and by the world's web development community. You can download the library and read its complete documentation at *http://developer.yahoo.com/yui*.

As this book was being completed, YUI 3 was in beta development. The information below pertains to versions prior to this. One of the big differences between YUI 2 and YUI 3 is the YUI object, which places YUI 3 features in their own namespace. This lets you transition from YUI 2 to YUI 3 without having to change all your code at once.

GET

The following method executes an Ajax GET request using the YUI Connection Manager. The method accepts three parameters: the request type, the destination for the request, and an object whose most common members are shown below. In the handler specified by success, you access o.responseText for responses in plain text. For XML responses, o.responseXML will have been populated with a DOM that you can access with JavaScript DOM methods. For JSON, you need to evaluate the result in o.responseText yourself. The argument member is used to pass whatever arguments you'd like to the handler methods. The timeout member is measured in milliseconds:

```
YAHOO.util.Connect.asyncRequest
(
    "GET",
    "service.php?key1=val1&key2=val2...",
    {
        success:   function(o)
        {
            // Do what is needed when the Ajax call returns successfully.
        },
        failure:   function(o)
        {
            // Do what is needed when the Ajax call returns on a failure.
        },
        timeout:   5000,
        argument:
        {
            key1:   val1,
            key2:   val2,
            ...
        }
    }
);
```

POST

The following method executes an Ajax POST request using the YUI Connection Manager. The parameters for the method are the same as described for GET except you set the first parameter to POST and add a fourth parameter containing a string of key-value pairs for the POST data:

```
YAHOO.util.Connect.asyncRequest
(
    "POST",
    "service.php",
```

```
{
    success:    function(o)
    {
        // Do what is needed when the Ajax call returns successfully.
    },
    failure:    function(o)
    {
        // Do what is needed when the Ajax call returns on a failure.
    },
    timeout:    5000,
    argument:
    {
        key1:    val1,
        key2:    val2,
        ...
    }
},
"key1=val1&key2=val2..."
);
```

On the Server

Once an Ajax request is executed in the browser, it's up to the server at the other end of the connection to handle the request. This section covers three important issues in writing the server's side of the transaction: choosing a data format, using a server proxy, and applying techniques that promote modularity.

Exchange Formats

The primary formats used to send data in Ajax responses are *plain text*, *XML*, and *JSON*. Of course, whichever format you choose, the JavaScript that you provide to handle responses must be prepared to work with that format, regardless of whether the library detects the format automatically or requires you to specify the format explicitly. In this section, we explore the various formats for data returned by the server and look at how to work with each of them in PHP.

Plain text

Ajax responses in plain text are simply strings returned by the server. Generally, a response from the server using plain text is not very useful, because it's largely unstructured. For anything but the simplest requests, this becomes unnecessarily difficult to deal with in the browser. Example 8-3 illustrates generating a plain-text response to an Ajax request in PHP.

Example 8-3. Returning an Ajax response in plain text using PHP

```
<?php
// Handle the inputs via $_GET or $_POST based on the request method.
...
```

```
// Assemble whatever data is needed to form the appropriate response.
...

$text = <<<EOD

...

EOD;

// Set the content type to specify that we're giving a text response.
header("Content-Type: application/text");

// For Ajax data that is very dynamic (which is often the case), you
// can set Expires: 0 to invalidate cached copies in future requests.
header("Expires: 0");

// Send the text response.
print($text);
?>
```

XML

Ajax responses in XML are highly structured; however, they can be verbose for the amount of real data that they actually contain. When you receive an XML response in the browser, the response is presented in the form of a DOM with which you can use all the normal DOM methods provided by JavaScript. For example, to get all the elements in the document with a specific tag, you can use `document.getElementsByTag Name`. Because DOM methods can have an impact on performance, it's important to structure your XML data with performance in mind. For example, keep the important data near the surface of the XML hierarchy or near a node that is accessible by ID (if you can get close to an element using `document.getElementById`, you only need to search that node's descendants). Example 8-4 illustrates generating an XML response to an Ajax request in PHP. You can find more about working with XML data in Chapter 6.

Example 8-4. Returning an Ajax response in XML using PHP

```
<?php
// Handle the inputs via $_GET or $_POST based on the request method.
...

// Assemble whatever data is needed to form the appropriate response.
...

$xml = <<<EOD
<?xml version="1.0"?>

...

EOD;

// Set the content type to inform that we're sending an XML response.
header("Content-Type: application/xml");
```

```
// For Ajax data that is very dynamic (which is often the case), you
// can set Expires: 0 to invalidate cached copies in future requests.
header("Expires: 0");

// Send the XML response.
print($xml);
?>
```

JSON

Ajax responses in JSON are also highly structured; however, since JSON is actually nothing more than just the normal JavaScript syntax for object literals, and a JavaScript object is exactly what we need in the browser, JSON is a great fit for Ajax. When you receive a JSON response in the browser, you evaluate it using `json_parse` (if the library hasn't done so already for you). After this, you access the data just like any other JavaScript object. Example 8-5 illustrates generating a JSON response to an Ajax request in PHP. You can find more about transforming a PHP data structure to JSON in Chapter 6.

Example 8-5. Returning an Ajax response in JSON using PHP

```
<?php
// Handle the inputs via $_GET or $_POST based on the request method.
...

// Assemble whatever data is needed to form the appropriate response.
...

$data = array
(

   ...

);

// Encode the PHP data structure so that it becomes a JSON structure.
$json = json_encode($data);

// Set the content type to inform that we're sending a JSON response.
header("Content-Type: application/json");

// For Ajax data that is very dynamic (which is often the case), you
// can set Expires: 0 to invalidate cached copies in future requests.
header("Expires: 0");

// Send the JSON response.
print($json);
?>
```

Server Proxies

When you specify the destination for an Ajax request, it's critical to remember that the destination *must be on the same server that served the original page*. In fact, some browsers will not allow you to specify a hostname within the destination at all, even if it's the same as the originating server. As a result, avoid the usual *http://hostname* prefix with Ajax URLs.

This *same-origin policy* prevents a type of security issue known as *cross-site scripting* (XSS), wherein code is injected by a malicious visitor into a page viewed by another visitor, unbeknownst to the initial visitor. Without such a policy for Ajax requests, malicious code could cause visitors of one page to interact unknowingly with an entirely different server. The issue is especially insidious for Ajax requests because they usually take place quietly behind the scenes.

Fortunately for benevolent developers, there is a safe and easy way to have Ajax requests handled by a different server from the one that sent the page: place a server proxy on the originating server through which all Ajax requests pass (i.e., you use the path of the proxy in the requests) before being routed to their true destination. This is permitted because requests first must pass through a server presumably under your control (the original server). If visitors trust your site, the assumption is that they are willing to trust other servers with whom you are communicating. Of course, others may contact your proxy server directly to use it as a pass-through. As a result, in many situations you'll want to examine who is making each request to determine whether or not it should be allowed to utilize the proxy. Example 8-6 is a server proxy for Ajax requests written using cURL in PHP.

Example 8-6. A server proxy for Ajax requests

```php
<?php
// Retrieve parameters passed to the proxy using GET. For this example,
// we're assuming that Ajax requests are being made using the GET method.
$query = "";

for ($_GET as $key => $val)
{
    if (!empty($query))
        $query .= "&";

    $query .= $key."=".$val;
}

if (!empty($query))
    $query = "?".$query;

// Set up the host and script that you really want for the Ajax request.
$host = "...";
$proc = "...";

$url = $host.$proc.$query;
```

```
$ch = curl_init();
curl_setopt($ch, CURLOPT_URL, $url);
curl_setopt($ch, CURLOPT_HEADER, false);

// Set the last value to true to return the output rather than echo it.
curl_setopt($ch, CURLOPT_RETURNTRANSFER, false);

header("Content-Type: application/json");
curl_exec($ch);

curl_close($ch);
?>
```

Modular Ajax

As the amount of data that you need to manage for an Ajax application increases, so does the need to have good techniques to manage the complexity on the server. Fortunately, the techniques we presented using data managers in Chapter 6 also work well when managing data for Ajax requests.

Recall from Chapter 6 that a data manager is an object that abstracts and encapsulates access to a specific set of data. Its purpose is to provide a well-defined, consistent interface by which you can get and set data in the backend, and to create a clear structure for the data itself. Chapter 6 also demonstrates how to combine and extend data managers using inheritance or aggregation. Recall that because a data manager is an object, anywhere you need to get the data it manages, you simply instantiate the data manager and call its get_data method. You can do this for Ajax, too.

Since data managers return data in associative arrays in PHP, one additional step that you need to perform for Ajax requests is to transform the data into a format suitable for Ajax responses. This is easy if the desired format is JSON, since all you need to do is pass the data structure returned by the data manager to json_encode. For XML, the process is not so simple. Because the steps required to transform data to XML are usually specific to the data itself, it often makes sense to encapsulate the support for this directly within the data manager and enable it with a parameter as you need it.

At times, you may want data marked up in HTML on the server. In this case, you can return the HTML within a member of a JSON object. Then, within the browser, insert it into the DOM using the innerHTML member of the node that you wish to make its parent. This approach may be beneficial when changes to the DOM resulting from an Ajax request are fairly complicated and you already have a lot of code on the server to construct the HTML. Rather than writing the code again in JavaScript, you can use the existing server code. Also, multiple calls to DOM methods in JavaScript, depending on the number and what they do, may result in slower performance than letting the browser rebuild the DOM for you after setting an element's innerHTML member.

Example 8-7 presents an example of an Ajax service that uses a data manager to return data for new car listings in the JSON format. The data manager follows the practices outlined for data managers in Chapter 6. For example, it uses the `new_car_listings` member to keep the inputs and outputs for the data manager uniquely identifiable should there be multiple data managers in use. The example first sets up the arguments for `NewCarListingsDataManager`, then calls the data manager's `get_data` method to populate `$load_data`. Once this method returns, it uses `json_encode` to convert the data in `$load_data` to JSON.

Example 8-7. Handling an Ajax request with a data manager

```php
<?php
require_once("..../datamgr/nwclistings.inc");
...

$load_args = array();
$load_data = array();
$load_stat = array();

// Handle inputs for the car query, starting point, total count, etc.
if (!empty($_GET["nwcqrymake"])
    $load_args["new_car_listings"]["make"] = $_GET["nwcqrymake"];
else
    $load_args["new_car_listings"]["make"] = "";

// There would likely be several other query parameters handled here.
...

// The following arguments presumably come from a pagination module.
if (!empty($_GET["pgnbeg"])
    $load_args["new_car_listings"]["begin"] = $_GET["pgnbeg"];
else
    $load_args["new_car_listings"]["begin"] = 0;

if (!empty($_GET["pgncnt"])
    $load_args["new_car_listings"]["count"] = $_GET["pgncnt"];
else
    $load_args["new_car_listings"]["count"] = 10;

// Call upon whatever data managers are needed to create the response.
$dm = new NewCarListingsDataManager();

$dm->get_data
(
    $load_args["new_car_listings"],
    $load_data["new_car_listings"],
    $load_stat["new_car_listings"]
);

...

// Confirm that no errors occurred; adjust the response accordingly.
...

// Encode the PHP data structure so that it becomes a JSON structure.
$json = json_encode($load_data);
```

```
// Set the content type to inform that we're sending a JSON response.
header("Content-Type: application/json");

// An Expires header set to 0 eliminates caching for future requests.
header("Expires: 0");

// Return the JSON data.
print($json);
?>
```

MVC and Ajax

Even with the help of Ajax libraries in the browser, large Ajax applications often have to manage complicated interactions. For example, changes to a single data source often require coordinated updates to several components in the user interface. In addition, the relationships between components in the user interface and their data sources may change over the lifetime of the application. MVC (Model-View-Controller) is a design pattern that can help address these issues. It does this by defining a system of distinct, loosely-coupled components: *models*, *views*, and *controllers*. Models are responsible for managing data, views are responsible for managing various presentations of the data, and controllers are responsible for controlling how the models and views change. In this section, we explore how MVC can help make the complexities of a large Ajax application more manageable. In the process, we'll also observe more of the Ajax operations presented earlier in action.

MVC is based on another design pattern, *Publisher-Subscriber*. The main idea behind Publisher-Subscriber is that a publisher maintains a list of subscribers that should be notified whenever something in the publisher changes. Publishers normally implement at least three methods: `subscribe`, `unsubscribe`, and `notify`. Subscribers call the `subscribe` method to register for notifications; subscribers call the `unsubscribe` method to tell publishers that they no longer want the notifications; and the publisher itself calls the `notify` method whenever the publisher needs to notify its list of subscribers about a change. The main method that subscribers implement is `update`. The publisher calls the `update` method within `notify` to give a subscriber the chance to update itself about a data change.

In the context of Publisher-Subscriber, models are *publishers* and views are *subscribers*. As publishers, models manage data and notify subscribed views whenever changes happen in the model. As subscribers, views subscribe to models and update the presentations they manage whenever they are notified by the models about changes to their data. The remarkable accomplishment of MVC, which it derives from Publisher-Subscriber, is that every time the data for a model changes, the views update themselves automatically. Furthermore, components responsible for the data and the presentations are loosely coupled—that is, one doesn't need to know about the other, so they are easier to maintain over an application's lifetime.

In the context of Ajax, models manage Ajax connections and store the resulting data. Views are notified of those changes and update themselves by modifying the parts of the DOM for which they are responsible. A good granularity for views is to make them correspond to modules (see Chapter 7). Interestingly, MVC is also helpful for DHTML applications that don't use Ajax but have other dynamic aspects to manage. The only difference is that changes to the model happen as a result of local data changes rather than from making an Ajax connection.

Using Ajax with MVC

To better understand how MVC specifically aids Ajax applications, let's look at a basic example for testing simple Ajax requests managed using MVC. In this example, we'll use one model, `TestModel`, to which two views are subscribed. Each view is an instance of `TestView`. For simplicity, the model manages a single piece of data: a timestamp that can be set via the server using an Ajax request or locally within the browser. Whenever the time is updated (either from the server or locally), each view updates itself to reflect the new timestamp in the model.

The implementation consists of three classes, shown in their entirety in this chapter, built on top of some libraries provided by YUI. Naturally, you can create the same basic structure using other JavaScript libraries.

Figure 8-1 shows the user interface for this application. The shaded area at the top of the figure is the first view; the shaded area at the bottom is the second. The lighter area in the middle is a control panel that contains several buttons that let you initiate various actions. In addition to the basic actions for making an Ajax request or local JavaScript call to set the time, the application lets you experiment with several other features, such as handling communication failures, data failures, timeouts, aborted requests, and collisions between concurrent requests. The following provides more detail about each of the actions in the application.

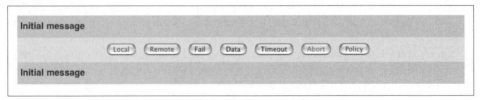

Figure 8-1. An application for testing simple Ajax requests managed using MVC

Local
> Sets the time in the model by making a local JavaScript call; no Ajax request is made. When you click this button, each view updates itself to display the message "Hello from the browser at *time*," which contains the current time in the browser. The Local button demonstrates the usefulness of MVC even for managing changes to a model without Ajax.

Remote

Sets the time in the model to the time on the server using an Ajax request to retrieve the time. When you click this button, each view updates itself to display the message "Hello from the server at *time*," which contains the current time on the server.

Fail

Simulates a communications failure (to show how the application would handle a bad URL, for example). When you click this button, the application responds with an alert.

Data

Simulates a failed attempt to get data (to show how the application would handle, for example, unexpected data from the server). When you click this button, the application responds with an alert.

Timeout

Causes the server to take too long to respond, which causes a timeout to occur. When you click this button, the application responds with an alert.

Abort

Aborts the current request. To test this, first click the button to test timeouts, then without giving it enough time to time out, click the button to abort the request; you won't get the alert for the timeout because the request is aborted before the timeout occurs.

Policy

Changes how collisions between concurrent requests are handled. The default state (Ignore) is to ignore subsequent Ajax requests within a model until the current one completes. Each time you click this button, you toggle between this policy and one that allows subsequent requests to cancel current ones (Change). A good example of the Change policy is an autocomplete application wherein a server is contacted for entries that match strings you type as you type them (e.g., type an entry into the Google or Yahoo! search box). If you type the next character of the entry before the server has a chance to respond with matches, only the latest request is needed (when typing pauses long enough). To test either policy, first click the button to test timeouts, then without giving it enough time to time out, make a remote request. If the Ignore policy is in place, you will see the alert for the first request that timed out. On the other hand, if the Change policy is active, you will get a response from the second request that canceled the first.

Example 8-8 presents the HTML for the Ajax application shown in Figure 8-1. Each button passes the appropriate action as a string argument (`loc` for Local, etc.) to the model using the `handleAction` method. You call `model.init` to initialize the model and notify the views that there is something to display. The `model` object is defined in Example 8-10.

Example 8-8. HTML for the Ajax example

```
<body>
<div id="testview1">
</div>
<div id="actions">
   <input id="loc" type="button" value="Local" onclick="handleAction
      ('loc');" />
   <input id="rmt" type="button" value="Remote" onclick="handleAction
      ('rmt');" />
   <input id="bad" type="button" value="Fail" onclick="handleAction
      ('bad');" />
   <input id="dat" type="button" value="Data" onclick="handleAction
      ('dat');" />
   <input id="tmo" type="button" value="Timeout" onclick="handleAction
      ('tmo');" />
   <input id="abt" type="button" value="Abort" onclick="handleAction
      ('abt');" />
   <input id="pol" type="button" value="Policy" onclick="handleAction
      ('pol');" />
</div>
<div id="testview2">
</div>

<script type="text/javascript">
// Initialize the model to a start value, which notifies the views too.
model.init();
</script>
</body>
```

Example 8-9 shows how to define the model and view objects for the example. The TestModel and TestView objects are derived from the prototype objects Model and View, respectively. You'll see more about these in a moment. For now, notice that the model implements three methods: init to set the initial state of the model and notify the views, abandon to handle timeouts, and recover to handle other failures. These methods are part of Model's abstract interface. The TestView object implements one method, update, to define what to update when the state of the model changes. This method is part of View's abstract interface.

Example 8-9. The model and views for the Ajax example

```
TestModel = function()
{
   MVC.Model.call(this);
};

// TestModel objects are derived from the Model object.
TestModel.prototype = new MVC.Model();

TestModel.prototype.init = function()
{
   // The state member of a model stores the current data for the model.
   this.state =
   {
```

```
    "message": "Initial message"
};

    // Only the setState method does notifications automatically for you.
    this.notify();
};

TestModel.prototype.abandon = function()
{
    // Implement this method to do whatever is needed to handle timeouts.
    alert("Called abandon to handle communications timeout.");
};

TestModel.prototype.recover = function()
{
    // Implement this method to do whatever is needed to handle timeouts.
    alert("Called recover to handle communications failure.");
};

TestView = function()
{
    MVC.View.call(this);
};

// TestView objects are derived from the View object.
TestView.prototype = new MVC.View();

TestView.prototype.update = function()
{
    // The id member is the containing element for the view in the DOM.
    var element = document.getElementById(this.id);

    // Whenever a view updates itself, it needs the state of its model.
    msg = this.model.getState().message;

    // Do the actual update for keeping this view current with the model.
    element.innerHTML = msg;
};
```

Example 8-10 shows how to use the model and view objects that we just defined. First, instantiate the model, then attach it to the views for which you would like to be notified of state changes. Any changes that take place in the model will cause a corresponding call to `TestView.update`. Example 8-10 also implements `handleAction`, which sets the state of the model based on buttons you click in the control panel. The `setState` method of `Model` lets you set the state of the model.

Example 8-10. Using the objects from Example 8-9

```
// This is the model that will keep track of the time last retrieved.
var model = new TestModel();

// Set a short connection timeout just to speed up the testing case.
model.setTimeout(2000);
```

```
// Create each view and attach the model. Attaching subscribes the view.
var view1 = new TestView();
view1.attach(model, "testview1");

var view2 = new TestView();
view2.attach(model, "testview2");

// This method handles the various actions by which you change the model.
function handleAction(mode)
{
    switch (mode)
    {
        case "loc":
            // Create a local timestamp without performing an Ajax request.
            var d = new Date();
            var h = ((h = d.getHours()) < 10) ? "0" + h : h;
            var m = ((m = d.getMinutes()) < 10) ? "0" + m : m;
            var s = ((s = d.getSeconds()) < 10) ? "0" + s : s;
            var t = h + ":" + m + ":" + s;

            // Update the model locally with the timestamp from the browser.
            model.setState({"message": "Hello from the browser at " + t});
            break;

        case "rmt":
            // Update the model with a remote timestamp via an Ajax request.
            model.setState("GET", "ajaxtest.php");
            break;

        case "bad":
            // Simulate a failure by giving an invalid URL for the request.
            model.setState("GET", "xxxxxxxx.php");
            break;

        case "dat":
        case "tmo":
            // Pass the mode to the server to test data or timeout problems.
            model.setState("GET", "ajaxtest.php?mode=" + mode);
            break;

        case "abt":
            // Tell the model to abort the current request if still running.
            model.abort();
            break;

        case "pol":
            // Toggle the policy for how to handle Ajax request collisions.
            if (model.collpol == MVC.Connect.Ignore)
            {
                model.setCollisionPolicy(MVC.Connect.Change);
                alert("Collision policy has been toggled to \"Change\".");
            }
            else
            {
                model.setCollisionPolicy(MVC.Connect.Ignore);
```

```
        alert("Collision policy has been toggled to \"Ignore\".");
    }

    break;
    }
}
```

To write your own Ajax application that uses MVC, derive your own models from `Model` and your own views from `View`. These are the prototype objects that we used for `TestModel` and `TestView` previously. Next, let's look at the interfaces for each of these objects and explore their implementations.

Public Interface for the Model Object

The `Model` object is the prototype object for all models. The public interface for `Model` contains the methods for which a default implementation is beneficial to most models. For example, the interface provides default methods for initializing the model, setting and getting the state of the model, subscribing and unsubscribing views, and notifying views of state changes in the model:

`init()`
> Initializes the model, which, by default, sets the state to an empty object and notifies the views for the first time. You can override this method to do something different to initialize your model.

`setState(mixed, url, post)`
> Sets the state of the model. If you pass only one argument to the method (`mixed`), the state for the model is set to the object passed in `mixed`. If you pass two arguments (`mixed` and `url`), the state for the model is fetched remotely using Ajax via the method in `mixed` (`GET` or `POST`) and the URL you specify in `url`. If you pass three arguments, the first must specify `POST`. The state for the model is fetched remotely via Ajax as in the case for two arguments, but the third argument passes POST data in the same format as that accepted by the YUI Connection Manager.

`getState()`
> Returns whatever data has been stored previously by `setState` as the current state of the model.

`subscribe(view)`
> Inserts the view specified by `view` into the list of views that will be notified about changes to the model.

`unsubscribe(view)`
> Deletes the view specified by `view` from the list of views that will be notified about changes to the model.

`notify()`
> Notifies all views that are subscribed to the model about changes to the model. This method is called automatically within the default implementations of `set`

`State` and `init`. Call this method whenever you need to trigger notifications your-self (for example, in your own implementations of `init` or `setState`).

Implementation of the Model Object

This section presents some of the implementation details for the `Model` prototype object. The `Model` object is responsible for managing views and handling updates from connections established by the YUI Connection Manager. The implementation for `Model` has one important method that we have not yet discussed:

update(o)
> This is different from the `update` method for subscribers called within `notify`. This method is the callback that the YUI Connection Manager calls when the connection from `setState` returns. The argument o is the status object passed into handlers by the YUI Connection Manager.

Example 8-11 presents the complete implementation for `Model`, including the default implementations for the methods outlined earlier for the public interface of `Model`.

Example 8-11. The Model prototype object for Ajax with MVC

```
// Place the Model object within its own namespace; create it if needed.
if (!window.MVC)
{
    MVC = {};
}

MVC.Model = function()
{
    MVC.Connect.call(this);

    this.state = {};
    this.views = new Array();
};

// Model objects are derived from the Connect object (to handle Ajax).
MVC.Model.prototype = new MVC.Connect();

MVC.Model.prototype.init = function()
{
    // Set up an empty state and notify the views for the first time.
    this.state = {};
    this.notify();
};

MVC.Model.prototype.setState = function(mixed, url, post)
{
    switch (arguments.length)
    {
        case 1:
            // One argument means the state for the model should be set
            // to the local object passed in mixed.
```

```
            this.state = mixed;
            this.notify();
            break;

        case 2:
            // Two arguments means set the state by fetching it remotely
            // using Ajax via the method in mixed (GET).
            this.connect(mixed, url);
            break;

        case 3:
            // Three arguments means set the state by fetching it remotely
            // using an Ajax POST; pass the POST data as the last argument.
            // If you do a GET with three arguments, the third is ignored.
            this.connect(mixed, url, post);
            break;
    }
};

MVC.Model.prototype.getState = function()
{
    return this.state;
};

MVC.Model.prototype.update = function(o)
{
    var r;

    // We're using JSON because the data stored as the state of the model
    // is an object.
    try
    {
        // This is where the response text is converted into a real object.
        r = json_parse(o.responseText);
    }
    catch(err)
    {
        // Handle if there is an issue creating the real JavaScript object.
        r = "";
    }

    if (typeof r != "object")
    {
        // If we don't get an object as a response, treat it as a failure.
        this.recover(o);
    }
    else
    {
        // Store the state and notify the views only when we're successful.
        this.state = r;
        this.notify();
    }
};

MVC.Model.prototype.subscribe = function(view)
```

```
{
    // Subscribe the view by inserting it into the list of subscribers.
    this.views.push(view);
};

MVC.Model.prototype.unsubscribe = function(view)
{
    var n = this.views.length;
    var t = new Array();

    // Unsubscribe the view by removing it from the list of subscribers.
    for (var i = 0; i < n; i++)
    {
        if (this.views[i].id == view.id)
            t.push(this.views[i]);
    }

    this.views = t;
};

MVC.Model.prototype.notify = function()
{
    var n = this.views.length;

    // Notifying all views means to invoke the update method of each view.
    for (var i = 0; i < n; i++)
    {
        this.views[i].update(this);
    }
};
```

Public Interface for the View Object

The View object is the prototype object for all views. Its public interface consists of just one method:

attach(m, i)
> Attaches the model specified by m to the view and subscribes the view to it. The argument i is the id attribute for the view's outermost div. The id attribute is stored with the view to make it easy to pinpoint where to modify the DOM; the view just needs to call document.getElementById.

Abstract Interface for the View Object

The abstract interface for View consists of a single method that specific views are expected to implement as needed:

update()
> Called by the Model object within its notify method to give a view the chance to update itself based on a state change in the model. Implement this method to

perform whatever updates are needed in your application based on a change to the model.

View Object Implementation

The implementation details of View focus on attaching models to views and prescribing an interface by which views update themselves. Example 8-12 presents the complete implementation for View.

Example 8-12. The View prototype object for Ajax with MVC

```
MVC.View = function()
{
   this.model = null;
   this.id = null;
};

MVC.View.prototype.attach = function(m, i)
{
   // Make sure to unsubscribe from any model that is already attached.
   if (this.model != null)
      this.model.unsubscribe(this);

   this.model = m;
   this.id = i;

   // Subscribe to the current model to start getting its notifications.
   this.model.subscribe(this);
};

MVC.View.prototype.update = function()
{
   // The default for updating the view is to do nothing until a derived
   // view can provide more details about what it means to update itself.
};
```

Public Interface for the Connect Object

The Model object presented earlier was derived from the Connect prototype object because it needed to support requests via Ajax. The Connect object is built on top of the YUI Connection Manager. The public interface for Connect provides default methods for making and aborting Ajax requests, as well as setting various connection options, such as the collision policy and timeouts:

connect(method, url, post)
> Establishes an asynchronous connection for making a request via Ajax. The method argument is the string GET or POST. The url argument is the destination for the request. When method is set to POST, pass the post data in post using the format accepted by the YUI Connection Manager. When the request returns, Connect calls the update method.

`abort()`

Terminates an Ajax request that is already in progress using this Connect object.

`setTimeout(value)`

Sets the number of milliseconds to use as the timeout when making Ajax requests with the Connect object.

`setCollisionPolicy(value)`

Sets the policy for handling collisions between concurrent requests. You can pass either MVC.Connect.Ignore or MVC.Connect.Change for value. With MVC.Connect.Ignore, new Ajax requests using the same Connect object are simply discarded while a connection is in progress. With MVC.Connect.Change, a new request replaces the one in progress.

Abstract Interface for the Connect Object

The abstract interface for Connect consists of methods that objects derived from Connect are expected to implement as needed. These methods allow a specific instance of Connect to define what should happen when requests succeed, time out, or fail. The nice thing about the structure of this object is that because the following are all methods of Connect, you can use the this reference inside each method to access members of your object. This offers a great opportunity for better encapsulation when managing Ajax requests:

`update(o)`

Called by Connect after an Ajax request is successful. Implement this method in your derived object in whatever way your application requires to handle successful requests. The argument o is the status object passed into handlers by the YUI Connection Manager.

`abandon(o)`

Called by Connect after an Ajax request exceeds its timeout. Implement this method in your derived object in whatever way your application requires to handle requests that have timed out. The argument o is the status object passed into handlers by the YUI Connection Manager. Example 8-13 does not invoke this method on requests terminated explicitly by calling abort, but you can easily modify the code to do so.

`recover(o)`

Called by Connect after an Ajax request experiences a failure. Implement this method in your derived object in whatever way your application requires to handle requests that have failed. The argument o is the status object passed into handlers by the YUI Connection Manager.

Implementation of the Connect Object

The implementation details of Connect focus on a number of tasks related to managing Ajax connections and prescribing an interface for handling various situations that can occur during the execution of an Ajax request. Example 8-13 presents the complete implementation for Connect.

Example 8-13. The Connect prototype object for Ajax with MVC

```
MVC.Connect = function()
{
    this.req = null;
    this.timeout = MVC.Connect.Timeout;
    this.collpol = MVC.Connect.Ignore;
};

// Set up a default for timeouts with Ajax requests (in milliseconds).
MVC.Connect.Timeout = 5000;

// These are the possible values used for setting the collision policy.
MVC.Connect.Ignore = 0;
MVC.Connect.Change = 1;

MVC.Connect.prototype.connect = function(method, url, post)
{
    // Allow only one connection through the YUI Connection Manager at a
    // time. Handle collisions based on the setting for collision policy.
    if (this.req && YAHOO.util.Connect.isCallInProgress(this.req))
    {
        if (this.collpol == MVC.Connect.Change)
        {
            this.abort();
        }
        else
        {
            return;
        }
    }

    // Use this as a semaphore of sorts to keep the critical section as
    // small as possible (even though JavaScript doesn't have semaphores).
    this.req = {};

    // This ensures access to the Connect (and derived object) instance in
    // the update, abandon, and recover methods. It generates a closure.
    var obj = this;

    function handleSuccess(o)
    {
        // Call the method implemented in the derived object for success.
        obj.update(o);
        obj.req = null;
    }
```

```javascript
    function handleFailure(o)
    {
        if (o.status == -1)
        {
            // Call the method provided by the derived object for timeouts.
            obj.abandon(o);
            obj.req = null;
        }
        else
        {
            // Call the method provided by the derived object for failures.
            obj.recover(o);
            obj.req = null;
        }
    }

    // Set up the callback object to pass to the YUI Connection Manager.
    var callback =
    {
        success: handleSuccess,
        failure: handleFailure,
        timeout: this.timeout
    };

    // Establish the Ajax connection through the YUI Connection Manager.
    if (arguments.length > 2)
    {
        this.req = YAHOO.util.Connect.asyncRequest
        (
            method,
            url,
            callback,
            post
        );
    }
    else
    {
        this.req = YAHOO.util.Connect.asyncRequest
        (
            method,
            url,
            callback
        );
    }
};

MVC.Connect.prototype.abort = function()
{
    if (this.req && YAHOO.util.Connect.isCallInProgress(this.req))
    {
        YAHOO.util.Connect.abort(this.req);
        this.req = null;
    }
};
```

```
MVC.Connect.prototype.setTimeout = function(value)
{
    this.timeout = value;
};

MVC.Connect.prototype.setCollisionPolicy = function(value)
{
    this.collpol = value;
};

MVC.Connect.prototype.update = function(o)
{
    // The default for this method is to do nothing. A derived object must
    // define its own version to do something specific to the application.
};

MVC.Connect.prototype.abandon = function(o)
{
    // The default for this method is to do nothing. A derived object must
    // define its own version to do something specific to the application.
};

MVC.Connect.prototype.recover = function(o)
{
    // The default for this method is to do nothing. A derived object must
    // define its own version to do something specific to the application.
};
```

Controllers

Up to now, we have touched on the idea of a controller only briefly. This is because the main job of a controller is to respond to messages or events, and the simplest controllers are just the event handlers for HTML elements. The event handler sets a new value in the appropriate model, which in turn causes the appropriate views to be updated. This might look something like the following in HMTL:

```
<input type="button" value="Preview" onclick="myModel.setState(...);" />
```

On the other hand, if setting the state of the model is more than a simple procedure, you can always implement a controller object. The typical interface for controller objects is to provide a handleMessage method that can call upon the appropriate methods to handle messages in a nicely encapsulated way:

```
YAHOO.util.Event.addListener
(
    element,
    "click",
    myController.handleMessage,
    MyController.SampleMessage,
    myController
);
```

Here, `myController` is an instance of `MyController` derived from `Controller`. `MyControl
ler.SampleMessage` is class data member (see Chapter 2) for the type of message to
handle. Class data members provide a good way to define possible message types.

An Example of Ajax with MVC: Accordion Lists

A good application of Ajax with MVC is to manage *accordion lists*. An accordion list is
a list or table for which you can show or hide additional items under the main items
displayed in the list. For example, Figure 8-2 shows a list of search results for cars that
have good green ratings. Each car in the table can be expanded to show additional trims
for the car by clicking on the View button. Once the list has been expanded, you can
hide the extra items again by clicking the Hide button.

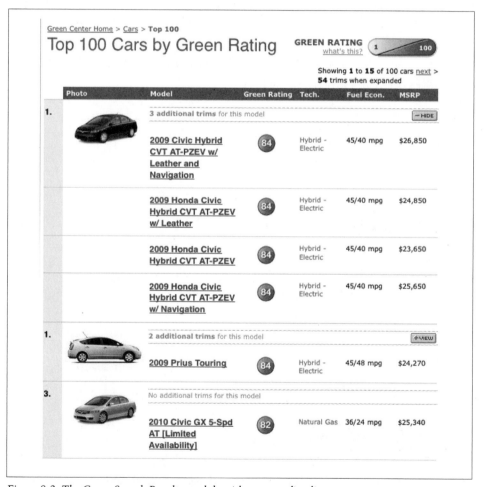

Figure 8-2. The Green Search Results module with an accordion list

The reason that Ajax and MVC work well for this example is that there's no need to load all the entries for each car in the expanded lists when the entire page loads. For a large list of cars, most of the extra entries will never be expanded. Ajax provides a good way to retrieve the expanded lists of entries only as you need them. MVC helps manage the changes that need to take place to show or hide the expanded lists for any of the cars.

The Green Search Results module defines one view and one model for each car in the main set of results. These models and views work with the items that must be loaded when each car is expanded. You embed the JavaScript for instantiating the models and views for the module using the get_js method. The JavaScript is embedded (as opposed to linked) because the module needs to create it dynamically at runtime. The module also specifies a number of JavaScript links using the get_js_linked method. This is the list of files to be linked for the page to ensure the rest of the JavaScript works properly. Example 8-14 illustrates how the module class encapsulates all of the pieces for this module. The example also illustrates the onclick handler in get_content, which sets the expansion for each list in motion.

Example 8-14. A class for the Green Search Results module with an accordion list

```
class GreenSearchResults extends Module
{
    protected $items;

    public function __construct($page, $items)
    {
        parent::__construct($page);

        $this->items = $items;
    }

    public function get_css_linked()
    {
        ...
    }

    public function get_js_linked()
    {
        return array
        (
            "yahoo-dom-event.js",
            "connection.js",
            "model-view-cont.js",
            "greencars.js"
        );
    }

    public function get_js()
    {
        $count = count($this->items);

        // This sets up the JavaScript array GreenSearchResultsModel.CarIDs
        // to embed. This holds the car ID for each item in $this->items.
```

```php
      // We need it in JavaScript too for access when initializing MVC.
      $js_ids_array = $this->get_js_ids_array();

      return <<<EOD
$js_ids_array

var i;
var GreenSearchResultsModel.MReg = new Array();
var GreenSearchResultsModel.VReg = new Array();

for (i = 0; i < $count; i++)
{
   // Instantiate a model for the item and set the associated car ID.
   // Store this in a static member of the model that holds all models.
   GreenSearchResultsModel.MReg[i] = new GreenSearchResultsModel(
      GreenSearchResultsModel.CarIDs[i]);

   // Instantiate a view for the item and set its position in the list.
   // Store this in a static member of the model that holds all views.
   GreenSearchResultsModel.VReg[i] = new GreenSearchResultsView(i);

   // Attach the model and view and set the ID of the expansion button.
   GreenSearchResultsModel.VReg[i].attach(GreenSearchResultsModel.MReg
      [i], "gsrexpbtn" + i);

   // Initialize the model for the item.
   GreenSearchResultsModel.MReg[i].init();
}

EOD;
   }

   public function get_content()
   {
      $count = count($this->items);
      $rows = "";

      for ($i = 0; $i < $count; $i++)
      {
         $exp_link = <<<EOD
<img src="http://.../view.gif" onclick="GreenSearchResultsModel.VReg
   [$i].show();" />
EOD;

         $main = $this->get_row($i, $exp_link);
         $rows .= $main;
      }

      $header = $this->get_header();

      return <<<EOD
$header
<table>
$rows
</table>
```

```
EOD;
  }

  protected function get_header()
  {
    // Return the HTML markup for the header region of the module.
    ...
  }


  protected function get_row($i, $exp_link)
  {
    // Return the HTML markup for a single car row at position $i.
    ...
  }

  protected function get_js_ids_array()
  {
    // Return all car IDs from $this->items as a JavaScript array.
    ...
  }
}
```

Example 8-15 presents the model and view objects, GreenSearchResultsModel and GreenSearchResultsView, that manage the accordion lists for this example. Whenever you click the View button, the event handler for the button click calls GreenSearchResultsView.show. This method calls setState for the model, which makes an Ajax request to get the expanded data for the car. Once the Ajax request returns, the model calls its notify method, which then invokes the update method for the view. The update method modifies the DOM to display the expanded list based on the data in the model.

Example 8-15. The model and view objects for the accordion list

```
GreenSearchResultsModel = function(id)
{
    MVC.Model.call(this);

    this.carID = id;
};

GreenSearchResultsModel.prototype = new MVC.Model();

GreenSearchResultsModel.prototype.recover = function()
{
    alert("Could not retrieve the cars you are trying to view.");
};

GreenSearchResultsModel.prototype.abandon = function()
{
    alert("Timed out fetching the cars you are trying to view.");
};

GreenSearchResultsView = function(i)
```

```
{
    MVC.View.call(this);

    // The position of the view is helpful when performing DOM updates.
    this.pos = i;
}

GreenSearchResultsView.prototype = new MVC.View();

GreenSearchResultsView.prototype.update = function()
{
    var cars = this.model.state.cars;

    // There is no need to update the view or show a button for one car.
    if (this.total == 1)
        return;

    if (!cars)
    {
        // When no cars are loaded, we're rendering for the first time.
        // In this case, we likely need to do different things in the DOM.
        ...
    }
    else
    {
        // When there are cars loaded, update the view by working with
        // the DOM to show the cars that are related to the main car.
        ...
    }
};

GreenSearchResultsView.prototype.show = function()
{
    // When we show the view, make an Ajax request to get related cars.
    // This causes the view to be notified and its update method to run.
    this.model.setState("GET", "...?carid=" + this.model.carID);
};

GreenSearchResultsView.prototype.hide = function()
{
    // When we hide the view, modify the DOM to make the view disappear.
    ...
};
```

In Chapter 9, we'll discuss how to add caching to this implementation so that once an expanded list is retrieved, it doesn't have to be fetched again when the View and Hide buttons for one car are clicked repeatedly.

Performance

Ultimately, none of the techniques presented in this book would be practical if they didn't provide a solid foundation on which to build large web applications that perform quickly and efficiently. This chapter shows how to use the foundation from the previous chapters to monitor and tweak the performance of your application.

You may well get a performance boost simply by following the practices already presented in this book. For example, the semantically meaningful HTML presented in Chapter 3 can speed up page display for several reasons. Likewise, modular techniques for large-scale PHP (see Chapter 7) generally create a faster site than jumping in and out of the PHP interpreter multiple times whenever needed.

But every professional web developer devotes time to performance as an end in itself, so this chapter shows how performance optimization interacts with the techniques in this book. To guide our discussion, we'll explore some of the recommendations presented in *High Performance Web Sites* (O'Reilly). This book, based on research conducted by Steve Souders at Yahoo!, suggests that for most websites, backend performance accounts for only 10 to 20 percent of the overall time required for a page to load; the remaining 80 to 90 percent is spent downloading components for the user interface. By following a set of 14 rules, many web applications can be made 20 to 25 percent faster.

These statistics emphasize the importance of paying close attention to the performance of how your HTML, CSS, JavaScript, and PHP work together. By utilizing a set of techniques for developing large web applications like the ones in this book, you can manage performance with relative ease and in a centralized manner.

> Tenet 9: Large-scale HTML, JavaScript, CSS, and PHP provide a good foundation on which to build large web applications that perform well. They also facilitate a good environment for capturing site metrics and testing.

We begin this chapter by looking at how the techniques for developing large web applications discussed in this book can help us manage opportunities for caching. Next, we'll explore some performance improvements that apply specifically to JavaScript. We then cover performance improvements related to ways we can distribute the various assets for an application across multiple servers. Finally, we'll look at techniques that facilitate capturing site metrics and performing testing.

Caching Opportunities

One of the biggest opportunities for improving performance is *caching*. Caching is the preservation and management of a collection of data that replicates original data computed earlier or stored in another location. The idea is to avoid retrieving the original data repeatedly and thus to avoid the high performance cost of retrieval. Some examples of resources that you can cache in a user interface are CSS files, JavaScript files, images, and even the entire contents of modules and pages. Whenever you encounter something that doesn't change very often (as is the case with CSS and JavaScript files especially), there is probably a good opportunity for caching.

Caching CSS and JavaScript

Whenever you can, you should place CSS and JavaScript in separate files that you can link on the pages that require them, as shown in Example 9-1. Not only does this allow you to share the contents of those files across multiple pages, it allows a browser to retrieve the files once over the wire, and then use them many times from the local cache.

Certainly, a browser can cache an HTML file that contains embedded CSS or JavaScript. However, the HTML is likely to change much more often than the CSS or JavaScript, so the browser may only cache it for a few moments. In contrast, you might go for months or even years without changing your CSS or JavaScript for a page. Separating the CSS and JavaScript into dedicated files therefore lets the browser store the CSS and JavaScript for repeated use, and just download the new HTML when needed.

In Chapter 7, you saw that modules and pages both define similar methods in their interfaces to specify the CSS and JavaScript files they require using `get_css_linked` and `get_js_linked`, respectively. Because each method results in links on the final page, as opposed to embedding CSS or JavaScript in the same page as the HTML, you get the benefits of caching.

Example 9-1. Linking JavaScript files for the benefits of caching

```
class PictureSlider extends Module
{
  ...

  public function get_js_linked()
  {
    // Specify the JavaScript files that must be included on the page.
    // This module needs YUI libraries for managing the DOM and doing
    // animation. The module's JavaScript is a part of sitewide.js.
    return array
    (
      "yahoo-dom-event.js",
```

```
            "animation.js",
            "sitewide.js"
        );
    }

    ...
}
```

Versioning CSS and JavaScript files

Anytime a browser caches a CSS or JavaScript file, it's important to ensure that the browser knows when a copy of the cached file is no longer up to date with changes you've made. Without this, your application is likely to be styled incorrectly or contain JavaScript errors as your HTML gets out of sync with your CSS and JavaScript. A simple way to ensure the browser knows when to fetch a new version of a file is to give each file a *version ID*. Whenever you change the file, simply advance the version ID. As a result, the browser does not find the new version in its cache and subsequently fetches it. A good method for constructing version IDs is to append the date to the name of the file or use the version number from your source control system. For example, you could have the following:

```
sitewide_20090710.js
```

If you need to update the file multiple times on a single day, you can append a sequence number or letter after the date:

```
sitewide_20090710a.js
```

Of course, you'll need to update references to the files wherever you link to them. Example 9-2 illustrates how easy this is to control in a centralized way using the `register_links` method presented in Chapter 7. Example 9-2 illustrates registering a JavaScript file with a version ID, and is based on the assumption that all pages in the web application have `SitePage` at some point in their class hierarchy. The `get_js_linked` method for pages and modules returns an array of keys. As files are linked for the page, these keys are used to look up the real path that was defined in `regis ter_links`. Each time you need to update the version ID for a file, you adjust it in one place, such as the `SitePage` class shown here. The process for CSS files is similar.

Example 9-2. Registering a JavaScript file with a version ID

```
class SitePage extends Page
{
    ...

    public function register_links()
    {
        ...

        $this->js_linked_info = array
        (
            "sitewide.js" => array
```

```
        (
            "aka_path" => $this->aka_path."/sitewide_20090710.js",
            "loc_path" => $this->loc_path."/sidewide_20090710.js"
        ),

        ...
    );

    ...
    }

    ...
}
```

Ideally, changes to a CSS or JavaScript file would apply wherever the file is accessed. But what if a dependency on one page prevents it from using the new version? Again, the `register_links` method provides an easy way to manage such fine-grained distinctions. The page class for the page containing the dependency defines a more specific version of `register_links` that first calls upon `register_links` in the parent to set up all the links as normal, then overwrites the name of the file for which the page requires the earlier version, as shown in Example 9-3.

Example 9-3. Overriding a version ID for just one page

```
class NewCarSearchResultsPage extends SitePage
{
    ...

    public function register_links()
    {
        // Call upon the parent class to set up all the links as normal.
        parent::register_links();

        // Alter the link for which this page needs a different version.
        $this->js_linked_info["sitewide.js"] = array
        (
            "aka_path" => $this->aka_path."/sitewide_20090709.js",
            "loc_path" => $this->loc_path."/sidewide_20090709.js"
        );
    }

    ...
}
```

Combining CSS and JavaScript files

One of the issues when placing CSS and JavaScript in dedicated files is determining a good way to divide the CSS (or JavaScript). On the one hand, if you place all your CSS within a single, large file, your application will become monolithic, lack modularity, and end up more difficult to maintain. On the other hand, if you place the CSS for each module within its own individual file, you'll end up with a large number of links on every page.

The section "Minimizing HTTP Requests" on page 238 discusses a good middle ground for dividing your CSS and JavaScript across a set of files to minimize HTTP requests. Once you have a good division of files, you can minimize the number of requests made for CSS or JavaScript files even further by combining multiple requests into one. To do this, you need to implement a server that understands combined requests. Such a request for CSS files might look like the following using a `link` tag:

```
<link href="http://.../?sitewide_20090710.css&newcars_20090630.css"
type="text/css" rel="stylesheet" media="all" />
```

Such a request for JavaScript files looks similar, but occurs in a `script` tag. A request for JavaScript files might look like the following:

```
<script src="http://.../ext/yahoo-dom-event_2.7.0.js&ext/yahoo-
animation_2.7.0.js&sitewide_20090710.js" type="text/javacript">
</script>
```

Once the server receives the request, it concatenates the files in the specified order and returns the concatenated file to the browser. It also caches a copy of the concatenated file on the server to use the next time a request with the same combination of files is made (for example, the next time the same page is displayed to any visitor). The browser receives the single, concatenated file for all the CSS (or JavaScript) via a single HTTP request. Furthermore, the next time a request is made from the same browser for the same set of files, the browser will already have the concatenated version cached and can avoid the request altogether.

To combine CSS and JavaScript files, you need to write some scripts on a server to do the combining and some code to assemble the requests for combining files as you generate pages. In this book, we won't examine the code to place on the server that does the combining, but the implementation is relatively straightforward. To build the requests for combining files, you need only make a few modifications to the `Page` class presented in Chapter 7. The modifications for combining JavaScript files are shown in Example 9-4. Combining CSS files is similar.

For CSS, just remember that you can only combine links that share the same media type (e.g., `all`, `print`), since all the concatenated files will form one file with one media type. Since media types other than `all` generally don't require multiple CSS files, a simple but effective approach is to ignore requests to combine CSS files that have a media type other than `all`.

Example 9-4. The Page class with support for combining JavaScript files

```
class Page
{
    protected $js_is_combined;

    ...

    public function __construct()
    {
        parent::__construct();
```

```
...

    // Default combining JavaScript to true; however, you can always
    // disable it in a derived page or by calling the setter method.
    $this->js_is_combined = true;
}

...

public function set_js_combined($flag)
{
    // Offer a way to enable or disable handling combined JavaScript.
    $this->js_is_combined = $flag;
}

...

private function create_js_combined_part($k)
{
    // Candidates for combining need to be from one server. Set that
    // here as a prefix to check. We'll log errors for other paths.
    $prefix = "...";

    // Look up the actual path for the file identified by the key k.
    $path = $this->js_linked_info[$k]["aka_path"];

    // Return a query part only if combining is supported for the path.
    $pos = strpos($path, $prefix);

    if ($pos === 0)
        return str_replace($prefix, "", $path);
    else
        return "";
}

private function create_js_combined_query()
{
    $combined_query = "";

    // We're making the assumption that local files are never combined
    // since normally alternative servers are used for the combining.
    if ($this->js_is_combined && !$this->js_is_local)
    {
        // Build an array of all the JavaScript keys in the order that
        // they were added by the page or modules created for the page.
        $all = array_merge
        (
            $this->js_common,
            $this->js_page_linked,
            $this->js_module_linked
        );

        $i = 0;
```

```
    // Build the combined query by appending each part one by one.
    foreach ($all as $k)
    {
        $part = $this->create_js_combined_part($k);

        if (empty($part))
        {
            // An empty part indicates that the path for the file is
            // not a path that supports combining. Log this issue.
            ...

            break;
        }

        $sep = ($i++ == 0) ? "?" : "&";
        $combined_query .= $sep.$part;
    }
}

    return $combined_query;
}

...
}
```

Caching Modules

Another opportunity for caching occurs each time you generate the CSS, JavaScript, and content for a module on the server. Caching for a module is especially useful when the module's content, styles, and behaviors require a fair amount of CPU work to generate and you don't expect them to change very often. A good approach to implementing cacheable modules is to provide the capabilities required by all cacheable modules within a base class called CacheableModule, derived from the Module class in Chapter 7. To make your own module cacheable, simply derive it from CacheableModule. Example 9-5 illustrates an implementation for the CacheableModule class.

Example 9-5. The implementation of a base class for cacheable modules

```
class CacheableModule extends Module
{
    protected $cache_ttl;
    protected $cache_clr;

    public function __construct($page)
    {
        parent::__construct($page);

        // The default time-to-live for entries in the cache is one hour.
        $this->cache_ttl = 3600;

        // The default is to check the cache first, but you can clear it.
        $this->cache_clr = false;
    }
```

```php
public function create()
{
    // Check whether data exists in the cache for the module at all.
    $cache_key = $this->get_cache_key();
    $cache_val = apc_fetch($cache_key);

    // Set the hash for the variables on which the new data is based.
    $hash = $this->get_cache_hash($this->get_cache_vars());

    if (!$this->cache_clr && $cache_val && $cache_val["hash"]==$hash)
    {
        // Whenever we can use the cached module, access the cache.
        $content = $this->fetch_from_cache($cache_val["data"]);
    }
    else
    {
        // Otherwise, generate the module as normal and cache a copy.
        $content = $this->store_into_cache($cache_key, $hash);
    }

    return $content;
}

public function set_cache_ttl($ttl)
{
    // Set the time-to-live to the specified value, in milliseconds.
    $this->cache_ttl = $ttl;
}

public function set_cache_clr()
{
    // Force the cacheable module to bust any cached copy immediately.
    $this->cache_clr = true;
}

protected function get_cache_vars()
{
    // Modules derived from this class should implement this method
    // to return a string that changes whenever the cache should be
    // discarded (the current microtime busts the cache by default).
    return microtime();
}

protected function fetch_from_cache($data)
{
    // Add cached CSS styles to the page on which the module resides.
    $this->page->add_to_css_linked($data["css_linked"]);
    $this->page->add_to_css($data["css"]);

    // Add cached JavaScript to the page on which the module resides.
    $this->page->add_to_js_linked($data["js_linked"]);
    $this->page->add_to_js($data["js"]);

    // Return the cached content for the module.
```

```
        return $data["content"];
    }

    protected function store_into_cache($cache_key, $hash)
    {
        $css_linked = $this->get_css_linked();
        $css = $this->get_css();

        $js_linked = $this->get_js_linked();
        $js = $this->get_js();

        $content = $this->get_content();

        // Set up the data structure for the data to place in the cache.
        $cache_val = array
        (
            "hash" => $hash,
            "data" => array
            (
                "css_linked" => $css_linked,
                "css" => $css,
                "js_linked" => $js_linked,
                "js" => $js,
                "content" => $content
            )
        );

        // Store the new copy into the cache and apply the time-to-live.
        apc_store($cache_key, $cache_val, $this->cache_ttl);

        // Add module CSS styles to the page on which the module resides.
        $this->page->add_to_css_linked($css_linked);
        $this->page->add_to_css($css);

        // Add module JavaScript to the page on which the module resides.
        $this->page->add_to_js_linked($js_linked);
        $this->page->add_to_js($js);

        // Return the content that was just generated using get_content.
        return $content;
    }

    protected function get_cache_hash($var)
    {
        // Hash the string used to determine when to use the cached copy.
        return md5($var);
    }

    protected function get_cache_key()
    {
        // This must be unique per module, so use the derived class name.
        return get_class($this);
    }
}
```

The CacheableModule class uses the APC (Alternative PHP Cache) cache of PHP to implement the caching between instantiations of the module. The class provides a good example of overriding create provided by Module (see Chapter 7). Instead of the default implementation of create, the implementation here inspects the APC cache before generating the module. If the module can use the cache, it fetches its CSS, JavaScript, and content instead of generating them from scratch. If the module cannot use the cache, it generates itself as normal and caches its CSS, JavaScript, and content for the next time. To be clear, there are four conditions under which the module will be generated from scratch:

- There is no copy in the cache at all.
- The variables from which the cached copy is derived have changed.
- The time-to-live has expired.
- The $cache_clr member is set.

One of the nice things about the implementation in Example 9-5 is that using a cacheable module is very similar to using a module that is not cacheable. For example, suppose NewCarSearchResults were a module derived from CacheableModule. The code to instantiate and create this module looks like what was presented in Chapter 7. The call to set_cache_ttl is optional, just to set a different time-to-live than the default for the cache. You can also call the public method set_cache_clr whenever you want to ensure that a fresh copy of the module is generated.

```
$mod = new NewCarSearchResults
(
    $this,
    $this->data["new_car_listings"]
);

$mod->set_cache_ttl(1800);
$results = $mod->create();
```

The main thing to remember when using a cacheable module is that your class derived from CacheableModule needs to implement get_cache_vars for how you want caching to occur. This method should return a string that changes whenever you no longer want to use the cached copy of the module. This string is typically a concatenation of the variables and values on which the cached module depends.

Notice that the default implementation for get_cache_vars in the base class returns the current time in microseconds. This value ensures the default behavior is never to use the cached copy, since the time in microseconds is different whenever you generate the module. This will be the case until you provide more informed logic about when the cache should be considered valid by overriding get_cache_vars within your own implementation in the derived class.

Caching for Pages

Just as you can cache the contents of individual modules that you don't expect to change frequently, you also can cache the contents of entire pages. The process for implementing this is similar to that for modules. You create a `CacheablePage` class and override the default implementations for the `create` and `get_page` methods. The start of `create` is a logical place to insert the code for generating the hash and searching the cache. At this point, you can inspect parameters for generating the page even before taking the time to load data for the page. If the page can use the cache, fetch the completely assembled page instead of generating it from scratch in `get_page`. If the page cannot use the cache, generate the page in the traditional manner (during which some caching may still be utilized by modules, remember) and cache the completely assembled page at the end of `get_page` for the next time.

A further opportunity for caching, of course, occurs when the data for the page is loaded. This type of caching is performed best by the backend since it has the visibility into how the data is stored, and ideally these details should be abstracted from the user interface. Therefore, we're not going to look at an example of this in this book, although it clearly plays an important part of most large web applications.

Whenever you expect to do a lot of caching, keep in mind that caching can cause its own performance issues as memory becomes too full. In this case, a system may begin to *thrash* as it begins to spend more time swapping virtual pages in and out of memory than doing other work. You can keep an eye on this by running `top` on Unix systems and monitoring the process in charge of swapping for your system.

Caching with Ajax

Ajax provides another opportunity for caching. In Chapter 8, we discussed the usefulness of the MVC design pattern in managing the separation between data, presentation, and control in an Ajax application. Here, we revisit Example 8-15 with caching in the model. The model in this example manages an accordion list of additional trims for one car in a list of cars with good green ratings. When the model is updated, a view that subscribes to changes in the model updates itself to show an expanded list of cars that are trims related to the main entry. Because many of the cars will never have their lists expanded, loading the lists of trims on demand via Ajax is a good approach. Because the list of trims doesn't change frequently, caching the list in the model once retrieved also makes a lot of sense. Example 9-6 illustrates caching trims in the model that we discussed in Chapter 8.

Example 9-6. Caching with Ajax added to Example 8-15

```
GreenSearchResultsModel = function(id)
{
    MVC.Model.call(this);

    this.carID = id;
```

```
};

GreenSearchResultsModel.prototype = new MVC.Model();

GreenSearchResultsModel.prototype.setCache = function()
{
   // This implements a caching layer in the browser. If other cars
   // under the main entry were fetched before, we don't refetch them.
   if (this.state.cars)
   {
      // Other cars under the main car were fetched before, so just
      // send a notification to each of the views to update themselves.
      this.notify();
   }
   else
   {
      // Cars under the main entry are not cached, so set the state of
      // the model by specifying the URL through which to make the Ajax
      // request. The setState method is responsible for notifying views.
      this.setState("GET", "...?carid=" + this.carID);
   }
};

GreenSearchResultsModel.prototype.recover = function()
{
   alert("Could not retrieve the cars you are trying to view.");
};

WineSearchResultsModel.prototype.abandon = function()
{
   alert("Timed out fetching the cars you are trying to view.");
};

GreenSearchResultsView = function(i)
{
   MVC.View.call(this);

   // The position of the view is helpful when performing DOM updates.
   this.pos = i;
}

GreenSearchResultsView.prototype = new MVC.View();

GreenSearchResultsView.prototype.update = function()
{
   var cars = this.model.state.cars;
   ...

   // There is no need to update the view or show a button for one car.
   if (this.total == 1)
      return;

   if (!cars)
   {
      // When no cars are loaded, we're rendering for the first time.
```

```
        // In this case, we likely need to do different things in the DOM.
        ...
    }
    else
    {
        // When there are cars loaded, update the view by working with
        // the DOM to show the cars that are related to the main car.
        ...
    }
};

GreenSearchResultsView.prototype.show = function()
{
    // When we show the view, check whether we can use the cache or not.
    this.model.setCache();
};

GreenSearchResultsView.prototype.hide = function()
{
    // When we hide the view, modify the DOM to make the view disappear.
    ...
};
```

To implement caching in the model, Example 9-6 adds the `setCache` method to `Green SearchResultsModel`. The event handler for showing the expanded list of cars invokes the `show` method of `GreenSearchResultsView`. This, in turn, calls `setCache` for the model. If the model already contains a list of cars, the cached list is used and no server request occurs. If the model does not contain the list, it makes a request back to the server via the `setState` method of `Model` and caches the returned list for the next time. To request the proper list of cars, the request uses the `carID` member of the model as a parameter. This is set in the constructor to identify the car for which we want additional trims. After the appropriate action is taken based on the state of the cache, the model calls `notify` (either directly or within `setState`), and `notify` calls `update` for each view subscribed to the model, which, in the list of search results, is just one view for each car.

Using Expires Headers

Another way to control caching for Ajax applications is to set an `Expires` header on the server. This header informs the browser of the date after which the result is to be considered stale. It's particularly important to set this to 0 when your data is highly dynamic. In PHP, set the `Expires` header to 0 by doing the following before you echo anything for the page:

```
header("Expires: 0");
```

If you have a specific time in the future at which you'd like a cached result to expire, you can use an HTTP date string:

```
header("Expires: Fri, 17 Jul 2009 16:00:00 GMT");
```

Managing JavaScript

We've already discussed some aspects of managing JavaScript performance in the various topics presented for caching. In this section, we look at other ideas for managing JavaScript, including its placement within the overall structure of a page, the use of JavaScript minification, and an approach for ensuring that you never end up with duplicates of the same JavaScript file on a single page.

JavaScript Placement

Whenever possible, you should place JavaScript at the bottom of the page. The main reason for this is because the rendering of a page pauses while a JavaScript file loads (presumably because the JavaScript being loaded could alter the DOM already in the process of being created). Given this, large files or network latency can cause significant delays as a page loads. If you've ever seen a page hang while waiting for an ad to load, you have likely suffered through this problem caused by JavaScript loading. If you place your JavaScript at the end of the page, the page will finish rendering by the time it encounters the JavaScript.

The Page class in Chapter 7 addresses this issue simply by defaulting all JavaScript to the bottom of the page where the page is assembled within the get_page method. That said, there are times when you may find it necessary to place your JavaScript at the top. One example is when the main call to action on a page requires JavaScript, such as a selection list or other user interface component that appears near the top and commands the user's attention. For these situations, Page provides the set_js_top method, which you can call after the page is instantiated to indicate that the JavaScript should be placed at the top of the page.

To preserve modularity, a module should not rely on a particular placement for its JavaScript beyond the order of the dependencies specified in its own get_js_linked method. So, for example, you shouldn't assume that the DOM will be ready to use when your JavaScript starts to run, even if you have placed the JavaScript at the bottom of the page. Here, it's better to rely on the YUI library's onDOMReady method for registering a callback to execute as soon as the DOM is stable.

JavaScript Minification

Minification removes whitespace, comments, and the like, and performs other innocuous modifications that reduce the overall size of a JavaScript file. This is not to be confused with *obfuscation*. Obfuscation can result in even smaller JavaScript files and code that is very difficult to read (thereby providing some rudimentary protection from reverse engineering), but its alteration of variable names and other references requires coordination across files that often makes the rewards not worth the risks. Minification, on the other hand, comes with very little risk and offers an easy way to reduce download times for JavaScript files.

To minify a JavaScript file, use Douglas Crockford's JSMin utility, which is available at *http://www.crockford.com/javascript/jsmin.html*, or you can use YUICompressor, available at *http://developer.yahoo.com/yui/compressor*, which minifies CSS, too. In addition, be sure that your web server is configured to gzip not only HTML, but CSS and JavaScript as well.

A common complaint among developers about minified JavaScript is how to gracefully transition between human-readable JavaScript within development environments and minified JavaScript for production systems. The register_links method of the Page class from Chapter 7 offers a good solution. As we've seen, register_links lets you define two locations for each file: one referenced using $aka_path (an "also-known-as" path intended for files on production servers), and the other referenced using $loc_path (a "local path" intended for files on development systems). Set the $js_is_local flag to select between them. Example 9-7 provides an example of managing minification.

Example 9-7. Managing minified and development JavaScript in a page class

```
class SitePage extends Page
{
    ...

    public function register_links()
    {
        $this->aka_path = "http://...";
        $this->loc_path = "http://...";

        $this->js_linked_info = array
        (
            "sitewide.js" => array
            (
                "aka_path" => $this->aka_path."/sitewide_20090710-min.js",
                "loc_path" => $this->loc_path."/sidewide_20090710.js"
            ),

            ...
        );

        // Access the minified JavaScript files on the production servers.
        $this->js_is_local = false;
    }

    ...
}
```

Removing Duplicates

Modular development intrinsically raises the risk of including the same file more than once. Duplicating JavaScript files may seem like an easy thing to avoid, but as the number of scripts added to a large web application and the number of developers working together increase, there's a good chance that duplications will occur if there's no procedure for managing file inclusion. Fortunately, the use of keys for JavaScript files, which we've already discussed, prevents the duplication of JavaScript files intrinsically. In fact, for a truly modular system, every module *is expected* to specify in its own `get_js_linked` method precisely the JavaScript files that it requires without concerns about which other modules might or might not need the files. The page will exclude the duplicates and link files in the proper order.

Example 9-8 shows how the `Page` class prevents duplicate JavaScript files from being linked within its `manage_js_linked` method. Managing duplicate CSS files is similar.

Example 9-8. Preventing duplicate JavaScript files from being linked

```
class Page
{
   ...

   private function manage_js_linked($keys)
   {
      $js = "";

      if (empty($keys))
         return "";

      // Normalize so that we can pass keys individually or as an array.
      if (!is_array($keys))
         $keys = array($keys);

      foreach ($keys as $k)
      {
         // Log an error for unknown keys when there is no link to add.
         if (!array_key_exists($k, $this->js_linked_info))
         {
            error_log("Page::manage_js_linked: Key \"".$k."\" missing");
            continue;
         }

         // Add the link only if it hasn't been added to the page before.
         if (array_search($k, $this->js_linked_used) === false)
         {
            $this->js_linked_used[] = $k;
            $js .= $this->create_js_linked($k);
         }
      }

      return $js;
   }

   ...
}
```

Distribution of Assets

Another method for improving the performance of a large web application is to distribute your assets across a number of servers. Whereas only very large web applications may be able to rely on virtual IP addresses and load balancers to distribute traffic among application servers, anyone can accomplish a distribution of assets to some extent simply by distributing CSS files, JavaScript files, and images. This section describes a few approaches for managing this.

Content Delivery Networks

Content delivery networks are networks like those of Akamai and a few other companies that are typically available only to very large web applications. These networks use sophisticated caching algorithms to spread content throughout a highly distributed network so that it eventually reaches servers that are geographically close to any visitor that might request it. Amazon.com's CloudFront, an extension to its S3 storage service, presents an interesting recent twist on this industry that may bring this high-performance technology within the reach of more sites.

If you work for a company that has access to a content delivery network and you employ an approach to developing pages using classes like those in Chapter 7, you can store the path to its servers within the `$aka_path` member used when defining CSS and JavaScript links in the `SitePage` class. Recall, `$aka_path` is intended to reference production servers when `$js_is_local` is false.

Minimizing DNS Lookups

As you distribute assets across different servers, it's important to strike a balance with the number of Domain Name Service (DNS) lookups that a page must perform. Looking up the IP address associated with a hostname is another type of request that affects how fast your page loads. Furthermore, even after a name has been resolved, the amount of time a name remains valid varies based on a number of factors, including the time-to-live value returned in the DNS record itself, settings in the operating system, settings in the browser, and the Keep-Alive feature of the HTTP protocol. As a result, it's important to pay attention to how many DNS requests your page ends up generating.

A simple way to manage this number is to define the paths (including hostnames) for the assets you plan to use across your large web application in a central place. The class hierarchy we discussed for pages in Chapter 7 provides some insight into where to place the members that define these paths.

Recall that a logical set of classes to derive from `Page` includes a sitewide page class, a page class for each section of the site, and a page class for each specific page. Considering this, the sitewide page class, `SitePage`, makes an excellent place to define paths that affect the number of DNS lookups. By defining the paths here, all parts of your large web application can access the paths as needed and you'll have a single, centrally located place where you can manage the number of DNS requests that your assets require. *High Performance Web Sites* suggests dividing your assets across at least two hosts, but not more than four. Many web applications use one set of hosts for static assets like CSS, JavaScript, and image files, and another set for server-side code.

Minimizing HTTP Requests

As we saw earlier in this chapter, the first step to minimizing HTTP requests is to take advantage of caching and combine multiple requests for CSS and JavaScript files into single requests for each. This section presents additional opportunities for minimizing the number of HTTP requests for a page. For the most part, this means carefully managing requests for CSS, JavaScript, and images.

Guidelines for CSS files

Just as we discussed with caching, one of the issues with minimizing HTTP requests for CSS files is determining a good division of files. A good starting point for managing the number of CSS files in a large web application is to define one CSS file as a common file linked by all pages across the site, one CSS file for each section of the site, and as few other CSS files as possible. However, you are likely to find other organization schemes specific to your web application. Naturally, as you start to need additional CSS files on a single page (to support different CSS media types, for example), you'll find that the number of CSS files that you may want to link can grow quickly. Therefore, whenever possible, employ the technique presented earlier for combining multiple CSS files into a single request.

Guidelines for JavaScript files

As with CSS files, a good starting point for managing the number of JavaScript files in a large web application is to use one common file containing JavaScript applicable to most parts of the site, a set of sectional files each specific to one section of the site, and as few other JavaScript files as possible. Of course, if you use a lot of external libraries, those will increase the number of files that you need to link; however, you can always take the approach of joining files together on your own servers in ways that make sense for your application.

This has the added benefit of placing the files directly under your control rather than on someone else's servers, and it reduces DNS lookups. In addition, many libraries provide files that contain groupings of library components that are most frequently used together. One example is *yahoo-dom-event.js* in the YUI library. Again, employ the techniques presented earlier for combining multiple JavaScript files into a single request.

Guidelines for image files

Surprisingly, you can also combine image files, although in a more complicated way than CSS and JavaScript files, using a technique called *spriting*. Spriting is the process of creating a single larger image that contains many smaller originals of the same type (e.g., GIF, JPEG, etc.) at known offsets in one file. You can use these offsets to position the larger image within an HTML element so that just its desired portion is visible. Spriting is a good way to reduce HTTP requests, but there are some practical considerations that limit how images can be combined.

One practical limitation occurs with images that will be used for repeating backgrounds. Only those images to be repeated in the same direction (i.e., the x or y direction) and with the same size in that direction can be combined. Otherwise, for all images smaller than the largest one, you'll see space between repeated images.

Another practical consideration is that sprites can change rather frequently because changes or additions for any individual image require the sprite file to change. When this happens, browsers that have an earlier version cached need to know to get the new version on the next request. Fortunately, using a version ID like we did for CSS and JavaScript files provides a good solution. That said, the management of version IDs for sprites is a little more problematic for two reasons: first, sprites are often referenced from CSS files, which usually are not run through the PHP interpreter (to manage the version IDs dynamically); and second, changes to images may require you to update offsets within the CSS as well as version IDs for files.

Considering these practical limitations, a good approach is to look for opportunities for spriting within scopes that are easy to manage. For example, if we create a sprite file with just the images for a specific module, it's easy to keep the module in sync with version ID and offset changes that take place as the sprite file changes. Example 9-9 illustrates spriting within a module for a navigation bar. The module uses five icons with two states (selected and unselected), which reside in one sprite file. The sprite is named after the module, which is a good practice for the purposes of documentation.

Example 9-9. Spriting for icons in a navigation bar

```
#navbar .ichome .selected
{
   width: 50px;
   height: 50px;
   background: url(http://.../navbar_20090712.jpg) 0px 0px no-repeat;
}
```

```
#navbar .ichome .noselect
{
   width: 50px;
   height: 50px;
   background: url(http://.../navbar_20090712.jpg) -50px 0px no-repeat;
}
#navbar .icrevs .selected
{
   width: 50px;
   height: 50px;
   background: url(http://.../navbar_20090712.jpg) -100px 0px no-repeat;
}
#navbar .icrevs .noselect
{
   width: 50px;
   height: 50px;
   background: url(http://.../navbar_20090712.jpg) -150px 0px no-repeat;
}

...

#navbar .icabout .selected
{
   width: 50px;
   height: 50px;
   background: url(http://.../navbar_20090712.jpg) ... 0px no-repeat;
}
#navbar .icabout .noselect
{
   width: 50px;
   height: 50px;
   background: url(http://.../navbar_20090712.jpg) ... 0px no-repeat;
}
```

Figure 9-1 illustrates positioning the sprite image for the first two icons in Example 9-9 (at positions 0px, 0px and −50px, 0px).

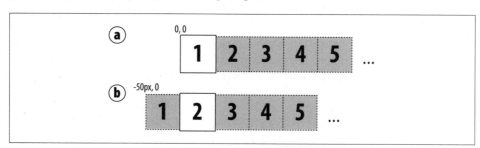

Figure 9-1. Positioning the sprite for the first two icons in Example 9-9

An additional approach for managing sprite files is to create one per CSS file. This way, whenever the sprite changes, you know that only its associated CSS file needs to be updated to reflect the new sprite file and changes to offsets. Again, a naming convention can help document this approach. For example, for the CSS file *newcars_20090731.css* (containing the CSS for one section of the application), you can create a sprite file called *newcars_20090731.jpg* that contains all the JPEG images for just that section.

Control Over Site Metrics

Although not directly related to performance from the standpoint of how fast a page loads, the ability to capture metrics about how visitors are using your web application does tell you a great deal about other aspects of how your application is performing with regard to the overall user experience. In this section, we'll look at an easy approach for adding Google Analytics to a large web application.

Google Analytics is a free service that provides great tools for analyzing how visitors are using your web application. Once you register for the service, enabling metrics for your site is simply a matter of adding a snippet of code to the right place on all pages that you want to track. As we have discussed several times throughout this chapter, the SitePage class that you define for use by all pages across your application offers a logical place to manage this code. Example 9-10 illustrates this.

Example 9-10. Adding Google Analytics across an entire web application

```
class SitePage extends Page
{
    protected $google_site_id;
    protected $google_site_nm;

    ...

    public function __construct()
    {
        // You get the ID for your site once you've signed up with Google.
        $this->google_site_id = "...";
        $this->google_site_nm = "...";
    }

    ...

    public function get_all_js()
    {
        // First, get all the JavaScript that was assembled for the page.
        $js = parent::get_all_js();

        // This is the snippet of Google Analytics code from registering.
        $analytics = <<<EOD
<!-- Google Analytics -->
<script type="text/javascript">
```

```
var gaJsHost = (("https:" == document.location.protocol)
    ? "https://ssl."
    : "http://www.");

document.write(unescape("%3Cscript src='" +
    gaJsHost + "google-analytics.com/ga.js'
    type='text/javascript'%3E%3C/script%3E"));

var pageTracker = _gat._getTracker($this->google_site_id);
pageTracker._setDomainName($this->google_site_nm);
pageTracker._trackPageview();
</script>
EOD;
    }

    // Append Google Analytics to the JavaScript that was assembled
    // otherwise for the page.
    return <<<EOD
$js
$analytics

EOD;
    }

    ...
}
```

Of course, your metrics won't be accurate if you include this code in environments for which you shouldn't be tracking pages. For example, you'll probably want to exclude development environments, testing environments, staging environments, and the like. To do this, simply define a flag that you set to the type of environment in which the page is being displayed, as shown in Example 9-11. The PHP code checks to make sure that it's generating a page within the production environment before including the Google Analytics code.

Example 9-11. Adding Google Analytics just for tracking on production systems

```
class SitePage extends Page
{
    protected $google_site_id;
    protected $google_site_nm;
    protected $op_environment;

    ...

    public function __construct()
    {
        $this->google_site_id = "...";
        $this->google_site_nm = "...";

        // Set this from a server config that indicates the environment.
        $this->op_environment = "...";
    }
```

```
    ...

    public function get_all_js()
    {
        // First, get all the JavaScript that was assembled for the page.
        $js = parent::get_all_js();
        $analytics = "";

        if ($this->op_environment == "production")
        {
            // Add the Google Analytics code here for production tracking.
            $analytics = <<<EOD
            ...

EOD;
        }

        // Google Analytics is not appended unless running in production.
        return <<<EOD
$js
$analytics

EOD;
    }

    ...
}
```

Modular Testing

Because the ability to test a large web application is closely related to performance, this section discusses how to use some of the techniques presented in this book to create pages that can easily utilize test data.

Using Test Data

Modularity makes adding and removing components easier. This is important for test data, too. The data for most web applications comes from databases or other backend systems. But while the backend is under development, you might have to test your modules in the absence of real data, or at least programming logic to retrieve the data. Therefore, you need a clean and simple way to inject invented data into your modules. Because data managers (see Chapter 6) define the interface for data exchange between the user interface and backend, they offer a good point at which to define hardcoded data that precisely matches the structure of the real data that you expect to exchange with the backend later. When you're ready to use the real data, it's easy to remove the test data manager and replace it with the real one.

To use a test data manager, require its include file in place of the include file for the real one, but use the same name for the data manager class. The only difference is something in the name of the include file to distinguish it, such as a *test* suffix. Example 9-12 illustrates the key goal: using the test data looks exactly like using the real data later, except for the name of the include file.

Example 9-12. Using a test data manager

```php
<?php
require_once(".../common/sitepage.inc");
require_once(".../common/navbar.inc");
require_once(".../common/subnav.inc");
require_once(".../common/nwcresults.inc");
...

require_once(".../layout/resultslayout.inc");
...

// Include the test data manager until the real data manager is ready.
require_once(".../datamgr/nwclistings_test.inc");
...

class NewCarSearchResultsPage extends SitePage
{
    ...

    public function load_data()
    {
        // This appears exactly like it will with the real data manager.
        $dm = new NewCarListingsDataManager();

        // The data members for loading are provided by the base class.
        // Populate them as needed by the data manager and call get_data.
        ...

        $dm->get_data
        (
            $this->load_args["new_car_listings"],
            $this->load_data["new_car_listings"],
            $this->load_stat["new_car_listings"]
        );

        // Check the status member and handle any errors, which often
        // require a redirect to another page using the header function.
        if ($this->load_stat != 0)
            header("Location: ...");

        ...
    }

    public function get_content()
    {
        ...
```

```
    // This appears exactly like it will with the real data manager.
    $mod = new NewCarResults
    (
        $this,
        $this->load_data["new_car_listings"]
    );

    $results = $mod->create();

    ...
    }

    ...
}
?>
```

Creating Test Data

An important aspect of creating test data managers is that they can actually serve as a contract of sorts between the user interface and backend for how the two will exchange data for real. Ideally, once the data manager is ready, you should be able to remove the test data manager, replace it with the real one, and have a working system with relatively minor tweaks.

Example 9-13 illustrates a simple test data manager, which populates a data structure with some hardcoded test values. This defines the data structure that will be used for the real data later.

Example 9-13. Defining a test data manager

```
class NewCarReviewsDataManager extends DataManager
{
    ...

    public function __construct()
    {
        parent::__construct();

        ...
    }

    public function get_data($load_args, &$load_data, &$load_stat)
    {
        // Populate the data structure explicitly with data for testing.
        // This also defines the contract between the backend and user
        // interface for how the real data eventually should be handled.
        $load_data = array
        (
            "0" => array
            (
                "name"  => "2009 Honda Accord",
                "price" => "21905",
                "link"  => "http://.../reviews/00001/"
```

```
        ),
        "1" => array
        (
            "name"  => "2009 Toyota Prius",
            "price" => "22000",
            "link"  => "http://.../reviews/00002/"
        ),
        "2" => array
        (
            "name"  => "2009 Nissan Altima",
            "price" => "19900",
            "link"  => "http://.../reviews/00003/"
        )
    );
  }
}
```

CHAPTER 10

Application Architecture

The architecture of a large web application has many facets, and we've already touched on many of these in previous chapters. In this chapter, we'll focus on one of the most prominent reflections of application architecture: organizing classes and files on the server so they reinforce the modularity established in your large-scale HTML, CSS, JavaScript, and server-side scripts. We'll also look at how this structure in a large web application helps with its maintenance down the road; you'll see how important it is to make sure the organization you choose reflects the scope in which you expect each class or file to be used. Tenet 10 (from Chapter 1) addresses this issue:

> Tenet 10: The organization of files on the server for a large web application reflects the architecture of the application itself, including clearly demarcated scopes in which each file will be used.

We'll begin by examining the design of a sample web page in terms of the modules it contains, because thinking modularly about web pages is a key part of envisioning the architecture for a large web application overall. We'll then go into more detail about how to organize the classes we presented in earlier chapters into files. Finally, we'll explore how the architectural discussion in this chapter, coupled with the techniques discussed earlier in the book, help you manage certain common situations that are likely to arise while maintaining a large web application. This will demonstrate further how a modular implementation improves reusability, maintainability, and reliability in a large web application over its lifetime.

Thinking Modularly

As mentioned in Chapter 3, when you develop a large web application, you should plan on ways to reuse as many of its components as possible. Even if you cannot find much that you expect to reuse, building a page as a set of individual components, or modules, will make a page easier to maintain and more reliable.

What constitutes a good module will often be fairly obvious; at other times, certain better divisions will reveal themselves as you build things. Figure 10-1 illustrates some examples of modules that appear to be rather natural divisions of the page into functional units: a search box, an ad unit, and a module for selecting new cars, for example. These are rather intuitive divisions. On the other hand, you might find it better in the end to break the module for selecting new cars into two modules: one including the Go button and everything above it, and the other including everything below this point. This division would give you flexibility to use each of the smaller units independently elsewhere.

Components that implement the overall structure for a page may not seem as easy to break into modules at first, but because components for this purpose offer a good means of abstraction and have a strong potential for reuse, they can be very good modules as well. Figure 10-2 shows a *layout*, which is the generic template that defines the overarching structure of a page. Figure 10-3 shows a *container*, which is a generic grouping of modules that you can place within layouts to support common organizations.

It's good to implement layouts and containers as modules because they each require their own HTML and CSS, and we shouldn't have to duplicate this code each time we need the same structure. Designers tend to think in terms of these reusable patterns as well, so layouts and containers also provide a good opportunity for engineers and designers to work together to establish standard guidelines for the overall structure of pages. Chapters 4 and 7 show how to implement layouts and containers using HTML, CSS, and PHP.

Organizing Components

As you build up a library of pages, modules, layouts, and containers in your architecture, it's important to look at how and where you intend to use each as you decide how to organize them. In the sections that follow, we'll explore a directory structure that presents one way to organize the components we've discussed for large web applications in previous chapters as an example. A reasonable place to start for most web applications is to decide where in the architecture each component belongs. Is it sitewide, section-specific, or page-specific?

Sitewide Architecture

In most large web applications, there are many components that you'll want to share across the entire application. These belong at a point in your directory structure that conveys this sitewide importance.

Figure 10-1. Some of the modules on a web page

Figure 10-2. A reusable layout for a web page

Figure 10-3. A reusable container for a web page

Pages and modules

The base classes for pages and modules are excellent examples of components that are used across an entire web application. By placing them in a directory called *common*, or something similar, at the top of the directory structure, you convey their sitewide scope. Each file is named after the class that it contains:

> *.../common/page.inc*
>
> *.../common/sitepage.inc*
>
> *.../common/module.inc*
>
> ...

You include these files whenever you implement your own classes for specific pages and modules. Example 10-1 shows `NavBar` derived from the `Module` base class, which requires *module.inc*.

 We're not going to examine the details of many of the classes in this chapter. You can learn more about their implementations in Chapter 7.

Example 10-1. Deriving the Navigation Bar module from Module

```php
<?php
require_once(".../common/module.inc");

class NavBar extends Module
{
   // You need to include module.inc to derive this class from Module.
   ...
}
?>
```

The top-level *common* directory is also a logical place to put classes for specific modules that you expect to use across the entire web application. Each file is named after the module class that it contains:

> *.../common/navbar.inc*
>
> *.../common/subnav.inc*
>
> *.../common/searchbox.inc*
>
> ...

Layouts and containers

Layouts and containers tend to be useful across an entire web application as well. Because layouts and containers fulfill a somewhat unique role, it may be helpful to place them in their own subdirectory, separate from the other common components. This directory contains files for specific layouts and containers as well as a file containing the Layout base class itself:

.../common/layout/layout.inc

.../common/layout/landinglayout.inc

.../common/layout/resultslayout.inc

.../common/layout/detailslayout.inc

.../common/layout/container4x1.inc

.../common/layout/container3x1.inc

...

In Chapter 7, you saw that layouts actually have a lot in common with modules. As a result, Layout is derived from Module, as shown in Example 10-2, and *layout.inc* requires *module.inc*. Example 10-3 shows how specific layouts are derived from Layout; these files all require *layout.inc*.

Example 10-2. Deriving a layout as a module

```php
<?php
require_once("../common/module.inc");

class Layout extends Module
{
    // You need to include module.inc to derive this class from Module.
    ...
}
?>
```

Example 10-3. Deriving a specific layout

```php
<?php
require_once("../common/layout/layout.inc");

class ResultsLayout extends Layout
{
    // You need to include layout.inc to derive this class from Layout.
    ...
}
?>
```

CSS and JavaScript

In Chapter 9, you saw that a good starting point for managing the organization of CSS and JavaScript files in a large web application is a common file containing CSS or JavaScript applicable to most parts of the site, a set of sectional files each specific to one section of the site, and as few other CSS or JavaScript files as possible. Sitewide CSS and JavaScript files go in their own top-level directories:

```
.../css/sitewide_20091011.css
.../css/printers_20091011.css
.../js/sitewide_20090929.js

...
```

Data management

In Chapter 6, you saw that data managers provide a clearly defined interface between the user interface and backend systems. We also discussed the fact that it is helpful to define data managers for fairly granular sets of data grouped logically from the backend perspective. After you have defined the data managers, the user interface can instantiate whichever of them are needed to load and save specific sets of data.

Because data managers are organized from the backend perspective, it's good to define a data manager directory under which you can create whichever subdirectories best reflect the backend architecture for data:

```
.../datamgr
```

Images and other resources

Images and other types of resources (PDF files, Flash files, etc.) used across the entire web application deserve dedicated areas, too:

```
.../images
.../docs
.../media

...
```

Recall from Chapter 9 that if you employ the techniques for spriting images, you'll end up with fewer image files to organize under the *images* directory.

Section Architecture

Most large web applications have some components that are specific to certain sections of the application, so it makes sense to place them at a point in the directory structure that reflects this. It's reasonable to make the directory structure for sections similar to the one for sitewide components.

Pages specific to one section

Pages within a certain section of a large web application often require similar capabilities that you can implement in a base class. By placing them in a directory called *common*, or something similar, at the top of the directory structure for the section, you convey their applicability to the entire section instead of the entire application. Each file is named after the class that it contains (e.g., "cpo" indicates Certified Preowned):

> *.../newcars/common/nwcpage.inc*
>
> *.../cpocars/common/cpopage.inc*
>
> *...*

You include these files whenever you implement your own classes for more specific pages. Example 10-4 shows `NewCarDetailsPage` derived from the `NewCarsPage` base class, which requires *nwcpage.inc*.

Example 10-4. The New Car Details page within the New Cars section

```php
<?php
require_once(".../newcars/common/nwcpage.inc");
...

class NewCarDetailsPage extends NewCarsPage
{
    // You need to include nwcpage.inc to derive this from NewCarsPage.
    ...
}
?>
```

A section-specific *common* directory is also a logical place to put classes for specific modules that you expect to use throughout that section. Each file is named after the module class that it contains:

> *.../newcars/common/nwcheader.inc*
>
> *.../newcars/common/nwccallout.inc*
>
> *...*

Other types of section files

Just as we defined a number of subdirectories for various other components used across the entire application, you can define similar directories for those components that are specific to a certain section:

> *.../newcars/css*
>
> *.../newcars/js*
>
> *.../newcars/images*
>
> *.../newcars/docs*
>
> *.../newcars/media*
>
> *...*

An alternative to placing CSS and JavaScript files for the section within the sections themselves is to place them within the sitewide directory for CSS or JavaScript and give them a section name:

.../css/newcars_20091009.css

.../css/cpocars_20091013.css

Architecture for Pages

The most specific points in the architecture address individual pages. As you navigate around a web application, a natural hierarchy among pages usually becomes evident. For example, at the highest level, there may be a series of landing pages that take you into sections of the application:

.../homepage

.../newcars

.../cpocars

.../usedcars

...

Once you navigate into these sections, there are often ways from those points to move deeper within each section. For example, within the New Cars section, you might have a page for new car search results:

.../newcars/search

When you select one of the results, it's likely that you'll need a page for displaying the details about that specific car:

.../newcars/details

Setting up a hierarchy like this for the directory structure on your server is a good reflection of the application architecture. These directories may be what you end up using for paths in the URLs to reach various parts of your web application, or you may end up creating rewrite rules on the server (to address the latest demands of the various search engines, for example). Even if you do end up creating rewrite rules, a hierarchy for pages provides solid underpinnings with which to work.

Files for implementing pages

In Chapter 7, you saw how to implement web pages as PHP classes that construct pages as sets of modules. To do this, you need only two files in the directory for each page: *index.html*, which instantiates the class for a specific page (see Example 10-5), and *index_main.inc* (see Example 10-6), which defines the page class itself.

Example 10-5. The index.html file for a page

```
<?php
require_once(".../homepage/index_main.inc");

$page = new Homepage(...);
$body = $page->create();
```

```php
print($page->get_page());
?>
```

Example 10-6. The index_main.inc file for a page

```php
<?php
// Include whatever files are needed for the page (e.g., usually files
// for the page base class, data managers, and all modules on the page.)
...

class Homepage extends SitePage
{
    ...
}
?>
```

Page-specific modules

In Chapter 7, you saw that everything a module needs is nicely encapsulated within a class as well. For modules used by just one page, the *index_main.inc* file for the page is a good place to define the module class. This reflects the fact that the scope for the module is just that page. In Example 10-7, the class for the Car Finder module is defined within the same file as the class for the home page.

Example 10-7. The home page, using a module specific to the home page

```php
<?php
...

class Homepage extends SitePage
{
    // This page is the only one that uses the Car Finder module below.
    ...
}

class CarFinder extends Module
{
    ...
}
?>
```

Modules on multiple pages

For modules used on multiple pages, define the module class in its own file (within one of the common locations discussed previously), and include the file wherever you use the module. In Example 10-8, the class for the Navigation Bar module is defined in its own file, named after the module itself (e.g., *navbar.inc*). The *index_main.inc* file for the home page includes *navbar.inc*.

Example 10-8. The home page using a module used by other pages, too

```php
<?php
require_once("../common/navbar.inc");
...

class Homepage extends SitePage
{
    // This page uses the Navigation Bar module defined in navbar.inc.
    ...
}
?>
```

Recall from Chapter 7 that each module has exactly one include file that you include to use it. If the module needs other files for its implementation, the module includes them itself. This is key to good encapsulation.

Pages of a similar type

Pages of a similar type that require similar capabilities may be derived from a common base class. In Example 10-9, the Homepage class is derived from LandingPage instead of the SitePage page class because it is one type of landing page and needs some of the same capabilities as others. LandingPage, in turn, is derived from SitePage (not shown here).

Example 10-9. The home page inheriting capabilities of a landing page

```php
<?php
require_once("../common/landingpage.inc");

class Homepage extends LandingPage
{
    // You need to include landingpage.inc to inherit from LandingPage.
    ...
}
?>
```

Architecture and Maintenance

Now that we have looked at a few ideas for organizing various components of a large web application, let's look at how a good architecture coupled with the techniques presented earlier in the book help address some common issues related to maintenance. In the end, it's an application's capability of adapting to changes that makes it truly maintainable.

Reorganizing Module Uses

One of the most common maintenance issues with large web applications is keeping the architecture organized as components are moved from one place to another. For example, suppose a module originally designed specifically for one page later is used on several pages across the entire application. Fortunately, with the architecture described earlier, the change is relatively easy.

Let's look at a module called `NewCarCallout`, originally designed for the New Car Details Page. Here are the steps to start using it across the entire application while keeping the architecture well organized:

1. Move the class `NewCarCallout` from its location within the *index_main.inc* file for `NewCarDetailsPage` to its own file, *.../common/nwccallout.inc*.

2. Add a `require_once` statement to include *.../common/nwccallout.inc* in the file *index_main.inc* for `NewCarDetailsPage`.

3. Add the module to whichever pages will use it by performing Step 2 for those pages and instantiating the module on those pages wherever the module should be added.

One of the most important things to notice about this process is that you don't have to move any CSS or JavaScript to use the module at its new location. Recall from Chapter 7 that links to CSS and JavaScript, as well as embedded CSS and JavaScript, are encapsulated by the class itself; the CSS and JavaScript effectively travel around with the module wherever it goes.

Example 10-10 is a reminder of the methods outlined in Chapter 7 that you might define for a module. As you can see, in addition to the **get_content** method, which returns the HTML for the module, there are methods to specify the linked and embedded CSS, and the linked and embedded JavaScript.

Example 10-10. A module specifying its CSS, JavaScript, and HTML

```
class NewCarCallout extends Module
{
    ...

    public function __construct(...)
    {
        // Do whatever is required to initialize the module instance.
        ...
    }

    public function get_css_linked()
    {
        // Return an array of CSS files you want linked for the module.
        return array
        (
            ...
        );
    }

    public function get_css()
    {
        // Return the string of CSS you want embedded for the module.
        return <<EOD
```

```
...
EOD;
    }

    public function get_js_linked()
    {
        // Return an array of JavaScript files that you wanted linked.
        return array
        (
            ...
        );
    }

    public function get_js()
    {
        // Return the JavaScript that you want embedded for the module.
        return <<<EOD
...
EOD;
    }

    public function get_content()
    {
        // Return the HTML markup to place on the page for the module.
        return <<<EOD
...
EOD;
    }
}
```

By defining the methods in Example 10-10, the module will work properly wherever it goes; however, it would be good to refactor its CSS and JavaScript into the sitewide files to reflect its new, more universal role in the architecture. This refactoring is easy to do because the CSS and JavaScript methods for a module also document exactly where the code to be refactored resides. In addition, the ID for the module's outermost `div` identifies exactly which block of CSS needs to move (see Chapter 4), and the namespace for the module's JavaScript identifies exactly what to change in the JavaScript (see Chapter 5).

It's worth noting that if a module that was used across an entire web application is reduced to being used on just one page or just one section, it's probably not worth moving the module from the common area to the more specific area, since the module has already demonstrated its relevance at a wider scope. However, even if you decide to make that change, it's a simple one since you will have already removed the module from where it was previously used, and you just need to refactor the CSS and JavaScript in the reverse direction.

Adding Module Variations

The more places you use a module within a large web application, the more likely you'll need different variations of it. When these variations require coordinated changes to a module's HTML, CSS, and JavaScript, they can become difficult to manage. Fortunately, the architecture we've described for modules makes handling such variations much easier. Because everything a module needs to function correctly is encapsulated inside the module class itself, you have a complete picture of what needs to change to support future variations.

Often, variations will require new parameters to configure the module, but you want to avoid altering code where the module is used already. There are a couple of ways to handle this: you can define additional parameters for the constructor of the module, and adapt the constructor to treat the parameters as optional; or you can define setter methods to handle the additional parameters after construction.

Let's revisit the Picture Slider module from Chapter 7 to examine how both of these alternatives work. Example 10-11 shows a small part of the implementation provided there. Suppose in a new variation of the module you want to allow the width of the pictures and the number of frames to be configured wherever the module is used. In Chapter 7, these were fixed at 65 and 8, respectively.

Example 10-11. The original implementation for the Picture Slider module

```
class PictureSlider extends Module
{
   var $gallery;
   var $type;
   var $picture_width;
   var $slider_frames;

   public function __construct($page, $gallery)
   {
      parent::__construct($page);

      $this->gallery = $gallery;
      $this->type = "default";
      $this->picture_width = 65;
      $this->slider_frames = 8;
   }

   ...
}
```

Again, the key is that you don't want to alter code at any of the points where the module is already being used. This is how existing instances of the module are created:

```
$mod = new PictureSlider($this, $gallery);
$slider = $mod->create();
```

Example 10-12 shows how you could use optional parameters within the constructor to support the new variation of the module.

Example 10-12. The Picture Slider module with a new constructor

```php
class PictureSlider extends Module
{
    var $gallery;
    var $type;
    var $picture_width;
    var $slider_frames;

    public function __construct($page, $gallery, $width="", $frames="")
    {
        parent::__construct($page);

        $this->gallery = $gallery;
        $this->type = "default";

        if (empty($width))
            $this->picture_width = 65;
        else
            $this->picture_width = $width;

        if (empty($frames))
            $this->slider_frames = 8;
        else
            $this->slider_frames = $frames;
    }

    ...

}
```

With this change, existing instances of the module work just as they did before; however, now you can also do the following:

```php
$mod = new PictureSlider($this, $gallery, $width, $frames);
$slider = $mod->create();
```

Example 10-13 shows how you can apply the alternative approach of defining setter methods to set optional parameters for the module.

Example 10-13. The Picture Slider module with setter methods

```php
class PictureSlider extends Module
{
    var $gallery;
    var $type;
    var $picture_width;
    var $slider_frames;

    public function __construct($page, $gallery)
    {
        parent::__construct($page);

        $this->gallery = $gallery;
        $this->type = "default";
        $this->picture_width = 65;
        $this->slider_frames = 8;
```

```
    }

    public function set_picture_width($width)
    {
        $this->picture_width = $width;
    }

    public function set_slider_frames($frames)
    {
        $this->slider_frames = $frames;
    }

    ...
}
```

With this change, existing instances of the module work just as they did before; however, now you can also do the following:

```
$mod = new PictureSlider($this, $gallery);
$mod->set_picture_width($width);
$mod->set_slider_frames($frames);
$slider = $mod->create();
```

Another common variation for modules is simply to affect a presentation change based on settings within the module. By changing these settings, either with a parameter passed to the constructor or via a setter method, you can apply different CSS classes to achieve different presentations using *presentation switching*. Chapter 4 discusses presentation switching in detail.

Making Widespread Changes

Over the lifetime of a large web application, it can become more and more difficult to make widespread changes so that they are consistent wherever they are applied. However, with a little forethought in your architecture, these changes don't have to be difficult to manage.

Base classes for pages and modules provide a good place to address this situation. As an example, let's suppose after some period of time your design team decides that you need a different header and footer on all the pages within a certain section of your web application. Recall from Chapter 7 that Page prescribes an interface for returning the HTML markup for the header and footer of pages. Normally SitePage, the base class for all pages across an entire web application, defines both of these methods, as shown in Example 10-14.

Example 10-14. Defining a header and footer for an entire site

```
class SitePage extends Page
{
    ...
```

```
   public function get_header()
   {
      // Return the HTML markup for the header across the entire site.
      return <<<EOD
<div id="sitehdr">
  ...
</div>

EOD;
   }

   public function get_footer()
   {
      // Return the HTML markup for the footer across the entire site.
      return <<<EOD
<div id="siteftr">
  ...
</div>

EOD;
   }

   ...
}
```

To change the header and footer within a certain section, define a page class from which to derive all pages for just that section and override the **get_header** and **get_footer** methods to return the section-specific header and footer, as shown in Example 10-15.

Example 10-15. Defining a special header and footer for the New Cars section

```
class NewCarsPage extends SitePage
{
   ...

   public function get_header()
   {
      // Return the HTML markup for the header of the New Cars section.
      return <<<EOD
<div id="nwchdr">
  ...
</div>

EOD;
   }

   public function get_footer()
   {
      // Return the HTML markup for the footer of the New Cars section.
      return <<<EOD
<div id="nwcftr">
  ...
</div>
```

```
EOD;
   }

   ...
}
```

How can you be sure the desired header and footer will be retrieved from the new definitions just created for `NewCarsPage` and not from `SitePage`? The correct methods are used because in the `create` method of the base class `Page`, `$this` now points to an instance of `NewCarsPage`. So, the `get_header` and `get_footer` methods of this class are invoked, as opposed to the methods in `SitePage`. Example 10-16 shows where this occurs in `Page`.

Example 10-16. Invoking get_header and get_footer within the Page class

```
class Page
{
   ...

   public function create()
   {

      ...

      // These invoke methods of the derived class, if defined there.
      $header = $this->get_header();
      $content = $this->get_content();
      $footer = $this->get_footer();

      ...
   }

   ...
}
```

If the header or footer defined in the section-specific page class requires CSS or JavaScript itself, you can place it in the CSS file or JavaScript file defined for that section of the site (if you're following the recommendations of Chapter 9). Page classes define an interface for specifying linked and embedded CSS and JavaScript exactly like that for modules. This way, whenever you add HTML within the page class, you can specify the CSS and JavaScript explicitly that you need.

The ideas mentioned in this section are very extensible. For example, you can define your own methods in a base class derived from `Page` and override these methods as needed. Another way to apply widespread changes is to make the changes directly within modules that are used in multiple places across your web application. Modules used in many places themselves inherently offer a central point for making widespread changes.

Changes in Data Sources

When the source behind a set of data changes, ideally the change should be abstracted from the user interface, provided the structure of the data is still the same. This demonstrates the key benefit of using data managers to establish a clearly defined interface between the user interface and backend systems. As mentioned in Chapter 6, the interface established by a data manager forms a contract of sorts between the user interface and the backend that prescribes the structure of the data to be exchanged. Example 10-17 illustrates this. As long as both parties work within the guidelines of the data structure, the source of the data can change however it needs to.

Example 10-17. The structure, or contract, for data managed via a data manager

```
array
(
    "0" => array
    (
        "name"  => "...",
        "price" => "...",
        "link"  => "..."
    ),

    "1" => array
    (
        "name"  => "...",
        "price" => "...",
        "link"  => "..."
    ),

    "2" => array
    (
        "name"  => "...",
        "price" => "...",
        "link"  => "..."
    ),

    ...
)
```

One example of a data source changing is when your application gets a new data provider for one of its services. For example, suppose your web application is going to start using a new company to provide periodic updates to new car inventories by way of a data feed. Changes to the user interface code are needed no further than in the get_data methods of the data managers that fetch data from the feed.

Another interesting example of a data source changing occurs when you have a content management system (CMS) managing some data. Imagine a control panel through which product managers can control which content will be retrieved by the backend at various times. This may be dynamic data for modules to display, or it might even be metadata that controls whether a module is displayed at all.

In a content management system, it's usually important to be able to preview how parts of the web application will look at scheduled times. To support previews, you can define a data manager base class that stores a time parameter with the other input arguments passed to a data manager. To set the preview time, look for a special value passed via GET or POST, or using a cookie (all retrieved in PHP via the `$_REQUEST` variable). Examples 10-18 and 10-19 illustrate handling previews for time-sensitive CMS data. The important thing to notice is that changes within the data source based on the preview time are abstracted from the user interface.

 Previewing is typically available in environments other than production systems, so that's how Examples 10-18 and 10-19 are implemented. In practice, the backend systems accessed for previews are typically different from those in the production environment as well to keep the data within the two environments isolated.

Example 10-18. A base class for data managers that access CMS data

```
class CMSDataManager extends DataManager
{
    protected $op_environment;
    protected $cms_preview_tm;

    public function __construct()
    {
        parent::__construct();

        // Set this from a server config that indicates the environment.
        $this->op_environment = ...;

        if ($this->op_environment != "production" && !empty($_REQUEST
            ["cmstime"]))
        {
            // Set the timestamp to use for the content management system.
            $this->cms_preview_tm = $_REQUEST["cmstime"];
        }
        else
        {
            // In production, or if no preview time was given, use the
            // current time as the time for which data is to be fetched.
            $this->cms_preview_tm = time();
        }
    }

    // No implementations are necessary for get_data and set_data here.
}
```

Example 10-19. A specific data manager accessing CMS data

```
class NewCarListingsDataManager extends CMSDataManager
{
    public function __construct()
    {
        parent::__construct();

        ...
    }

    public function get_data($load_args, &$load_data, &$load_stat)
    {
        // Explicitly add the timestamp for the content management system.
        $load_args["cms_preview_tm"] = $this->cms_preview_tm;

        // Do whatever else you would normally do to retrieve the data.
        // The timestamp is passed automatically with the other arguments
        // so that it can be used as needed to fetch time-sensitive data.
        ...
    }

    ...
}
```

Exposing Modules Externally

Clearly, the classes presented in Chapter 7 are designed to work together, but an important attribute is that they can also work independently. The same interface that you use to create modules on pages derived from Page lets you extract everything a module needs (e.g., its HTML, CSS, and JavaScript) so that it can be placed on pages generated within a different environment, as shown in Example 10-20. Modules do need some instance of Page passed to the constructor, but you can ignore the page after you construct it and pass it to the modules. For this, you may want to define a special page class (e.g., TransPage) with empty implementations for methods that modules call but that aren't needed in this context. For example, modules call add_to_js_linked, add_to_js, add_to_css_linked, and add_to_css, but it's more efficient to have these do nothing if the page instance is just a placeholder.

Example 10-20. Accessing the components of a module

```
// You do need some instance of Page for modules, but then ignore it.
$page = new TransPage();

...

// Anyone can extract a module's HTML, CSS, and JavaScript like this.
$mod = new PictureSlider($page, ...);
$html = $mod->create();

$css_linked = $mod->get_css_linked();
$css = $mod->get_css();
```

```
$js_linked = $mod->get_js_linked();
$js = $mod->get_js();
```

The important thing here is that this lets you build systems in an evolutionary way. Large web applications take a lot of time to build and modify, so it's important to have a truly modular architecture that has the potential to work within other systems while different parts are in different states.

Index

We'd like to hear your suggestions for improving our indexes. Send email to *index@oreilly.com*.

D

data action (MVC), 202
data interfaces, 15, 18, 115, 120
data managers, 117–123
    accessing XML data, 127–130
    creating, 120, 254
    extending, 121–123
    handling data source changes, 266–268
    modular Ajax and, 198
    passing flags to, 133
    using cURL inside, 131
databases, connecting to, 121, 123–126
date stamps, 53, 88
degrading gracefully, 37
dependencies in class diagrams, 14
descendants (CSS), 56
DHTML, and MVC, 201
directory structure, 252
display attribute (CSS), 73
diversity of web interfaces, 2
divisions of modules, 63
DNS lookups, 237, 239
document flow (CSS), 67
Document Object Model (see DOM)
Dojo JavaScript library, 94, 189
DOM (Document Object Model)
    common methods, 91, 92
    and faster rendering, 35, 234
    JavaScript libraries for, 93–98
    and request handling, 186
    XHTML and, 42
    XML responses in, 195
Domain Name Service (DNS) lookups, 237, 239
double margin bug (IE), 73
DTD, strict, 45
Dublin Core vocabulary, 46
duplicate files, removing, 235
dynamic data, 115, 145
dynamic modules, 116

E

edges, 10
elements (CSS), 56
elements (DOM), 92
embedding (CSS), 53
embedding (JavaScript), 89
empty tags (XHTML), 43

encapsulation, 3, 90, 140, 211, 258
eval (JSON), 186
event handling, 89, 98–102
exchange formats, 194
Expires headers, 233
extending a class in PHP, 19, 122

F

factory methods, 136
fail action (MVC), 202
faster rendering, 35
final keyword (PHP), 21
final methods (PHP), 21
fixed-width layouts/containers (CSS), 71
Flanagan, David, 22
Flash, JavaScript alternatives to, 102
floating elements (CSS), 70
font normalization across browsers, 85–86
footers, 63, 77, 146, 264
forms, 133, 134
forward compatibility (HTML), 36

G

general page information, 147
generalization, 10
$_GET array (PHP), 134
GET requests (Ajax), 189–194
getElementById method (DOM), 91, 195
getElementsByTagName method (DOM), 93, 186, 195
getState (MVC), 206
get_all_css (PHP), 142
get_all_js (PHP), 143
get_cache_vars (PHP), 230
get_content (PHP page class), 137
get_content (PHP), 146, 162, 164, 216
get_css (PHP), 144, 162, 163, 181, 182
get_css_common (PHP), 144, 157, 163
get_css_linked (PHP), 144, 161, 163, 222
get_data (PHP), 117, 121, 123, 198, 266
get_doctype (PHP), 142
get_footer (PHP), 146, 157, 161, 264
get_header (PHP), 146, 157, 161, 264
get_js (PHP), 145, 162, 164, 182, 216
get_js_common (PHP), 143, 145, 157
get_js_linked (PHP), 145, 161, 164, 216, 222, 234, 236
get_meta (PHP), 142

get_page (PHP), 136, 141, 143, 231, 234
get_section (PHP Layout class), 177
get_title (PHP), 142
global data in event handlers, 98
Google Analytics, 158, 241–243
Google Maps, 87
grid-based layouts/containers (CSS), 71
grouping selectors (CSS), 57

H

handleConnect method (Ajax), 186
handler method (YUI JavaScript), 99
handleRequest method (Ajax), 186
"has-a" relationship, 10
headers, 63, 72, 75, 146, 264
height property (CSS), 67
High Performance Web Sites (Souders), 221,
        238
hooks, 31
hostnames, 237
HTML
    aggregating in PHP, 137
    and Ajax, 202
    bad tags, 37
    benefits of good, 35
    caching, 222
    chained selection lists, 105
    class attribute, 40
    embedding/inlining JavaScript into, 89
    good and bad examples of, 28–32
    good tags, 38–40
    ID attribute, 40
    and JSON, 198
    name attribute, 41
    overview, 27
    retrieving header, footer, content markup,
        146
    semantically meaningful, 31
    versions, 41, 45, 49
    and XHTML, 41
HTTP requests, 225, 238

I

icons, spriting, 239
ID
    HTML/CSS, 40, 55, 58, 91
    version, 223, 239
iframe element (Ajax), 188

Ignore policy (MVC), 202
image files, 239, 254
importance (CSS), 57
information architecture, 27
information hiding (JavaScript), 24
information hiding (PHP), 16
inheritance (JavaScript), 25
inheritance (PHP), 19, 122, 258
init (MVC), 206
inlining (CSS), 54, 67
inlining (JavaScript), 89
innerHTML property (HTML DOM), 93
input element (CSS), 32
instance of a class, 8
interfaces, 15, 18, 115, 120
internationalization, 36
interoperability issues, 27, 188
"is-a" relationship, 10

J

JavaScript, 108
    (see also JSON)
    aggregating in PHP, 137, 147
    caching, 222–227
    chained selection lists, 105–114
    combining with CSS files, 224–227
    cookies, 133
    creating an object in, 22
    duplicate files, 235
    dynamic, 182
    embedding, 44, 89, 163
    establishing server connections, 186
    HTTP requests for, 225, 238
    information hiding in, 24
    inlining, 89
    linking, 88, 161, 163, 222
    managing through PHP, 143, 145, 163,
        167
    methods in, 24, 90
    minification, 234
    modularity, 88, 101
    object orientation in, 7, 22–26
    overview, 87
    for Picture Slider example, 171–176
    placement of, 234
    refactoring, 260
    scoping, 90–92
    stubs, 89
    using events instead of method calls, 101

About the Author

Kyle Loudon is a software developer at Yahoo!, where he leads a group doing user interface development. Some of Kyle's experiences prior to joining Yahoo! include working on the user interface for the original Apple iPod, writing software for other mobile devices, and leading the user interface group at Jeppesen DataPlan (a Boeing company) in the development of a flight-planning system used by airlines around the world. He also spent a small amount of time with IBM in the early 1990s. For several years, he has taught object-oriented programming part-time at the University of California, Santa Cruz, while working as a software developer in Silicon Valley.

Kyle received a B.S. in computer science from Purdue University in 1992 with a minor in French, and was elected there to the Phi Beta Kappa honor society. He has also done some advanced education in computer science at Stanford University.

Colophon

The animal on the cover of *Developing Large Web Applications* is a Newfoundland. Also known as a "Newf" or "Newfie," this massive dog is 26–28 inches tall at the shoulder and weighs 100–150 pounds. As its name implies, it originated in Newfoundland, Canada, where it was used by fishermen to haul nets, carry boat lines to shore, and retrieve items that fell overboard. An agile swimmer, the Newfoundland has webbed feet and a water-resistant coat, which can be black, brown, gray, or white and black (Landseer).

Newfoundlands are "gentle giants" known for their sweet, loyal dispositions and obedience to their masters. They rarely bark, but are protective when necessary. They are generally very good with children and other animals. They are well suited for apartment dwellers, as they tend to be relatively inactive indoors; for exercise, a daily walk is usually sufficient, though they do enjoy opportunities to play and swim. In keeping with their heritage, Newfoundlands prefer colder climates and do not do well in hot weather; they should never be left in the heat without water and shade. They are prone to certain health problems, including hip and elbow dysplasia, cystinuria (a hereditary defect indicated by calculi stones in the kidney or bladder), and subvalvular aortic stenosis, a common heart defect that can cause sudden death at an early age. Their average life expectancy is 10 years.

Thanks to its muscular build and swimming prowess, the breed is frequently used in water rescues. Indeed, it seems to have an innate lifesaving ability in general: Newfoundlands have been credited with saving shipwreck survivors (the 1863 wreck of the *Dispatch*, which carried more than 100 Irish immigrants, and the 1919 wreck of the SS *Essie*); navigating through blizzard conditions in Alaska and the Aleutian Islands during World War II to provide ammunition and supplies to soldiers; and, according to legend, keeping Napoleon Bonaparte afloat when rough seas knocked him overboard following his escape from exile on the island of Elba in 1815. One particularly heroic story involves the Newfoundland mascot of the Royal Rifles of Canada, called Sergeant Gander. During the Battle of Lye Mun on Hong Kong Island in December 1941, the courageous dog retrieved a grenade thrown at the battalion and carried it off, saving several lives and sacrificing his own in the process. In 2000, nearly 60 years after his heroic act, Sgt. Gander was posthumously awarded the Dickin Medal, given to animals displaying "conspicuous gallantry" in times of war.

The cover image is from Wood's *Animate Creation*. The cover font is Adobe ITC Garamond. The text font is Linotype Birka; the heading font is Adobe Myriad Condensed; and the code font is LucasFont's TheSansMonoCondensed.